Speaking with One Voice

This book explores the dynamics and challenges that underlie the ability of organizations to speak with one voice. Contributions by experienced and emerging scholars shed light on the nature and regulation of the communication processes whereby the many and diverse voices of a collective can unite, act, and speak as a distinct entity, thus contributing to its organizing.

By focusing on communicational events, whether in the context of for-profit and non-profit organizations, political protests, or social movements, chapters guide the reader through the diverse manifestations and concrete ways of dealing with the imperative for organizations of all kinds to speak with one voice. In doing so, the book creates bridges between different perspectives with regard to the notion of voice and its significance for the study of organizing, between fields of study, and between theory and empirical research aimed at investigating organizing beyond the boundaries of the formal organization.

Offering a thorough and comprehensive investigation of the dynamics between multivocality and univocality in the organizing of various collectives, this book will be an important resource for scholars and students of organizational communication, management studies, media studies, and rhetorical studies.

Chantal Benoit-Barné is Associate Professor in the Department of Communication at the Université de Montréal, Canada.

Thomas Martine is Associate Professor in the Communication & Culture Department at Audencia Business School, France.

ROUTLEDGE STUDIES IN COMMUNICATION, ORGANIZATION, AND ORGANIZING
Series Editor: François Cooren

The goal of this series is to publish original research in the field of organizational communication, with a particular—but not exclusive—focus on the constitutive or performative aspects of communication. In doing so, this series aims to be an outlet for cutting-edge research monographs, edited books, and handbooks that will redefine, refresh and redirect scholarship in this field.

The volumes published in this series address topics as varied as branding, spiritual organizing, collaboration, employee communication, corporate authority, organizational timing and spacing, organizational change, organizational sense making, organization membership, and disorganization. What unifies this diversity of themes is the authors' focus on communication, especially in its constitutive and performative dimensions. In other words, authors are encouraged to highlight the key role communication plays in all these processes.

For a full list of titles in this series, please visit www.routledge.com.

Authority and Power in Social Interaction
Methods and Analysis
Edited by Nicolas Bencherki, Frédérik Matte and François Cooren

Organizing Inclusion: Moving Diversity from Demographics to Communication Processes
Edited by Marya L. Doerfel and Jennifer L. Gibbs

Whistleblowing, Communication and Consequences
Lessons from The Norwegian National Lottery
Edited by Peer Jacob Svenkerud, Jan-Oddvar Sørnes and Larry Browning

Speaking with One Voice
Multivocality and Univocality in Organizing
Edited by Chantal Benoit-Barné and Thomas Martine

Speaking with One Voice

Multivocality and Univocality
in Organizing

Edited by Chantal Benoit-Barné and
Thomas Martine

Routledge
Taylor & Francis Group

NEW YORK AND LONDON

First published 2022
by Routledge
605 Third Avenue, New York, NY 10158

and by Routledge
2 Park Square, Milton Park, Abingdon, Oxon, OX14 4RN

Routledge is an imprint of the Taylor & Francis Group, an informa business

Library of Congress Cataloging-in-Publication Data
Names: Benoit-Barné, Chantal, editor. | Martine, Thomas, editor.
Title: Speaking with one voice : multivocality and univocality in
organizing / edited by Chantal Benoit-Barné and Thomas Martine.
Description: Milton Park, Abingdon, Oxon ; New York, NY :
Routledge, 2022.
| Series: Routledge studies in communication, organization, and
organizing | Includes bibliographical references and index.
Subjects: LCSH: Communication in social action.
| Communication--Social aspects. | Communication--Political aspects.
| Social movements.
Classification: LCC HM1206 .S67 2022 (print)
| LCC HM1206 (ebook) | DDC
361.2/4--dc23
LC record available at https://lccn.loc.gov/2021019872
LC ebook record available at https://lccn.loc.gov/2021019873

ISBN: 9780367264529 (hbk)
ISBN: 9781032040004 (pbk)
ISBN: 9780429297830 (ebk)

DOI: 10.4324/9780429297830

Typeset in Sabon
by KnowledgeWorks Global Ltd.

Contents

Contributors

Helle Kryger Aggerholm holds a position as Head of Research at the Danish School of Media and Journalism, Denmark. Her research examines the role of strategic communication in change processes in public and private organizations, strategy communication within a strategy-as-practice context, organizational communication, and language as social interaction. Her most recent work in these areas has been published in *Journal of Management Inquiry, International Journal of Strategic Communication, Journal of Management Communication, Public Relations Review, Business Ethics: A European review,* and *Corporate Communication: An International Journal.*

Birte Asmuß is Associate Professor at the Department of Management at Aarhus University, Denmark. Her research interests are on interactional processes of organizational work including both strategy and leadership processes as well as issues related to identity work and organizational communication in general. Her work has been published in leading international journals like *Journal of Communication Management, Journal of Management Inquiry, Culture and Organization,* and *Economic and Industrial Democracy.*

Nicolas Bencherki is Associate Professor of Organizational Communication at TÉLUQ Montréal, Canada. His work investigates the way communication and materiality constitute organizational reality, including classic notions such as strategy, authority or membership. His work has been published, among others, in *Academy of Management Journal, Organization Studies, Journal of Communication,* and *Communication Theory.* He co-edited *Authority and Power in Social Interaction: Methods and Analysis* (2019).

Chantal Benoit-Barné is Associate Professor in the Department of Communication at the Université de Montréal in Canada. Her research draws on rhetorical theories and Communication as Constitutive of Organization (CCO) perspectives to explore the constitutive dimensions of communication in work interactions, public deliberations, and sociotechnical controversies. Her work appears in academic journals such as *Quarterly Journal of Speech*, *Communication Monographs* and *Management Communication Quarterly*.

Erna Bodström is an affiliated researcher at The Centre for Research on Ethnic Relations and Nationalism CEREN, University of Helsinki, Finland. Her research focuses on migration, especially on asylum and integration. She draws on theories of borders, citizenship and discourse, and is an expert on text and image analysis, particularly specialising in policy texts. She is also a human rights activist working through, among others, the Right to Live network in Helsinki, Finland.

Kat Davis is Sustainability Coordinator at Boise State University, United States of America and is currently working to coordinate campus and community action around climate change solutions. Her thesis project focuses on methods of art-marking and narrative as a tool for working through climate anxiety and instilling a sense of personal resilience and collective action toward a sustainable future.

Clément Decault is a PhD student in the Department of Communication at the Université de Montréal in Canada. He received his M.Sc. in communication science from the Université de Montréal in 2017. His master's thesis aims to examine ongoing mechanisms and strategies of colonial power in the United States and to explore how social activism is shaped by rap artists involved within the Black Lives Matter movement.

Annis Grover Golden is Associate Professor in the Department of Communication at the University at Albany, SUNY, United States of America. Her research is concerned with intersections of communication, organizations, and health and well-being, including discourse analytic approaches to understanding processes associated with community-based health promotion. Her work has appeared in such journals as *Communication Monographs*, *Management Communication Quarterly*, *Human Relations*, *Health Communication*, and *Social Science & Medicine*.

Camilla Haavisto is University Lecturer in Communication at the Swedish School of Social Science at the University of Helsinki, Finland. Her research relates to the claims-making of ethnic and cultural minorities and focuses on such topics as the politics of listening and the role of media for conflict resolution. She is also interested in media pedagogy, particularly from the perspective of inequalities.

Salla-Maaria Laaksonen is a postdoctoral researcher at the Centre for Consumer Society Research. University of Helsinki, Finland. She received her PhD in media and communication studies, but her research intersects with technology studies and organization studies, focusing on topics such as organizing on and with digital platforms, uses of data and analytics in organizations, and organization-stakeholder relations in the hybrid media system. Further, she is an expert of digital and computational methods.

Thomas Martine is Associate Professor of Communication at Audencia Business School, France. He received his PhD from Troyes Technology University. His research focuses on the communicative nature of phenomena such as authority, creativity, and objectivity as well as on the development of methods to evaluate these phenomena. His work has been published in journals such as *Communication Management Quarterly*, *Journal of Creative Behavior*, *Communication Theory* as well as in several book chapters published by Springer, Sage, and Routledge.

erin daina mcclellan is Associate Professor at the Department of Communication, Boise State University, United States of America. She has pursued research over the past decade focused on how official and vernacular rhetorics are embedded in and influence (1) inclusive teaching and learning; (2) urban public places and spaces; and (3) community engagement with discourses of sustainability. Her research and teaching aim to help inspire diverse communities to better work together across various articulations and understandings of what is meaningful in everyday life.

Alessandro Poroli is a PhD candidate in Communication at Hong Kong Baptist University, Hong Kong. His research explores how communication constitutes, defines, and constrains corporate social responsibility practices, organizational societal commitment processes, and employee engagement. His studies span organizational communication, environmental communication, and public relations.

Khaoula Zoghlami is a PhD candidate in Communication Studies in Université de Montréal, Canada. Among her research interests are intersectionality, participative and democratic forms of organizing and minorized group practices of political representation. She is a member of the Research Group on Language, Organization and Governance (LOG) and *Institut de recherche et d'études féministes* (IREF). She is also a lecturer at Université du Québec à Montréal where she teaches "Feminisms and Islam."

Acknowledgements

The idea of this book came during ICA 2018 preconference titled "Voice and Voices: Exploring tensions between plurivocity and univocity" that we co-organized with François Cooren and Laurence Kaufmann. We are very indebted to the speakers and participants whose exchanges and insights during the preconference greatly influenced the making of this book. We thank them all.

List of abbreviations

a.k.a.	Also known as
COVID-19	Disease caused by the new coronavirus SARS-CoV-2
e.g.,	Exempli gratia (for example)
etc.	et cetera (and so on)
i.e.,	id est (that is)
IPCSR	Independent popular consultation on systemic racism
p. and pp.	Page(s)
US	United States
ALFA	Fictitious name for national organization responsible for communal marketing, product quality monitoring, and standards compliance
CCO	Communicative constitution of organizations
(C)SR	(Corporate) social responsibility; also SR (social responsibility)
DELTA	Fictitious name for fieldwork office, sectoral organization with representative and coordinating roles for network of consumer co-operatives (NOVA)
GM	Genetically modified
GMOs	Genetically modified organisms
NGOs	Non-governmental organizations
NOVA	Fictitious name for network of consumer co-operatives
CBO	community-based organizations
WHP	Women's Health Project
RTL	Right to Live
SMOs	Social movement organizations

1 Voice

A Metaphor and Its Significance for Organizational Communication

Chantal Benoit-Barné and Thomas Martine

This book explores the dynamics and challenges that underlie the ability of organizations to *speak with one voice*. It takes as a starting point the idea that organizations are both united and diverse (Robichaud, Giroux, & Taylor, 2004; Taylor & Van Every, 2011), at times acting and speaking as one yet remaining fundamentally heterogeneous (i.e., distinct people with distinct identities, interests, roles, fields of expertise, authority, tasks, etc.). Hence, organizations have always faced a fundamental challenge: how to create the conditions of unity necessary for their existence despite the multiplicity of elements and processes that compose them. In our pluralistic societies, this problem takes on new importance, as the diversity of voices becomes not only more prevalent but also more valued. Our society and the organizations that compose it are in search of both unity and diversity, striving for integration without losing sight of the fact that they are heterogeneous and multisided. As pointed out by Robichaud, Giroux, and Taylor (2004), "[I]t appears that organization, as we usually conceive of it, is simultaneously pluralistic and unitary, multivocal and univocal, polyphonic and monophonic, many and one" (p. 618) To exist and be recognized as such, organizations have at some point to be able to *speak with one voice*.

To say that an organization has a voice and that it is speaking with one voice is not trivial. What exactly do we mean by this and what are the empirical manifestations of the phenomenon in question? Consider the following two examples. In December 2019, Greta Thunberg, the Swedish environmental activist, was named *Time* magazine's Person of the Year, becoming the youngest individual to earn this honour. In the editorial justifying this choice, *Time*'s editor-in-chief Edward Felsenthal (2019) explained:

> Meaningful change rarely happens without the galvanizing force of influential individuals, and in 2019, the earth's existential crisis found one in Greta Thunberg. Marshaling "Fridays for Future" protests throughout Europe; thundering, "How dare you!" at the world's most powerful leaders in her viral U.N. speech; leading some 7 million

DOI: 10.4324/9780429297830-1

climate strikers across the world in September and tens of thousands more in Madrid in early December, Thunberg has become the biggest voice on the biggest issue facing the planet.

(para. 2)

He concluded his editorial: "For sounding the alarm about humanity's predatory relationship with the only home we have, for bringing to a fragmented world a voice that transcends backgrounds and borders, for showing us all what it might look like when a new generation leads, Greta Thunberg is TIME's 2019 Person of the Year" (para. 10).

Other media have variously called Greta Thunberg "the voice of the future" (see the documentary *Greta Thunberg: The Voice of the Future*, Hill, 2020), "the voice of the planet" (Tait, 2019), "the voice of a generation" (Lubs, 2019), or "the voice of climate activism" (Fleming, 2019). Whether Greta Thunberg is *the biggest voice*, as stated by *Time*, or *the* voice (of a generation, of the future, etc.), as claimed by others, is, of course, subject to discussion. By mobilizing the metaphor of voice, commentators are making explicit her key role in the organization of a global climate movement.

As a second example of the manifestation of voice, on March 20, 2020, in the early months of the COVID-19 pandemic, the international president of Médecins Sans Frontières (MSF), Dr. Christos Christou (2020), published a letter addressed to MSF staff and supporters on the MSF website. The letter was said to convey the organization's priorities that will guide its activities during the crisis. It presented MSF's unique perspective on the situation, stressing the importance of supporting ongoing efforts against the pandemic while also maintaining its other regular medical programs "for the hundreds of thousands of patients we care for and for the extremely vulnerable communities we help around the world" (para. 4). This letter can be conceived as MSF's voice with regard to the COVID-19 crisis, as expressed by Dr. Christou, an official spokesperson for the organization. It voices, in the sense that it puts into words and makes visible, MSF's unique perspective at this particular moment in time (its priorities, the challenge it faces, what it has done so far, what it plans to do next), both for the members of the organization and for its many publics—a perspective rooted in MSF's long-standing commitment to provide assistance to populations in need.

These two cases illustrate what *speaking with one voice* may mean with regard to organizations. Throughout this book, the reader will uncover many other ways of making sense of this idea which has been described as one of the main utopias that conditions the field of organizational communication (see Grosjean, Mayère, & Bonneville, 2018). For instance, they will read about how managers involved in strategic decision-making about downsizing can find a common voice through the use of idiomatic formulations, such as "one cannot keep up with everything" (see Chapter 2);

they will learn about the efforts of a community health initiative to combine a plurality of voices rather than unite them as a way to adapt how it conceives of and talks about health issues to those it serves (see Chapter 3); they will also read about the process by which political protesters can unite and develop a common voice by formulating demands and communicating about the protest online (see Chapter 4).

As a whole, the chapters in this book call attention to the notion of voice and its significance for organizational communication. *Voice* is particularly interesting for organizational communication scholars because it places communication at the forefront of the organizational process by which a collective actor (a corporation, a non-governmental organization, a social movement, a political protest, etc.) is constituted and can be conceived as the collective subject of a voice. By focusing on the meanings of voice and on how the notion has been mobilized and investigated in organizational communication studies, we hope this introduction will do justice to the metaphorical power of the idea of voice and the richness of the concept, the two being obviously linked. Voice, as we will demonstrate throughout this chapter, is both a common way of talking about organizations and a fruitful concept for theorizing organization by emphasizing the organizing property of communication, in particular with regard to issues of collective agency, representation, and empowerment.

Understanding the Metaphorical Power of Voice

The metaphor of voice is ubiquitous throughout the humanities and social sciences, from anthropology (Magnat, 2018; Weidman, 2014) to composition studies (Bowden, 1995), psycholinguistic studies (Bertau, 2007), media and communication studies (Couldry, 2010), industrial relations (Benson, 2000; Bryson, 2004), and political science (Kunreuther, 2014). In organizational communication, voice has been a key metaphor for well over 30 years. Back in 1996, voice was described as one of four key problematics that define the field of organizational communication (Mumby & Stohl, 1996). According to Mumby and Stohl (1996), organizational communication scholars have built a sense of community and identity through investigating problematics of voice. In doing so, they have "problematize[d] and contest[ed] the monolithic managerial voice that tends to dominate other areas of organizational studies" (p. 55), providing "insight into the practices of traditionally marginalized groups or forms of organizing" (p. 58). This focus on voice also led organizational communication scholars toward studying alternative organizational structures and conceiving of organizations as social and political phenomena, rather than strictly economic ones. As a whole, *voice*, as a key term of organizational communication studies, "emphasizes the multi-layered, world making possibilities of communication" (Dempsey, 2017, p. 1).

The Different Meanings of Voice

Although the metaphor of voice is prevalent in organizational communication, what the notion means remains difficult to pinpoint. There is no such thing as a general definition of voice. Furthermore, the vast majority of authors do not define the term when they employ it, so one cannot easily understand precisely what they mean by it. As a way to further our investigation of how the metaphor has shaped our understanding of organizations, we first propose to consider the different meanings of the term *voice* based on the full entry of *The Oxford English Dictionary* ("Voice," 2020). We focus on four related meanings of the term, each of which manifests to varying degrees in organizational communication studies: voice as sound, voice as style of expression, voice as discourse, and voice as agency.

Voice as Sound

First, voice is a sonic phenomenon that is bodily produced and perceived. From that standpoint, voice refers to the sound made as air passes through the vocal organs, for instance when a person is speaking, singing, shouting, etc. The tone and quality of this sound (high, low, soft, loud, nasal, quavering, etc.) are conceived as individual characteristics closely linked to one's individuality. We can, for instance, recognize a person simply by hearing their voice over the phone.

Voice as Personal Style of Expression

Voice also refers to a personal tone or style of expression. We can say, for instance, that a rhetor has a voice that is unmistakably their own. This typically implies a unique combination of vocal tone and qualities, style of expression, opinions, aspirations, etc. The phrase "to find one's own voice" relates to this meaning, which is particularly important in composition studies, where the metaphor of voice has been widely used since the late 1960s (Bowden, 1995).

Voice as a Discursive Standpoint

The notion of voice can also be detached from vocality and its originating body and be conceived as discourse with meaning(s). A voice then refers to a discursive standpoint, whether in the form of opinions, narrations, experiences, etc. In this context, *to have a voice* can be conceived as a value associated with free speech, as "a right to express a preference or opinion, a say" ("Voice," 2020). As we will emphasize later, voice as a discursive standpoint can be attributed to an individual (i.e., the voice of an employee) or a group (i.e., the employees' collective voice).

Voice as Agency

Finally, a voice is also « the agency or means by which something ... is expressed, represented, or revealed» ("Voice," 2020). It is linked to a capacity to act and related to the verb *to voice*. From this standpoint, to have a voice is to have agency, and to be a voice is to be an agent able to speak as and for something or someone. To say that something or someone is the voice of reason in a debate is also part of that meaning (s/he voices reason in that debate and, as such, is the means by which it appears). So is the idea that an individual can act as a representative of a group, hence speaking for them and acting as their voice.

These four established meanings intersect and overlap when we use the term *voice*, giving the metaphor a strong evocative power. The notion of employee voice is a great example in that regard. *Employee voice*, commonly defined "as any type of mechanism, structure or practice, which provides an employee with an opportunity to express an opinion or participate in decision-making within their organization" (Lavelle, Gunnigle, & McDonnell, 2010, p. 396), has been a steady focus of investigation for organizational scholars, especially those studying employment relations. *Employee voice* is said to be direct when employees are personally involved in the decision-making process, or it is said to be indirect when voice is achieved through some form of collective employee representation (i.e., trade unions). Thus, the term *employee voice* evokes the four related meanings we have just described: It implies a sonic phenomenon, that is to say, an employee's ability to speak up and be heard. It also evokes a particular discursive standpoint and style of expression, for this ability to speak up implies a distinctive contribution (i.e., the expression of a particular point of view, expressed in a unique way by a speaking subject). Finally, the employee may be speaking on their own behalf or on behalf of others, which evokes the fourth meaning of voice as agency.

Given these overlapping meanings, how can we make sense of how voice is used in organizational communication studies? Our review of the literature indicates that voice is a normalized way of speaking about and thinking about organizations that carry with it a set of ideas and values with regard to issues of communication. According to Bowden (1995), voice is a metaphor fundamentally linked to orality that presumes and perpetuates the power of speech and co-presence. She explains the appeal of this metaphor in composition studies as follows:

> The voice comes from the body; the body is utterly personal and this personableness somehow ... is powerful. Spoken language is naturally closer than writing to the life spring, to consciousness, and to presence—all significant attributes of an orientation in which spoken voice is the privileged term. Speech (conveyed by the human voice) gets closest to what's real, genuine, legitimate, or in other words, the endpoint

or final objective of our meaning-making or communicating and does so in the most powerful way, through personal presence.

(p. 182)

One can certainly find traces of this deeply rooted preference for oral communication and co-presence in organizational communication studies—see Dempsey (2017) for a treatment of this issue. That said, our overview of the ways in which the voice metaphor is mobilized indicates a concern to broaden this conception to include various forms of communication and a reflection on how organizing occurs beyond face-to-face interaction. The section that follows highlights different ways in which the voice metaphor reveals itself within the field of organizational communication, thus documenting and explaining its appeal for this particular field of inquiry.

Voice(s) in Organizational Communication Studies

The most common and general idea about voice in organizational communication studies is that it somehow relates to discourse. The term is often used as a synonym for a wide range of discursive forms, from talk in interaction to public speeches, written texts, interview accounts, and more. This trend is particularly marked in discursive approaches to organizational communication, but it cuts across different perspectives on discourse. Voice can signify language in use when it refers to a local and context-dependent form of discourse—what Alvesson and Karreman (2000) have termed small-d discourse. It can also refer to established and sustainable ways of thinking and speaking—a.k.a. big-D discourse. In both instances, the metaphor of voice emphasizes the fact that a discourse can somehow be linked back to a speaking body, whether individual or collective. Consider the following two examples from the organizational communication literature.

Tracy and Rivera's (2010) article, "Endorsing Equity and Applauding Stay-at-Home Moms: How Male Voices on Work-Life Reveal Aversive Sexism and Flickers of Transformation," relies on the term *voices* to mean interview accounts or, more specifically, "talk about employees, wives, children, the division of domestic labor, and work-life policy" (p. 3) gathered during interviews. According to the authors, these male executive voices both reveal and constitute an implicit gendered script that is inscribed in and sustained by the current organization of labour and the male executive way of life. As such, their voice is a form of local talk, a specific manifestation of a gendered script and the means by which it is (re)produced. It is a link between talk and ideology.

Another telling example of this reliance on voice to emphasize the connection between small-d and big-D discourse can be found in Broadfoot and Munshi's (2007) article about postcolonial approaches to organizational communication. The authors rely on the notion of voice to call attention to the different rationalities that exist within the field, the need to find a way to open up to them, and the challenges such a postcolonial project entails. By relying on the metaphor of voice, they invite organizational scholars to look beyond the local talk of speaking subjects, toward a better understanding of the historically and culturally situated standpoints from which speaking subjects can act or speak.

Beyond this general idea that voice is a form of discourse that can inform our understanding of the connections between talk and ideology, the literature we have reviewed addresses a heterogeneous set of issues pertaining to voice that we broadly group into three themes: (1) the organizing properties of *speaking for* a collective, (2) voice in relation to power, and (3) the tensions between multivocality and univocality.

The Organizing Properties of Speaking for a Collective

Voice has been employed to emphasize the speaking subject as a driving force of the organizational process, in particular, with regard to issues of representation and collective agency through the practice of speaking for a collective. The idea that an organization is partly constituted by and through the activities of spokespersons who *stand for, act for,* and *speak for* it is at the heart of *communication as constitutive of organization* (CCO) research, particularly in studies relying on a Montreal School approach (Benoit-Barné & Cooren, 2009; Robichaud et al., 2004; Robichaud & Benoit-Barné, 2010; Taylor & Cooren, 1997; Taylor & Robichaud, 2004).

For instance, in "What Makes Communication Organizational? How the Many Voices of a Collectivity Become the One Voice of the Organization," Taylor and Cooren (1997) ground organizational communication in pragmatics, specifically speech act theory, and the agent-to-principal relationship(s) that a speaking subject constitutes by their speech: the speaking subject is engaging in organizational communication and constituting the organization as s/he is speaking as an agent for a principal. One of the examples by which they highlight the organizing effects of this process is the Speaker of the House of Commons, the president of the Parliament of Canada, whose roles entail, among others, to manage exchanges in the House and ensure decorum. When the Speaker of the House claims, "I hereby recognize the Leader of the Opposition" (p. 427), s/he is implicitly invoking both this function and the institution that authorizes it (« in my function as speaker of the house, I hereby ») so that it is not *I* who speaks but the House through its representative. Taylor and Cooren (1997) explain:

> "The house is not, and cannot be, an actor in the usual sense, in that the House is a collective, not a single entity, and its voice can *only* be expressed through an agent ... [T]he speaker constitutes himself as such a voice, and therefore comes to give expression to the organization

itself, i.e., the House. This is how the *many* voices of a collective become, institutionally, the *one* voice of an organization" (p. 482, emphasis in original).

As a whole, the work of James R. Taylor and Elizabeth J. Van Every (2000) has drawn our attention to the constitutive effects of representation through the communicative practices of speaking for, or voicing, the organization. *Speaking for* is constitutive of organizations in two fundamental ways. First, speaking on behalf of a collective can be conceived as a communicative practice involved in situated conversations and interactions whereby a speaker voices an organization's or a collective's identity and interests. The communicative act of representing, Taylor and Van Every argue, brings the community "into a state of collective identity as a pragmatic occurrence—its realization in the practices of communication" (p. 238). Second, the constitutive dimension of the act of *speaking for* follows also from the fact that it involves the production of a *text*, that is, *a* representation in the form of a "collective identity as a semantic or ideational occurrence—its conceptual realization" (p. 238). In line with the general framework of their thought, Taylor and Van Every thus consider representation as a process whereby the organization emerges both as a situated performance (or, in their words, a conversation) *and* as a text that objectifies the multiple practices and the distributed collective knowledge that make up the organization.

Of course, any text representing the organization will inevitably constitute a reduction of the organization's daily conversational world. This is so not only because complex organizations are constellations of communities of practice, each involving their own perspectives and world views, but also because any practice itself is made of layers of tacit knowledge and pre-reflexive habits that can never be fully accounted for and textualized. This fundamental indeterminacy of a representation is what makes it inherently unstable by nature and so consequential from a constitutive standpoint. It must be constantly presented, maintained, and stabilized and can always be contested. The speaking subject and the practices of speaking for the organization are driving forces in this process.

The emphasis on the speaking subject as a driving force of the organizing process through the act of *speaking for* was later nuanced in Cooren's ventriloquial approach to organizational communication (Cooren, 2010, 2012, 2014; Cooren, Matte, Benoit-Barné, & Brummans, 2013; Cooren & Sandler, 2014). Drawing from the works of Latour (1996, 2005), Greimas (1987), and Derrida (1988), Cooren uses the metaphor of the ventriloquist to emphasize the fact that communication is always a shared accomplishment, in other words, that people are never the sole authors of what they do and say. For instance, when someone says that "wearing a mask is a matter of public safety," this person positions him- or herself as speaking on behalf of public safety, which also means that public safety is supposed to animate this person when they say that. In this case, at least two entities can be regarded as the co-authors of the utterance "wearing a mask is a matter of public safety": the person who says it and public safety itself.

Far from being an isolated case, Cooren argues that this distributed or shared authorship is at play in virtually any act of communication. To the extent that it is always possible to identify a specific reason (or set of reasons) that makes us say what we say (or do what we do), we are never the sole authors of our saying and doing. We are always, to some extent, the mediator or translator of other things or beings that speak through us, whether they are values, rules, policies, emotions, situations, tools, people, cultures, identities, etc. This does not mean that the speaking subject is devoid of any real agency. This means that this agency is always shared with other things and beings. Therefore, the question of the (speaking) subject's agency can never be answered a priori: it always depends on the entities that s/he happens to be connected with. In other words, it is always an empirical question.

Through the metaphor of the ventriloquist, Cooren thus significantly broadens the meaning of "speaking" or "having a voice." From this perspective, anything that makes a difference in a specific situation can be regarded—at least metaphorically—as "throwing its voice," that is, as acting as a ventriloquist that makes someone or something do or say something. Thus, for something or someone to make its/his/her voice heard, one does not need to have a "real" voice, since someone or something else can do the talking on its/his/her behalf, and the voice does not even need to make any sound: what matters is that the voice somehow makes a difference.

Voice in Relation to Power

The idea that voice is power and that to make one's voice heard is to exercise power is well established within critical approaches to organizational communication. Dempsey (2017) provides an overview of critical studies that focus on issues of voice. She explains that one of their main contributions has been to shed light on the many different ways by which voices in organizations can be silenced, colonized, manipulated, distorted, devalued, or dismissed. Questions pertaining to who can or cannot speak and whose voice matters are particularly salient. Silence is also important because it can indicate a lack of power or a restriction of power (see, for instance, Bell, Özbilgin, Beauregard, & Sürgevil, 2011). Critical investigations have also called attention to ways to empower and provide equal opportunity for voice through feminist and participatory forms of organizing (see, for instance, Ashcraft, 2001; Stohl & Cheney, 2001). Dempsey (2017) draws attention, however, to "the danger of considering voice as intrinsically positive" (p. 6), arguing that we need to account for the fact that more opportunities for voice do not always translate into more power. She proposes the notion of *bounded voice* as a way to recognize this possibility (Dempsey, 2007). *Bounded voice* refers to the process of strategically limiting opportunities for voice as a way to possibly advance broader empowerment goals. This could mean, for example, that stakeholders with significant resources would remain silent and temporarily limit their opportunities to express themselves in order to give other stakeholders an opportunity to speak.

In her analysis of a two-year lockout at the Staley Manufacturing plant in Decatur, Illinois, Dana Cloud (2005) goes one step further, arguing that voice is simply not enough because it is essentially symbolic power, and "voice is seldom accompanied by material equality in which workers reap the full reward of their labor" (p. 513). In developing this argument, her article offers a strong critique of discursive approaches toward voice as power and what she refers to as a generalized "overemphasis on discursive power in organizational communication" (p. 511).

In line with a critical agenda, Couldry (2010) makes a convincing case for the notion of voice and its theoretical fruitfulness to investigate sociological, political, and organizational issues alike. Relying on the work of French philosopher Paul Ricoeur, Couldry conceives voice as a fundamentally narrative process. To voice is to narrate things about oneself and about one's unique perspective on and knowledge about the world. From this standpoint, "what matters is less the Sonic aspect of voice (deaf people's language of signing is just as much voice, in our sense, as spoken language); more important is voice's role as the means whereby people give an account of the world in which they act" (p. 91). However, Couldry insists, having a voice is not enough. It ought to matter as well, so voice has to be conceived as a value. "By voice as a value, I shall refer to the act of valuing, and choosing to value, those frameworks for organizing human life and resources that themselves value voice (as a process). Treating voice as a value means discriminating in favour of ways of organizing human life and resources that, through their choices, put the value of voice into practices" (p. 2). Couldry's work, although still relatively little used by organizational communication researchers, has the potential to enrich the thinking around issues of voice and their relationship to organizational processes. Two of the chapters in this book demonstrate this potential as they mobilize Couldry's work to reflect on the organizing of the Black Lives Matter movement (Chapter 5) and an intersectional consultative process about systemic racism (Chapter 8).

The Tensions between Multivocality and Univocality

Finally, one of the most common and enduring ideas with regard to voice in organizational communication is that multivocality is a normal condition of organizational life and that organizations are composed of heterogeneous

voices. From this general idea stems another one, namely that the existence of a monolithic organizational voice (the fact that an organization can
speak with one voice) is a communicative achievement that deserves to be
explained, not the normal state of affairs. These two related propositions
are most often associated with Bakhtin's philosophy of dialogism and his
related notions of polyphony, multivoicedness, and heteroglossia (Bakhtin,
1981, 1984, 1986).

According to Bakhtin, polyphony or multivoicedness is a basic condition
that characterizes any social phenomenon from words to subject to organizations and beyond. Although voice is at the core of his thinking, Bakhtin
does not explicitly define the notion. Bertau (2007) understands Bakhtin's
conception of voice in this way:

> In my reading of Bakhtin, a voice has the function of a carrier as it
> carries the speaking subject out of himself, decentering and orienting
> him toward the other(s), supporting and leading the contact. What a
> voice carries and expresses at the same time is that the utterance is as
> well "mine" as "other's" (Bakhtin, 1986, p. 89). A voice carries the
> individual expression of contact with the other which is always min-
> gled with some alien components. It supports the necessary multiplicity
> belonging to the living language in the world.
>
>   (p. 154)

Thus, voice is a vector of relationships and change. The speaking subject
cannot be conceived as a stable point of origin, in control and autonomous,
that can dictate these relationships. S/he is, as stated by Bertau, "decen-
tered" and oriented toward others, and as such, exists through and by his
or her relationships to the world. Robinson (2011) explains: "To exist is to
engage in dialogue, and dialogue must not come to an end. Dialogues do
not occur between fixed positions or subjects. People are also transformed
through dialogue, fusing with parts of the other's discourse" (para. 21).

Bakhtin is the most prevalent theoretical inspiration within organizational communication with regard to issues of multivocality or polyvocality. As Sullivan and McCarthy (2008) wrote, polyphony has become
a metaphor in its own right and it "has clearly caught the imagination
of organizational studies" (p. 525). This influence is evident in narrative
approaches to organizational communication, particularly studies that
take a critical stance (Belova, King, & Sliwa, 2008). Because Bakhtin's
perspective accounts for the tensions that arise from multivoicedness and
heteroglossia, his thinking is also congruent with a tension-centred perspective on organization. For instance, Aggerholm, Asmuß, and Thomsen
(2012) and Aggerholm and Thomsen (2015) have relied on the notions of
multivocality and polyvocality to conceptualize the ambiguous nature of
strategizing. Relying on a ventriloquial perspective, Cooren et al. (2013)
have shed light on how tensions emerge in interactions out of multivocality,

that is, out of the many voices that conflict with each other in the enactment of a situation.

Overall, the three themes just reviewed establish the significance of the voice metaphor for organizational communication studies. Our overview also draws attention to three different understandings of the idea of *speaking with one voice*. First, on the basis of Taylor and Cooren (1997), Taylor and Van Every (2011), and Cooren (2010, 2012, 2014), *speaking with one voice* through the act of *speaking for* is fundamentally organizational. It is a driving force of the organizing process by which organization emerges both as a situated performance and as a text that objectifies the multiple practices and the distributed collective knowledge that make up an organization. Second, from the point of view of critical scholars, such as Mumby and Stohl (1996), Dempsey (2007, 2017), and Couldry (2010), organization is as much a political phenomenon as it is a social and economic one. Speaking with one voice is a possibility, but it is neither a necessity for an organization to exist nor an end in and of itself. Rather, what deserves our scholarly attention are the conditions (symbolic, material, economic, etc.) that allow (or impede) the members of an organization to speak as one. Who can speak, who is silenced, how marginalized groups can (or cannot) speak for themselves, and how they can do so in their own words to relate their specific experiences and knowledge are all salient issues that need to be considered. Third, based on Bakhtin's perspective, multivocality is the normal state of affairs *and speaking with one voice* (a.k.a. univocality) should be regarded as an ephemeral achievement filled with tensions, one to be viewed with great skepticism. It is probably useful to view Bakhtin's conception of a fundamentally polyphonic world, where tensions and multivoicedness are desirable circumstances, in light of the political situation in Russia during his lifetime. From that standpoint, speaking with one voice takes on an eminently negative connotation, linked to propaganda, suppression of voices, and lack of freedom. Bakhtin famously wrote: "A single voice ends nothing and resolves nothing. Two voices is the minimum for life, the minimum for existence" (Bakhtin, 1984, p. 252).

Overview of the Book's Chapters

The remaining chapters of this book illustrate these different stances toward the idea of speaking with one voice quite eloquently. The contributors took up our call to investigate how organizations can speak with one voice, thus creating the conditions of unity necessary for their existence on the basis of the multiplicity of voices that compose them. In doing so, they mobilized many of the authors and addressed many of the issues we have reviewed so far.

Chapter 2, titled "Authority-in-Action: How Voices Are Negotiated through Idiomatic Formulations during Organizational Downsizing," examines how managers legitimize decisions to lay off employees at a large public organization in Denmark. Drawing from conversation analysis and the CCO perspective, Kryger, Aggerholm, and Asmuß analyze the role that idiomatic formulations (such as "one cannot keep up with everything") play in these legitimization efforts. Their analysis shows that the interactional efficacy of these formulations notably lies in their anonymity and generality, which make them difficult to oppose.

Chapter 3, titled "'I'm just saying': Multivocal Organizing in a Community Health Initiative," studies a non-profit organization whose purpose is to encourage women from underserved minorities in New York State to obtain reproductive health screenings. Drawing from the CCO perspective and Bakhtin's writings, Gorver Golden and Bencherki demonstrate that a key aspect of this organization's job involves combining a plurality of voices. As the authors show, the organization's members must be able to combine voices from the clinical world (e.g., by showing they understand how specific contraception devices work) with that of the community they serve (e.g., by using the language of the everyday life in the community). This chapter contributes to a growing body of research showing that multivocality is a key resource of organizing rather than an impediment to it.

Chapter 4, titled "Finding the Voice of a Protest: Negotiating Authority among the Multiplicity of Voices in a Pro-refugee Demonstration," examines the constitution of a grassroots movement in Helsinki to help asylum-seekers threatened with deportation. Drawing from the CCO perspective, Laaksonen, Bodström, and Haavisto analyze how the protesters (mainly Afghan and Iraqi refugees and Finnish activists) progressively developed a common voice by formulating demands and communicating about the protest online. Their analysis shows that while protesters were often torn between celebrating the diversity of the movement and maintaining consistency, certain concerns progressively prevailed over others by federating a large coalition of voices.

Chapter 5, titled "Amplifying Voices: Hip Hop as a Mode of Engagement for Community Organizing in the Context of the Black Lives Matter Movement," studies how hip-hop artists involved in the Black Lives Matter movement conceive of their role of artist-activist. Inspired by Couldry's writings, Decault analyzes the many facets (and voices) that these artists aim to combine through their art: analyst of situated experiences of power, teller of the civil rights movement legacy, developer of youth imagination, and disrupter of racist narratives among others. This analysis illuminates the specific ways hip-hop artists contribute to energizing and unifying the Black Lives Matter movement.

Chapter 6, titled "Taking a Relational Approach to Rhetoric and Discourse: (Re)Considering the Voices of Recycling and Sustainability," examines the rhetorics of various actors involved in a recycling initiative that took place during a concert at a US university. Drawing on the works of Burke (1969) and Hauser (1999), mcclellan and Davis analyze, in particular, the tensions and incongruities between the various rhetorics of recycling developed in connection to the planning, unfolding, and coverage of the event. This lens allows them to complicate the shared narrative of the initiative's success and illuminate how specific rhetorics of recycling are related to a larger shared discourse of sustainability.

Chapter 7, titled "Tensional Dynamics in Discussions of Social Responsibility: Voice Mobilization, Concern Negotiation, and Organizational Boundaries Co-creation," examines how members of a network of cooperatives negotiate common positions on various matters of social responsibility. Drawing from the CCO perspective and Cooren's ventriloquial perspective, Poroli analyzes how the network's members give authority to their respective positions by showing the various voices that speak through them. The author also shows how these struggles of authority contribute to the shaping of the organization's boundaries.

Chapter 8, titled "'Centering [Voices from] the Margins': Negotiating Intersectionality as a Consultative Framework," addresses the organizational challenges surrounding the implementation of an intersectional framework to organize an independent popular consultation on systemic racism in the province of Quebec, Canada. Although the consultation did not make it through the design process, it was the subject of many discussions and debates spread over two years and involving dozens of activists from various organizations (unions, student organizations, grassroots organizations, cultural and religious minority associations, feminist groups, etc.). Drawing from Couldry (2010), Zoghlami explains how the idea of "centering the margins" was put forward as a consultative approach and how it allowed the stakeholders to reframe their understanding of what it meant to consult, taking their attention away from questions like "how can we include the greatest number of racialized communities?" to focus instead on questions like "how can we maximize the possibilities of voice for the most marginalized and silenced racialized communities?" This chapter contributes to a growing body of research on what "having a voice" through public consultation may mean for minority groups.

Chapter 9, titled "Conclusion: Speaking with One Voice Is a Specific Form of Multivocality," provides an overview of the book's main contributions while advancing the argument that univocality is not the opposite of multivocality but rather a *specific re-ordering* of multivocality. Martine and Benoit-Barné discuss different aspects of this relationship using examples from each chapter.

As a whole, by focusing on communicational events, whether in the context of for-profit or non-profit organizations, political protests, or social movements, these chapters guide the reader through the diverse and concrete ways organizations of all kinds deal with the imperative to speak with one voice. In doing so, this book creates multiple bridges between different perspectives on voice and its significance for the study of organizing: between different fields of study (in particular, organizational communication, rhetoric, and political science); and between theory and empirical research aimed at investigating organizing beyond the boundaries of the formal organization. As the various chapters demonstrate, the tensions between multivocality and univocality are as much a part of the agreement-reaching process within a team of managers involved in strategic decision-making about downsizing as they are a part of the negotiations among political activists regarding their shared purposes; they are as much a part of the talks that surround the choice of a spokesperson able to speak for a political movement as they are a part of the efforts of a community health initiative to adapt its ways of conceiving of and talking about health issues to those it serves. By offering concrete illustrations of the way tensions are managed in corporate, non-profit, and political organizations alike, this book documents the dynamics between multivocality and univocality in the organizing of collectives of all kinds and origins.

References

Aggerholm, H. K., Asmuß, B., & Thomsen, C. (2012). The role of recontextualization in the multivocal, ambiguous process of strategizing. *Journal of Management Inquiry*, 21(4), 413–428. https://doi.org/10.1177/1056492611430852

Aggerholm, H. K., & Thomsen, C. (2015). Strategic communication: The role of polyphony in management team meetings. In D. R. Holtzhausen & A. Zerfass (Eds.), *The Routledge handbook of strategic communication* (pp. 172–186). New York, NY: Routledge.

Alvesson, M., & Karreman, D. (2000). Varieties of discourse: On the study of organizations through discourse analysis. *Human Relations*, 53(9), 1125–1149. https://doi.org/10.1177/0018726700539002

Ashcraft, K. L. (2001). Organized dissonance as hybrid form: Alternatives to bureaucracy from feminist organization. *Academy of Management Journal*, 44, 1301–1322.

Bakhtin, M. M. (1981). *The dialogic imagination: Four essays* (C. Emerson & M. Holquist, Trans.). Austin, TX: University of Texas Press

Bakhtin, M. M. (1984). *Problems of Dostoevsky's poetics* (C. Emerson, Trans.). Minneapolis, MN: University of Minnesota Press.

Bakhtin, M. M. (1986). *Speech genres and other late essays*. Austin, TX: University of Texas Press.

Bell, M. P., Özbilgin, M. F., Beauregard, T. A., & Sürgevil, O. (2011). Voice, silence, and diversity in 21st century organizations: Strategies for inclusion of gay, lesbian, bisexual, and transgender employees. *Human Resource Management*, 50(1), 131–146. https://doi.org/10.1002/hrm.20401

Belova, O., King, I., & Sliwa, M. (2008). Introduction: Polyphony and organization studies: Mikhail Bakhtin and beyond. *Organization Studies*, 29(4), 493–500. https://doi.org/10.1177/0170840608088696

Benoit-Barné, C., & Cooren, F. (2009). The accomplishment of authority through presentification: How authority is distributed among and negotiated by organizational members. *Management Communication Quarterly*, 23(1), 5–31. https://doi.org/10.1177/0893318909335414

Benson, J. (2000). Employee voice in union and non-union Australian workplaces. *British Journal of Industrial Relations, 38*, 453–459.

Bertau, M. C. (2007). On the notion of voice: An exploration from a psycholinguistic perspective with developmental implication. *International Journal for Dialogical Science, 2*(1), 133–161.

Bowden, D. (1995). The rise of a metaphor: "Voice" in composition pedagogy. *Rhetoric Review, 14*(1), 173–188.

Broadfoot, K. J., & Munshi, D. (2007). Diverse voices and alternative rationalities: Imagining forms of postcolonial organizational communication. *Management Communication Quarterly, 21*(2), 249–267. https://doi.org/10.1177/0893318907306037

Bryson, A. (2004). Managerial responsiveness to union and nonunion worker voice in Britain. *Industrial Relations, 43*, 213–241.

Burke, K. (1969). *A grammar of motives.* Berkeley, CA: University of California Press.

Christou, C. (2020, March 20). In the midst of COVID-19, "we're getting down to work." Médecins Sans Frontières. https://www.msf.org/msf-president-highlights-priorities-during-covid-19-response

Cloud, D. (2005). Fighting words: Labor and the limits of communication at Staley, 1993 to 1996. *Management Communication Quarterly, 18*, 509–542.

Cooren, F. (2010). *Action and agency in dialogue: Passion, incarnation and ventriloquism.* Amsterdam, the Netherlands: John Benjamins Publishing Company.

Cooren, F. (2012). Communication theory at the center: Ventriloquism and the communicative constitution of reality. *Journal of Communication, 62*(1), 1–20. https://doi.org/10.1111/j.1460-2466.2011.01622.x

Cooren, F. (2014). Pragmatism as ventriloquism: Creating a dialogue among seven traditions in the study of communication. *Language under Discussion, 2*(1), 1–26.

Cooren, F., Matte, F., Benoit-Barné, C., & Brummans, B. H. J. M. (2013). Communication as ventriloquism: A grounded-in-action approach to the study of organizational tensions. *Communication Monographs, 80*(3), 255–277. https://doi.org/10.1080/03637751.2013.788255

Cooren, F., & Sandler, S. (2014). Polyphony, ventriloquism, and constitution: In dialogue with Bakhtin. *Communication Theory, 24*(3), 225–244. https://doi.org/10.1111/comt.12041

Couldry, N. (2010). *Why voice matters: Culture and politics after neoliberalism.* London, UK: Sage. https://doi.org/10.4135/9781446269114

Dempsey, S. E. (2007). Negotiating accountability within international contexts: The role of bounded voice. *Communication Monographs, 74*(3), 311–332. https://doi.org/10.1080/03637750701543485

Dempsey, S. E. (2017). Voice. In C. Scott & L. K. Lewis (Eds.), *The international encyclopedia of organizational communication* (pp. 1–8). Hoboken, NJ: John Wiley & Sons. https://onlinelibrary.wiley.com/doi/abs/10.1002/9781118955567.wbieoc216

Derrida, J. (1988). *Limited Inc.* Evanston, IL: Northwestern University Press.

Felsenthal, E. (2019, December 23–30). Time 2019 Person of the Year: The choice. Time.com. https://time.com/person-of-the-year-2019-greta-thunberg-choice/

Fleming, S. (2019, September 23). Greta: The voice of climate activism who says 'listen to the scientists.' World Economic Forum. https://www.weforum.org/agenda/2019/09/greta-thunberg-climate-change-strikes/

Greimas, A. J. (1987). *On meaning: Selected writings in semiotic theory*. London, UK: Frances Pinter.

Grosjean, S., Mayère, A., & Bonneville, L. (2018). *Les utopies organisationnelles*. London, UK: ISTE Édition.

Hauser, G. A. (1999). *Vernacular voices: The rhetoric of publics and public spheres*. Columbia, SC: University of South Carolina Press.

Hill, J. (2020). *Greta Thunberg: The voice of the future* [Motion picture]. Films for Change.

Kunreuther, L. (2014). *Voicing subjects: Public intimacy and mediation in Kathmandu*. Berkeley, CA: University of California Press.

Latour, B. (1996). On interobjectivity. *Mind, Culture, and Activity, 3*(4), 228–245.

Latour, B. (2005). *Reassembling the social: An introduction to actor-network theory*. London, UK: Oxford University Press.

Lavelle, J., Gunnigle, P., & McDonnell, A. (2010). Patterning employee voice in multinational companies. *Human Relations, 63*(3), 395–418. https://doi.org/10.1177/0018726709348935

Lubs, Q. (2019, December 16). Greta Thunberg: The voice of a generation [Editorial]. *The Paw Print*. https://www.wrpawprint.com/opinions/2019/12/16/greta-thunberg-the-voice-of-a-generation/

Magnat, V. (2018). A traveling ethnography of voice in qualitative research. *Cultural Studies ↔ Critical Methodologies, 18*(6), 430–441. https://doi.org/10.1177/1532708617742407

Mumby, D., & Stohl, C. (1996). Disciplining organizational communication studies. *Management Communication Quarterly, 10*, 50–72.

Robichaud, D., & Benoit-Barne, C. (2010). L'épreuve de la conversation: Comment se négocie la mise en œuvre des normes dans l'écriture d'un texte organisationnel. *Études de communication, 34*, 41–60.

Robichaud, D., Giroux, H., & Taylor, J. R. (2004). The meta-conversation: The recursive property of language as the key to organizing. *Academy of Management Review, 29*, 617–634.

Robinson, A. (2011, July 29). Bakhtin: Dialogism, polyphony and heteroglossia. *Ceasefire*. https://ceasefiremagazine.co.uk/in-theory-bakhtin-1

Stohl, C., & Cheney, G. (2001). Participatory processes/paradoxical practices: Communication and the dilemmas of organizational democracy. *Management Communication Quarterly, 14*, 349–407.

Sullivan, P., & McCarthy, J. (2008). Managing the polyphonic sounds of organizational truths. *Organization Studies, 29*(4), 525–541. https://doi.org/10.1177/0170840608088702

Tait, A. (2019, June 6). Greta Thunberg: How one teenager became the voice of the planet. *Wired*. https://www.wired.co.uk/article/greta-thunberg-climate-crisis

Taylor, J. R., & Cooren, F. (1997). What makes communication organizational? How the many voices of a collectivity become the one voice of the organization. *Journal of Pragmatics, 27*(4), 409–438.

Taylor, J. R., & Robichaud, D. (2004). Finding the organization in the communication: Discourse as action and sensemaking. *Organization, 11*(3), 395–413. https://doi.org/10.1177/1350508404041999

Taylor, J. R., & Van Every, E. J. (2000). *The emergent organization: Communication as its site and surface*. Mahwah, NJ: Lawrence Erlbaum.

Taylor, J. R., & Van Every, E. J. (2011). *The situated organization: Studies in the pragmatics of communication research*. New York, NY: Routledge.

Tracy, S. J., & Rivera, K. D. (2010). Endorsing equity and applauding stay-at-home moms: How male voices on work-life reveal aversive sexism and flickers of transformation. *Management Communication Quarterly*, 24(1), 3–43. https://doi.org/10.1177/0893318909352248

Voice. (2020). OED Online. Oxford, UK: Oxford University Press. https://www.oed.com/view/Entry/224334?rskey=0xFlMN&result=1

Weidman, A. (2014). Anthropology and voice. *Annual Review of Anthropology*, 43, 37–51.

2 Authority-in-Action

How Voices are Negotiated through Idiomatic Formulations during Organizational Downsizing

Helle Kryger Aggerholm and Birte Asmuß

Introduction

Over the years, there has been a movement towards increased restructuring of organizations. One dominant strategic practice in relation to this increased focus on restructuring is downsizing, which recurrently presents a managerial as well as a communicative challenge in terms of legitimizing strategic decisions among employees and other stakeholders (Erkama & Vaara, 2010; Hirsch & DeSoucey, 2006; Johnson et al., 2007). Traditionally, downsizing has narrowly been formulated as "an intentional reduction in the number of people in an organization [...] accomplished via a set of managerial actions" (Freeman, 1999, p. 1507). This view is based on an understanding that it is the management's responsibility to ensure rational planning and allocation of resources. Within this mechanistic and financially grounded conceptualization, downsizing is seen as a tool available to management with the purpose of making the organization more efficient (Aggerholm, 2014).

However, from a postmodern organizational perspective, which defines organizations as social constructs created through discursive interactions, downsizing can also be defined as "the planning, implementation and management of dialogical communication processes and activities in relation to various actors and stakeholders with the aim of deliberately reducing the number of employees" (Aggerholm, 2014, p. 475). Such a postmodern conceptualization focuses on processual and communicative elements of authority, power, and strategic thinking, hence inevitably making interactions and communication relevant during the strategically sensitive situation of a downsizing process. Despite the fact that downsizing often is a key element in strategic decision-making, how and by what means downsizing decisions actually are taken remains largely unstudied.

Therefore, the current chapter seeks to better understand how managers—during these polyphonic communication processes where managerial authority, power, and differing interests are at stake—balance between multivocality and univocality in the pursuit to reach a strategic decision about who to lay off. In doing so, we build upon recent calls from strategy

DOI: 10.4324/9780429297830-2

research to investigate in greater detail the processual aspects of strategic actions in real life (Langley, 2007).

In the context of downsizing, communication comes to play a pivotal role in the organizing practices and in the creation of univocality in a multivocal situation where organizational members naturally have different and often opposing views. In previous studies (Aggerholm & Thomsen, 2015), we have studied how polyphony, defined as a "multiplicity of independent and unmerged voices ..." (Bakhtin, 1984, p. 208) occurs in management team meetings, and what the implications are for the subsequent strategic communication at an organizational level. In this chapter, we want to study the actions taken for creating a position of authority that, in turn, allows for univocality and multivocality in the pursuit of making strategic decisions. In specific, we will analyze three instances where a group of top managers in a large public organization articulate multiple and at times opposing voices in relation to a downsizing decision. We will explore how the meeting participants acquire a position of authority by use of idiomatic formulations that allow them to direct or re-direct the ongoing discussion in a preferred way. Hence, from a multivocal perspective and by means of conversation analysis, the chapter explores the discursive micro-level practices involved in creating and managing authority.

In a bigger picture, we are concerned with the relationship between institutionalized strategic decision-making and in-situ discursive meeting practices. The study contributes to an empirically grounded understanding of how discursive micro-level practices in the form of idiomatic formulations make way for the acquisition of authority by certain participants, leading to consensus and eventually decision-making. Thus, we propose that the use of idiomatic formulations in the management meeting serves as an interactional resource available to the participants in the process of accomplishing a position of authority in a strategically sensitive and potentially stressful situation of deciding who to lay off.

The structure of this chapter is as follows: first we describe our theoretical framework focusing on authority, multivocality, and idiomatic formulations. After having specified the research purpose, we account for our research design. This section is followed by the analysis. We end the chapter by summarizing and discussing our analytical findings in relation to multivocality and univocality and the role of idiomatic formulations, and the implications for our theoretical and empirical understanding of authority and its role for strategic decision-making about downsizing.

Authority in Action

Modern sociologists (Sennett, 1980; Weber, 1968) and management scholars (Benoit-Barné & Cooren, 2009; Boström, 2006; Casey, 2004) have pointed to authority as a fundamental feature in order to create univocality and thus make organizational members act in agreement. Authority is often linked to legitimacy, in that it is a form of power that creates "a sense of integration, predictability, and order" (Benoit-Barné & Cooren, 2009, p. 6). Moreover, it is perceived to be in agreement with already established roles, rules, and practices, and therefore, authority "is an act of influence perceived to be "right" because it is in accordance with existing and accepted organizational structures" (Benoit-Barné & Cooren, 2009, p. 6). Benoit-Barné and Cooren argue that authority has traditionally been seen as something pertaining to a hierarchical structure (i.e., status), a trait (i.e. charisma) or the obedient consent of others (Kahn & Kram, 1994). By introducing the concept of authority, we acknowledge that aspects such as power, position, status, and leadership play a role in organizational interactions, however, it is important to underline that these qualities do not necessarily originate with a person *in authority*, i.e., the CEO, but can also be *acquired* during an interaction (Benoit-Barné & Cooren, 2009). Authority is thus a key dimension of an agent's capacity to influence the unfolding of an event and to make a difference (Benoit-Barné & Cooren, 2009; Giddens, 1984). In keeping with the perspective presented by Benoit-Barné and Cooren (2009), we propose to rely on the notion of authority to explain how a certain agent (the CEO) is making a difference in-situ by creating univocality through his/her use of idiomatic formulations. Thus, the current chapter applies a processual lense towards authority (Langley, 2007) and it relies on an interactional understanding of authority (Benoit-Barné & Cooren, 2009) to investigate how it emerges processually as a consequence of micro-level discursive resources in form of idiomatic formulations.

Polyphony, Multivocality, and Voice

Bakhtin introduced the polyphonic notion when he defined the term as the "multiplicity of independent and unmerged voices and consciousnesses ... each with equal right and its own world" (Bakhtin, 1984, p. 208). With this definition, he unveiled the complexity of human interactions, and hence, paved the way for an alternative understanding of communication away from the simplistic idea of organizational communication as message exchange between sender and receiver (Shannon & Weaver, 1949) to an understanding of communication as a much more complex, multivocal process constituted and sustained by the fact that speakers are continuously switching into different voices of their own (Bakhtin, 1981; Goffman, 1981; Klewitz & Couper-Kuhlen, 1999; Kotthoff, 1998). The multivocal setting can be seen as a metaphor for the situated contexts in which the various organizational actors act, communicate, and encompass both sender and receiver communication, in that the actors constantly assume both roles and enter into relations with one another as they communicate to, with, against, about, and past each other. In regards to strategic communication, there is a predominant understanding of strategic communication as a one-way directed event seeing the management team members as one homogenous, passive stakeholder group. This traditional understanding disregards the fact that all members of a management team communicate from within their individual, situated context and thus are part of a multiplicity of different and at times opposing voices.

According to Belova et al. (2008), the concept of multivocality is useful to analyze organizations as discursive spaces shaped by a multiplicity of dominant as well as peripheral voices "which together make up a contested and ever-changing arena of human action" (2008, p. 495). Thus, in their work, Belova et al. (2008) advocate the application of a polyphonic lens in organization studies in order to understand strategic practice as a multi-centred, non-linear, and intersubjective discursive activity. As such, the concept of polyphony assists us in viewing organizations as spaces with no universally agreed-upon central voice (Gergen & Whitney, 1996). Far from being a sum of free-will and free-flowing points of view, organizations are constituted by complex webs of activities between groups and individuals whose understandings intersect, clash, and interfere with each other (Cooren et al., 2013). In the multivocal view of organizations, there is no overarching meaning of what is going on, but only partial, non-linear, elusive, and constantly changing understandings that change depending on one's relation to others. Hence, Carter, Clegg, Hogan, and Kornberger (2003) claim the omnipresence of polyphony in organizations even if it is often silenced by dominant voices, stating, "in most organizations, there is a persistent plurality of different linguistic constructions that shape organizational reality" (2003, p. 295) Along these lines, Tretheway and Ashcraft (2004) argue for a "tension-centered" view of organizations that builds on the premise that "organizations are conflicted sites of human activity"(2004, p. 82).

As suggested by Kornberger et al. (2006), organizational polyphony is constituted by the various discourses that embody and reinforce differences between disparate groups and members of an organization. Consequently, an important managerial task becomes the translation of these heterogeneous discourses by conveying the message with its context and underlying meanings without having to unify or erase differences that enrich organizational life. These multiple points of view that at times may lead to some degree of tension are often studied by means of tropes. Oswick, Putnam, and Keenoy. (2004) identify four master tropes: metaphor, metonymy, synecdoche, and irony. The first three are seen as "resonance tropes" as they use resemblance through contrast, substitution, representation, and reduction, whereas irony is characterized as a "dissonance trope" because of its use of ambiguities and contradictions (Cooren et al., 2013; Oswick et al., 2004).

In this chapter, we want to build on the existing literature on tropes, in specific idiomatic formulations. Instead of looking at them as static markers of either resonance or dissonance, we seek to pursue their role as an interactional resource available to the members in their individual attempts to acquire authority. The acquisition of authority by one member can be a powerful discursive resource, which helps the group to move from disagreement in the form of multivocal positionings towards agreement and univocality. By doing so, we link to research on the concept of "voice" (Taylor & Cooren, 1997) as we try to empirically show how multiple voices can develop into one organizational voice. In specific, we shed light on how the discursive micro-practices—i.e., tropes, enable participants to acquire a position of authority, and we will show how authority is locally accomplished by means of an idiomatic formulation that due to its generality is difficult to challenge and, therefore, invites for affiliation in the here and now of the interaction by the other participants. Grounded in our ethnographic data, we argue that idiomatic formulations can serve as a strategic resource for the interlocutors to create a unified voice and consensus in an environment of potential disagreement due to multiple opposing voices.

The Power of Idioms

Idiomatic formulations have been defined as formulaic constructions of a word or phrase, sometimes even a sentence that have a figurative meaning (Drew & Holt, 1988, p. 398). Sacks (1992) talks about "idiom-like things" and points out that due to their generality, they are difficult to contradict. Moreover, he highlights the fact that contradicting an idiomatic formulation might be consequential for the flow of the ongoing talk, as this might be interrupted in case of disagreement (p. 25).

In line with the prior, several studies have indicated that idiomatic formulations are often successful in creating agreement and affiliation (i.e., Drew & Holt, 1988; 1995). In terms of moving from multiple voices to one unified voice, idiomatic formulations are very effective, as they are hard to challenge both because their generality makes them independent of the specific details of any particular person or situation (in this case, the downsizing selection process) and because they invoke and constitute the taken-for-granted knowledge shared by all competent members of the organizational setting. Previous conversation-analytic work by Drew & Holt (1988) or Kitzinger (2000), for instance, on idioms have shown how they are powerful rhetorical forms of talk that are hard for participants to question, challenge, or contradict precisely because of their characteristic vagueness and their encapsulation of social norms. Moreover, idiomatic formulations have the capacity to sum up the gist of the prior talk in a way that enhances legitimacy of the speaker producing the idiomatic formulation (Drew & Holt, 1988, p. 395). The speaker's ability to sum up the talk by means of the idiomatic formulation makes her able to *acquire* authority (Benoit-Barné & Cooren, 2009), and this–perhaps newly–gained authoritarian capacity makes her able to influence the unfolding of the interaction and make a difference in terms of creating univocality and agreement in relation to a potentially problematic decision-making process, i.e., downsizing.

Research Design and Methodology

The data for the current chapter was collected in a public, knowledge-based organization during an extensive one-year period of ethnographic data collection, for the purpose of following a strategy process from development to implementation with a focus on the management communication taking place in the different phases of the strategy process.

The dataset consists of more than 45 hours of videotaped meeting data, formal and informal interviews with the management team, participant observations, organizational fieldwork, and a large number of documents (e.g., meeting minutes, PowerPoint slides, emails, official reports, etc.). While conducting this ethnographic fieldwork, the organization was forced to implement serious budget cuts, which consequently resulted in the initiation of a downsizing process. As we were already allowed access to the organization and the management meetings, we were also granted access to videotaping the meetings related to the downsizing process, which are the ones in focus in the present study. For the current study, we focus on a five-hour meeting in which the upper management group is in the initial phase of discussing the specific employee-related issues of downsizing. Before starting the "naming" of potentially redundant employees, the CEO introduces what needs to be done and how they should go about doing it, thus outlining the procedural frame for the meeting. In this meeting, we have identified 41 instances of idiomatic formulations that are directly related to the downsizing decision.

The method applied to study the meeting is a conversation analytic approach (Sacks, Schegloff, & Jefferson, 1974; Sidnell, 2010). This method has been chosen as it enables us to focus on discursive micro-level aspects of strategic decision-making processes (Langley, 2007) by investigating the interactional patterns that serve as resources for the actions in question. That way, we are able to make visible the interactional micro-processes involved in potentially moving from a plurivocal situation in terms of disagreement to a univocal situation in terms of agreement. As these interactional micro-processes do not consist of verbal actions only, we have included embodied and material resources in the transcripts in cases where they were deemed relevant for the accomplishment of authority and subsequently either uni- or multivocality. All information in the data that could lead to the identification of the involved company or individuals has been anonymized in accordance with international ethical procedures (Statement of Ethical Practice from the British Sociological Association).

Data Analysis

Looking through our data it became apparent that the meeting participants made use of idiomatic expressions during open or latent disagreements concerning the downsizing decision. Here, we found expressions like "he does not really pull his own weight," "who is going to get their marching orders," "now there are no holds barred," "a hill you can't climb," and "a piece to move with."

Our analysis presented in this chapter is based on a collection of 41 instances of idiomatic formulations related to the act of downsizing. All of these formulations were used in the sequential context of open or latent disagreements concerning the downsizing decision about which employee should be layed off. We found this interesting and decided to look closer at the interactional patterns in these meeting sequences. We are going to focus on three examples of the phenomenon in question in this chapter, to shed light on the discursive micro-practices that enable participants to acquire a position of authority. Authority here is locally accomplished by means of an idiomatic formulation that due to its generality is difficult to challenge and therefore invites for affiliation in the here and now of the interaction by the other participants. Thus, the idiomatic formulation creates a kind of common baseline that authorizes its producer to set the scene and enables her to pursue her individual objective and allows her to reinforce either multi- or univocality in the process of strategic decision making.

We indicate the start and end of embodied and material actions and provide a two line glossing, where the first line is the original Danish transcript and the second line consists of an intelligible English translation in italics. The idiomatic formulations in focus are marked in bold. Further information about the transcription conventions is provided at the end of the chapter.

In the data, there were eight meeting participants, who were seated in the following way (see Figure 2.1):

All the meeting participants are part of the upper management team and are gathered to discuss how to react to the current need for downsizing. Participants A, B, C, E, F, and H are heads of department, D, who is the CEO, is formally in charge of the meeting, and G is the HR-manager of the organization, and thus closely involved in and responsible for the strategic process of downsizing. We can, thus, see that the meeting participants have different formal positions of authority. However, in our analysis, we will show how a position of authority can be acquired not only due to pre-assigned formal positions like CEO and HR-manager but also by means of specific micro-level discursive practices in form of idiomatic formulations.

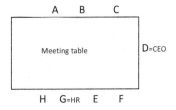

Figure 2.1 The meeting setting.

Example 1: No Holds Barred

Below, you can see a first example of the phenomenon; we are interested in, namely how meeting participants can locally acquire a position of authority by relying on idiomatic formulations. We will show how this process unfolds by focusing on when and how one meeting participant in times of multiple divergent voices makes use of an idiomatic expression and how this consequently puts her/him in a position of authority by steering the discussion into a position of univocality.

In the below example, the upper management group is in the initial phase of discussing the specific employee-related issues of downsizing. Before starting the identification of who should be layed off, the CEO makes a suggestion for how to go about the meeting. Despite several attempts, this suggestion does not get support from the other meeting participants. The CEO, D, then uses an idiomatic formulation that creates the opportunity for group affiliation at a point in his presentation where signs of affiliation by the other meeting participants are lacking. That way, he is able to steer the occurrence of multiple, opposing voices towards one univocal voice of affiliation.

Excerpt (1)

```
1      D:    jeg tror vi kom- (.) nødt til- vi kommer til o' o'
             I believe we come  have to   we will come to

2            (0.5)

3      D:    springe lidt rundt;
             jump a bit around

4            (0.4)

5      D:    tror jeg. og så må vi samle sammen til sidst.
             I think. and then we have to collect everything together
             in the end.

6            (0.5)

7      D:    [jeg er også nødt til at sige
             I also have to say
             [((D looks around at participants))
             [((A, B, C, E, F look down))
             [((H looks at D))

8      D:    [.hh vi kommer til o' [have nogle
             we will come to have some
             [((D looks around at participants))
             [((A, B, C, E, F look down))
                                   [((A, B, H look at D))

9      D:    [meninger om hinandenss: (.).hh medarbejdere;
             opinions about each others' employees
             [((D looks around at participants))
             [((C, E, F look down))   [((C, E, F, G look down))
             [((A, B, G, H look at D))
```

```
10    D:   [og >sån noget<; (.) som kan v- (.) [jah
           and the like that can w- yes
           [((D looks around at participants))  [((D looks down))
           [((C, E, F look down ))              [((C, E, F, G look
           down))
           [((A, B, G, H look at D))

11         (.)

12    D:   [men [sån >det det tror jeg jeg synes< nu må
           but then this this I believe I think now
                [((A, B, C, E, F, G look down))
           [((D looks down))
           [((H looks at D))
13    D:   [vi [have (.). h fisken på disken som det
           there are no holds barred so to
                [((D looks around))
           [((H looks at D))
           [((A, B, C, E, F, G look down))

14    D:   [hedder.. tshh (.) æh
           say.
           [((D looks around))
           [((H looks at D))
           [((A, B, C, E, F, G look down))
15    H:   jo [altså jeg mener vi er nødt [ti' det i den her
           right well I think we have to this in this
16    D:        [ja                            [ja
                yes                            yes

17    H:   pro[cess hvis [der er nogle øh (.)
           process if there are any uh
18    F:      [(god idé)
              (good idea)
19    D:                 [ja
                         yes

20    H:   hvis der er nogle (.) s:vage punkter rundt
           if there are any (.) weak points around
21    H:   omkring [så vi nødt til at Thage dem med=
           then we have to take them out
22    D:          [ja
                  yes

23    H:=[om man så må sige; (fordi) vi kan ikke (.) forsvare
           so to say; we can not defend
24    D:=[ja
           yes

25    H:   overfor medarbejderne, fordi hvis vi
           towards the employees, because if we

26    H:   ved der er nogle svage punkter så ved
           know there are some weak points then they

27    H:   de det altså endnu mere; det er dem
           know it even more; it is them
```

```
28   H:   der er tættest på.
          who is closest by.

29   E:   °mm°,
          mm
```

In line 1, the CEO, D launches a new topic, which is how to go about the meeting. He does so by proposing a procedure ("jump a bit around," line 3). After a 0.4 second gap (line 4) where the other meeting participants could mark their support for the proposal, no one comes in and shows her/his support. After a turn expansion (line 5) and another gap (line 6), the CEO continues to elaborate on his proposal (lines 7–10). Despite him trying to establish gaze contact with the meeting participants, less than half of the group responds his eye gaze and none of the co-present meeting participants takes the turn to mark some kind of support. In this environment of lack of agreement and, thus, latent divergent positions, the CEO now reframes his proposal by use of an idiomatic expression, which sums up the gist his prior suggestion (lines 10–14).

In lines 10–12, the CEO, D, marks a discontinuation with the prior turn by starting with the construction "yes (.) but" (Steensig & Asmuß, 2005) followed by a number of restarts. He then reformulates his proposal about the meeting going to be different because they will have to cross each other's areas of responsibility. He does so by means of an idiomatic expression: "there are no holds barred" (line 13). The literal translation in the Danish original means "to put a fish on the counter," which indicates that the relevant thing should not be hidden away, but needs to be put up front. In this way, the CEO, D, reformulates his prior proposal by means of this idiomatic formulation, which sums up the gist of what he suggested before. While D does so, he starts to gaze up from the table towards the meeting participants (line 13), thus inviting the other participants to respond. While he in his prior attempts to receive a response to his suggestion was not successful, he now receives a number of supportive responses. H takes the lead in marking his agreement with D's suggestion by first using a marker of affiliation ("right," line 15), and then framing the following as his personal opinion. Some of the other meeting participants now also join into marking support (F in line 18, E in line 19).

Thus, the use of the idiomatic formulation recruits affiliative responses from the co-present participants, who also previously had the opportunity to mark affiliation, but who had not done so. The use of the idiom enables D to finally recruit univocal responses at a place in the interaction, where these were not forthcoming, and he succeeds in ensuring support for his prior suggestion. In that way, he manages to acquire an in-situ position of authority and power to direct the ongoing interaction by means of an idiom as a micro-level discursive resource.

The first excerpt provided evidence for the fact that idiomatic formulations are consequential for the ongoing interaction. We could also see that they are seldomly challenged due to the generality of the idiom (Drew & Holt, 1988, 1995). It empowers the user of the idiomatic formulation to recalibrate the ongoing interaction.

We have now seen that the indisputable nature of the idiomatic formulation helps the CEO to accomplish a base for affiliation which consequently enables him to recruit a supportive response at a place in the interaction, where no support has been voiced previously. The generic nature of the idiom seems here to enable the respondent to directly and supportedly progress the discussion without first having to clarify or account for the actual meaning of the prior. That way, the idiom helps to progress the interaction at point of time, where progression was at risk due to the lack of support from the other co-participants. Hence, an idiomatic formulation can be seen as a powerful micro-level discursive resource that allows the speaker to acquire a position of authority in terms of being able to steer the interaction into a preferred and prior non-accomplished direction.

Example 2: To Keep Pace

In the second excerpt, we are going to show another example of how the use of an idiomatic formulation can assist the producer of the idiom in influencing the unfolding of an interaction, thus contributing to establishing his or her authority.

In contrast to the prior excerpt, the user of the idiomatic formulation here does not hold a formal position of authority; instead she acquires a form of authority *in-situ* through the use of an idiom, which enables her to navigate opposing voices into one single voice. In keeping with our theoretical framework, this indicates that authority is accomplished in and through action just as well as it is shaped through pre-established categories, and that the study of specific discursive micro-level practices helps understand the underlying dynamics of these processes.

In this excerpt, meeting participant A is raising her concern about budget issues. She starts out questioning whether there are enough resources in order to deal with all the necessary tasks.

Excerpt (2)

1	A:	.h og spørgsmål er oss' jamen: HAr vi råd til det
		and the question is also, well can we afford this
2	A:	i en periode at der ligger så mange (0.6) ressourcer
		for a certain period of time that there are so many resources
3	A:	derude til at løfte de her opgaver.
		out there to cope with all these tasks
4		(1.4)

5   A: ø:hm.
           uhm

6   (0.2)

7   A: Og de:t jo en besl<u>u</u>tning o' s- s<u>i</u>ge (.) NhEj
           And it is a decision to say no

8   A: det er der <u>i</u>kke.
           there is not.

9   (0.2)

10   A: Eller j<u>a</u> det <u>e</u>r det.=Men så >er der bare <u>a</u>ndre ting
           Or yes there is. But then there are simply other things

11   A: vi <u>I</u>kke< kan l<u>a</u>ve.
           we cannot do.

12   (3.5)

13   E: .H Men (.) du t<u>a</u>ler så for o' o' skære n<u>e</u>d (.) på
           konfer<u>e</u>ncer
                   But you argue for cutting down on conferences

14   E: o':*.* m<u>ø</u>der.
           and meetings.

15   (0.4)

16   E: j- eller t<u>a</u>ler du f<u>or</u> o' centralis<u>e</u>re?
           y- or do you argue to centralize?

17   (0.2)

18   E: *a::*dministrat<u>I</u>on[en?
           the administration?

19   A: [Det ka' være <u>A</u>lt.
                                  It could be everything.

20   (0.2)

21   A: Jeg t<u>a</u>ler bare på, vi [sk<u>a</u>l jo have fundet de her
           ress<u>o</u>urcer,=
                                  I just talk about, we need to find these ressources,

22   E: [j<u>a</u>,
                                    yes,

23   A: =ikk?=Vi ka' jo ikk', [vi ka' <u>i</u>kke blive v<u>e</u>d med o' k<u>ø</u>re=
           right? We cannot, we cannot continue to drive
           We cannot, we cannot continue to keep pace

24   E: [J<u>o</u> jo.
                                  Yes yes.

25   A: i det [s<u>a</u>mme gear. med [<u>A</u>lt.
           in the same gear. with everything.
           with everything.

26   E?:   [hm.   [hm.
                          hm   **hm**

27   (1.8)

28   D: N<u>e</u>[j ( )
           No

```
29   F:   [Det vil jo ku' mærkes at vi:*[:* reduce[rer dem.
          It should be noticeable that we reduce those.
30   E:                                  [ja.       [hr hrm
                                          yes.       hr hrm

31        (0.2)

32   F:   altså er [det ikk', (.) er det ikk' [det?
          actually is this not, is this not true?
33   D:            [Jah ja.                   [ja.
                   Yes yes                     yes.

34        (0.8)
35   D:   .H[h
          Hh
36   G:   [Ja[(jeg håber) da at det kan mærkes.
          Yes (I hope) really that it is noticeable.
```

In lines 1–3, A raises her concern about the match between resources on the one hand and tasks to be dealt with on the other. Despite a significant gap in line 4, none of the co-participants take over, which can be seen as a first indication of upcoming interactional problems or disagreements (Pomerantz & Fehr, 1997), thus potentially divergent positions toward the issue raised by A.

In lines 5–8, A continues to express her concern. She marks her turn as a direct continuation of the prior by use of the conjunction "and" at the beginning of the turn (line 7), which can be seen as a way to minimize the delicacy of not having received a response to her prior turn. She elaborates by pointing out that even though there is an agreement that there are enough resources to cope with the tasks, there will be other things that cannot be dealt with (lines 10–11). This turn by A is again followed by a significant gap (3.5 seconds), where none of the co-participants marks any sign to take over. That way, no support for her concern is provided by the other participants, and thus we can see a plurivocal situation represented by A on the one hand and the remaining participants on the other. This lack of support continues in the following lines, where E after the 3.5 seconds long pause (line 12), takes over in lines 13–18 with a request for clarification, which A in response treats as irrelevant (line 19). We can now see that E and A are openly not aligned in terms of what to talk about and how to deal with the problem of saving costs.

At this point, where there is a clear emergence of opposing positions, A takes over and produces an idiomatic formulation, which topicalizes an effort to reduce costs ("cannot keep pace with everything") (lines 21–25). She starts by mitigating what she has said before ("I just talk about," line 21), and then she recycles her point ("to find these resources," line 21). She ends this turn construction unit by means of a tag question ("right," line 23), which invites for agreement from the other participants. E marks minimal agreement ("yes yes," line 24) in overlap, while A has started to produce an idiomatic formulation ("we cannot continue to keep pace with everything," lines 23–25). Literally, this formulation means "to continue to drive in the same gear," and thus it has a metaphorical quality. As in the excerpt before, we see the production of an idiomatic formulation after several unsuccessful attempts to create agreement. At the same time, we also see that the generic nature of the idiomatic expression makes it difficult to counter or challenge the argument that it is part of without risking to set the interaction on hold. Consequently, the use of the idiomatic formulation empowers A to steer the conversation in a preferred way, thus reinforcing her authority.

In line with the previous excerpt, several of the co-participants now take over and mark their agreement. D produces a token agreement ("no," line 28), and the other co-participants join in and mark agreement. In line 29, F produces a revised version of the idiomatic formulation pointing out that a reduction of resources would be noticeable in terms of the tasks that can be dealt with. In overlap with F and in support with A, E produces minimal acknowledgement tokens in line 30. After a 0.8 seconds long pause in line 34, F, D, and G produce more supportive turns for A's overall statement.

As such, despite of participant A being a head of department with no formal authority in this group setting, she succeeds in locally accomplishing a position of authority by relying on an idiomatic expression that allows her to pursue her goal of establishing affiliation with her prior suggestion. This position of authority allows her to create a univocal, supportive environment in a sequential context, where this support was not provided earlier.

Example 3: To Get the Marching Orders

In the final excerpt, we are going to show an example of an idiomatic formulation that enables a head of department to locally set a baseline for joint understanding. In contrast to the prior excerpts, where the use of an idiom sustained the creation of an univocal environment of agreement and support for the proposed suggestion, in the following example the reliance on an idiom creates a plurivocal environment that allows for an ongoing discussion of divergent positions.

In excerpt (3), the head of department, H, is summing up his presentation of employees in his department who according to him could be candidates to be layed-off as part of the downsizing process.

Excerpt (3)

```
1     H:    Ja. Men jeg tror, [er vi ikke >sådan
            Yes. But I think, have we not like
2     D:                      [ja,
                              yes

3     H:    nået ordentligt igennem?<=
            come properly through everything?
```

```
4    H:    =alt[så, I- I har=
           right, you (PL) have
5    D:         [Jo.
                Yes.

6    H:    =[forhåbentligt I har <[forstået=
           hopefully you (PL) have understood
7    A:                          [Jo::.
                                 Yes.
8    F:                          [Jo.
                                 Yes.

9    H:    =princippet,> ikk' og=æ:
           the principles, right and uh

10   H:    og [de:r altså nogen, der [kan spares.=
           and there are some, that can get sacked.
11   F?:       [ja.
               yes.
12?:                               [Hhhh
                                   Hhhh

13   H:    [=men de:t j- nogen=æ:
           but these are some uh
           [((E moves back in chair and looks at H))
14   D:    [(*i virk*[eligheden,)
           in reality
15   G:    [.hja
           yes.

16   E:                    [((points with 1. hand in the air))

17   E:    Æ- jam- hvis [vi lige, [nu:*:*
           Uh yes but if we right now
18   D:                  [Ja,
                         yes,
19   H:                            [(( ))=

20   E:    = altså je- jeg=æhm:: (.) alts*å* (.) [Peter (.)
           right I I uhm right Peter
                                 [((E moves forw.
                                   and turns head 1. to H))

21   E:    Møller Christensen,
           Møller Christensen

22   H:    ja,=
           yes,

23   E:    =.HHh Ø::hm,
           HHh Uhm,

24         (1.2)

25   E:    Hh er jeg faktisk ikke helt enig i skal
           do I actually not quite agree shall
           I do actually not agree that he should
```

26   E: ud af kl<u>a</u>ppen.
           out of the hatch
           get his marching orders.

27   H: N<u>e</u>j. Men det sa- s<u>a</u>gde jeg os[se.
           No. But this I also said.

28   E?:   [HRmm=
                                            HRmm

29   E?:   H[rm   [hrm
            Hrm hrm

30   B: [J<u>a</u>. ((smile))
           Yes.

31   H: [der v- der var vi <u>i</u>kke helt <u>e</u>nig i.
                           this we- this we did not fully agree upon.

32   E: Nh<u>e</u>jhha[ha. N<u>e</u>j.=æhm (.) men <u>a</u>ltså:: j<u>a.</u>
           Nho ha ha. No uhm but right yes.

33   H: [heh<u>a</u>
                Heha

34   E: de mel- m<u>e</u>lder jo <u>o</u>gså at han måske <u>u</u>dnytter syst<u>e</u>met
           they announce also that he perhaps exploits the system

35   E: l<u>i</u>dt [en-
           a bit

In lines 1–3, H sums up his presentation about who in his department could be laid off by posing a polar question to the rest of the meeting participants. There is no uptake from the other meeting participants, and H continues to address the whole group directly in line 4 ("you" (PL)), which can be seen as a more targeted attempt to generate a response. In response, several of the participants (D, A, F) display verbal agreement (lines 5, 7, 8) in the form of minimal acknowledgement tokens. Nevertheless, the agreement is still only a partial one, as neither B, C, nor E has verbally or by means of embodied moves indicated their agreement or disagreement with H's position. As a consequence of this partial agreement, H continues his summing up of his proposal with tags that appeal to joint understanding (line 9 "right"), still without getting further supportive responses.

At this point, participant E starts making embodied moves that indicate she is not going to take part in smooth agreement, but rather that her upcoming turn might be a less supportive one. E, who has not yet responded to H's question yet, moves backwards in her chair which opens up the opportunity for her to establish eye contact with H (line 13). Shortly after, she raises her left hand forward in order to mark that she is ready to take a turn (line 16). E takes over, starts her turn with hesitation markers ("uh," line 17) and restarts (lines 17, 20), which are indicative of a dispreferred, in this case non-supportive move. And this is precisely what happens: E opposes that a specific person presented by H as being in the group of people who could be laid off should actually be laid off.

She does so by first topicalizing the person in question by mentioning his full name "Peter Møller Christensen." While she produces the name, she moves her body forward on the table and establishes eye gaze with H. She continues a dispreferred turn design with hesitation markers ("uhm," line 23) and a pause (line 24), while still holding the turn. She then completes her turn by making use of an idiomatic expression ("get his marching orders," line 26). The literal translation of the Danish original is "to get out of the hatch," which is used to explicate in an informal way that someone is forced to leave a place or position by means of pressure (Den Danske Ordbog).

In line with excerpts (1) and (2), the generality of the claim made by the idiom makes it difficult to challenge the idiomatic formulation as such, and it locally establishes an environment of joint understanding within the management team about the nature of the delicate task of laying off employees. However, this enables E to redirect the discussion, which puts her in a position of authority that is locally and discursively accomplished. Instead of now pursuing a univocal position as in the prior excerpts, the redirection of the discussion helps her to reinforce multivocality, as it enables her to redirect the interaction and to question whether the discussion about the member of H's department who is potentially to be laid off should actually be closed.

In response to the idiomatic expression, H steps in and marks agreement with E's prior turn.

First, H produces an acknowledgement token "no" (line 27), which here marks alignment with the prior turn and in line with the prior excerpts, this supports Kitzinger's finding about the difficulty to disagree with an idiom. H then continues by specifying what his agreement is about. He first builds an aligning turn construction unit, where he points out that what E said before (she does not agree with H's suggestion about whom to lay off) is in line with what he had said initially. He then continues in line 31 by specifying what this agreement actually is about, which is to respect divergent positions. In response, E affiliates by means of laughter (line 32), which H joins (line 33). This locally accomplished affiliation in response to an idiomatic formulation enables E to reopen the discussion about the adequateness of laying off this person (line 34), thus enabling for the emergence of multivocality more than for striving towards a univocal positioning.

As in the prior excerpts, this excerpt has shown how idiomatic formulation can serve as a recalibration of the ongoing discussion locally empowering the speaker to direct the discussion in a projectable and preferred way. While the preferred way in excerpts 1 and 2 was to locally acquire univocality in an environment of plurivocality, in the final excerpt, the strive toward univocality was replaced by means of an idiomatic formulation to pave the grounds for the exchange of plurivocal positions.

Findings and Discussion

Our study sheds light on how discursive, micro-level practices like idiomatic formulations can play a decisive role in accomplishing a position of authority that in consequence allows the speaker to direct or re-direct the ongoing discussion about strategic decisions. Authority here, is not a stable, pre-assigned position that can be employed strategically in the interaction, instead, the study reveals that authority, as a way to control future actions, is accomplished by means of locally situated, discursive practices in form of idiomatic formulations.

So, why are idiomatic formulations so powerful? Based on our data, we can firstly see that their generality (and their figurative rather than literal quality) makes them independent of the specific details of any particular person or the delicate downsizing situation in question. As such, they are particularly well-suited to diffuse the inherent tension of a difficult and sensitive situation. Secondly, their status as commonplace both invokes and sustains the taken-for-granted knowledge shared by all meeting members. Therefore, it becomes clear that the participants' use the idiomatic formulations to locally accomplish affiliation when divergent and opposing voices have been raised about the downsizing decision.

In Figure 2.2, we try to illustrate our findings with regard to the use of idiomatic formulations in order to create authority leading to either multi- or univocality.

As can be seen in the figure, authority is locally accomplished by means of an idiomatic formulation that due to its generality is difficult to challenge and therefore invites for affiliation in the here and now of the interaction by the other participants. The idiomatic formulation, thus, creates a kind of common baseline that empowers its producer by means of in-situ acquired authority to set the scene and enables her to pursue her individual objective. In terms of navigating different voices, the individual objective can consist of reinforcing either multi- or univocality in the process of

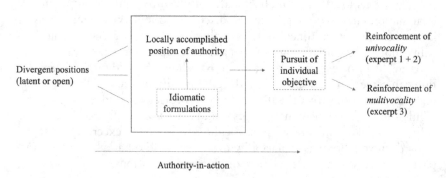

Figure 2.2 Authority-in-action by means of idiomatic formulations.

decision making. Consequently, authority is grounded in discursive actions and accomplished through interaction.

The study indicates that it is important to acknowledge the interactive nature of discursive micro-practices, as it is by and through interaction that the function of these discursive micro-practices to create authority can be fully understood. In a setting, which is unusual and potentially socially sensitive for the involved participants (such as a downsizing decision-making process), the use of a specific interactional micro-practices, i.e., idiomatic formulations, helps create a joint platform of agreement that contributes to the normalization of an activity like downsizing, which is typically not a "normal" and usual task for those involved in the process.

As such, our chapter contributes methodologically to the growing research on micro-foundations of authority (i.e., Benoit-Barné & Cooren, 2009; Bourgoin et al., 2020; Cooren et al., 2013). It demonstrates that it is useful to rely on video-based micro-ethnography to advance our understanding of the relationship between the interactional establishment of authority, the reliance on idiomatic formulations, and the dynamics between multivocality and univocality. Video-ethnographic work has allowed us to describe how the achievement of authority is locally achieved through the mobilization of idioms that generate either the interactional conditions conducive to the emergence of a strong voice (univocality) or the possibilities for different voices to coexist (multivocality) without undermining the decision-making process.

References

Aggerholm, H. K. (2014), Communicating Organizational Change Reactions: Downsizing Survivors' Discursive Constructions of Flexible Identities. *Business and Professional Communication Quarterly*, 77(4), 473–498.

Aggerholm, H. K. and Thomsen, C. (2015). Strategic Communication: The Role of Polyphony in Management Team Meetings. In Holtzhausen I. D. and Zerfass A. (red.), *The Routledge handbook of strategic communication* (pp. 172–189). New York: Routledge.

Atkinson J. M. and Heritage J. (eds) (1984). *Structures of social action: Studies in conversation analysis*. Cambridge: Cambridge University Press.

Bakhtin, M. M. (1981). *The dialogic imagination*. Austin, TX: University of Texas Press.

Bakhtin, M. M. (1984). *Problems of Dostoevsky's poetics* (C. Emerson, Trans.). Minneapolis, MN: University of Minnesota Press.

Belova, O., King, I., and Sliwa, M. (2008). Introduction: Polyphony and organization studies: Mikhail Bakhtin and beyond. *Organization Studies*, 29(4), 493–500.

Benoit-Barné, C. and Cooren F. (2009). The accomplishment of authority through presentification: How authority is distributed among and negotiated by organizational members. *Management Communication Quarterly*, 23(1), 5–31.

Boström, M. (2006). Regulatory credibility and authority through inclusiveness: Standardization organizations in cases of eco-labelling. *Organization*, *13*(3), 345–367.

Bourgoin, A., Bencherki, N., and Faraj, S. (2020). And who are you?": A performative perspective on authority in organizations. *Academy of Management Journal*, *63*(4), 1134–1165.

Carter, C., Clegg, S., Hogan, J., and Kornberger, M. (2003). The polyphonic spree: The case of the Liverpool Dockers. *Industrial Relations Journal*, *34*(4), 290–304.

Casey, C. (2004). Bureaucracy re-enchanted? Spirit, experts and authority in organizations. *Organization*, *11*(1), 59–79.

Cooren, F., Matte, F., Benoit-Barné, C., and Brummans, B. H. J. M. (2013). Communication as ventriloquism: A grounded-in action approach to the study of organizational tensions. *Communication Monographs*, *80*(3), 255–277.

Drew, P. and Holt, E. (1988). Complainable matters: The use of idiomatic expressions in making complaints. *Social Problems*, *35*, 398–417.

Drew, P. and Holt, E. (1995). Idiomatic expressions and their role in the organization of topic transition in conversation. In M. Everaert, E. J. van den Linden, A. Schenk, and R. Schreuder (Eds.), *Idioms: Structural and psychological perspectives* (pp. 117–132). Hillsdale, NJ: Lawrence Erlbaum Associates, Inc.

Erkama, N. and Vaara, E. (2010). Struggles over legitimacy in global organizational restructuring: A Rhetorical perspective on legitimation strategies and dynamics in a shutdown case. *Organization Studies*, *31*(7), 813–839.

Fatigante, M. and Orletti, F. (2013). Laughter and smiling in a three-party medical encounter: negotiating participants' alignment in delicate moments. In P. Glenn and E. Holt (Eds.), *Studies of laughter in interaction* (pp. 161–184). London: Bloomsbury Academics.

Freeman, S. J. (1999). The gestalt of organizational downsizing: Downsizing strategies as packages of change. *Human Relations*, *52*, 1505–1541.

Gergen, K. and Whitney, D. (1996). Technologies of representation in the global corporation: Power and polyphony. In D. Boje, R. Gephart, and T. Thatchenkery (Eds.), *Postmodern management and organization theory* (pp. 331–357). Thousand Oaks, CA: Sage.

Giddens, A, (1984). *The constitution of society: Outline of the theory of structuration*. Cambridge, UK: Polity.

Goffman, E. (1981). *Forms of talk*. Philadelphia, PA: University of Pennsylvania Press.

Hirsch, P.M. and DeSoucey, M. (2006). Organizational restructuring and its consequences: Rhetorical and structural. *Annual Review of Sociology*, *32*, 171–189.

Johnson, G., Langley, A., Melin, L., and Whittington, R. (2007). *Strategy as practice: Research directions and resources*. Cambridge: Cambridge University Press.

Kahn, W. A. and Kram, K. E. (1994). Authority at work: Internal models and their organizational consequences. *Academy of Management Review*, *19*(1), 17–50.

Kitzinger, C. (2000) How to resist an idiom, research on language and social interaction. *Research on Language and Social Interaction*, *33*(2), 121–154.

Klewitz, G. and Couper-Kuhlen, E. (1999). Quote-unquote? The role of prosody in the contextualization of reported speech sequences. *Interaction and Linguistic Structures*, *12*, 1–32.

Kornberger, M., Clegg, S., and Carter, C. (2006). Rethinking the polyphonic organization: managing as discursive practice. *Scandinavian Journal of Management,* 22, 3–30.

Kotthoff, H. (1998). Irony, quotation, and other forms of staged intertextuality: double or contrastive perspectivation in conversation. *Interaction and Linguistic Structures,* 5, 1–27.

Langley, A. (2007). Process thinking in strategic organization. *Strategic Organization,* 5(3), 271–282.

Oswick, C., Putnam, L. L., and Keenoy, T. (2004). Tropes, discourse and organizing. In D. Grant, C. Hardy, C. Oswick, and L. L. Putnam (Eds.), *The Sage handbook of organizational discourse* (pp. 105–127). Thousand Oaks, CA: Sage.

Pomerantz, A. and Fehr, B. (1997). Conversation analysis: An approach to the study of social action as sensemaking practices. In T. A. Van Dijk (Ed.), *Discourse as social interaction* (pp. 64–91). London: Sage.

Sacks, H. (1992). *Lectures on conversation.* Oxford, England: Blackwell, vol. I.

Sacks H., Schegloff, E. A., and Jefferson, G. (1974). A simplest systematics for the organization of turn-taking for conversations. *Language,* 50(4), 696–735.

Shannon, C. and Weaver, W. (1949). *The mathematical theory of communication.* Urbana, IL: University of Illinois Press.

Sennett, R. (1980). *Authority.* New York, NY: Knopf.

Sidnell, J. (2010). *Conversation analysis. An introduction.* Southern Gate: Wiley-Blackwell.

Steensig, J. and Asmuß, B. (2005). Notes on disaligning 'yes but' initiated utterances in Danish and German conversations. In A. Hakulinen and M. Selting (Eds.), *Syntax and lexis in conversation: Studies on the use of linguistic resources in talk-in-interaction* (pp. 349–373). Amsterdam, the Netherlands: John Benjamins Publishing Company.

Taylor, J. R. and Cooren, F. (1997). What makes communication "organizational"? How the many voices of a collectivity become the one voice of an organization. *Journal of Pragmatics,* 27, 409–438.

Tretheway, A. and Ashcraft, K. L. (2004). Practicing disorganization: The development of applied perspectives on living with tension. *Journal of Applied Communication Research,* 32(2), 119–146.

Weber, M. (1968). *Economy and society: An outline of interpretative sociology.* In G. Roth and C. Wittich (Eds.), New York, NY: Bedminster (Original work published in 1922).

Transcription Glossary

Based on the Jefferson transcription conventions as described in Atkinson and Heritage (1984: ix–xvi).

right	Speaker emphasis
YES	Noticeably louder than surrounding talk
u:	Stretched sound
ka-	Sharp cut-off of the prior sound
?	Rising intonation
,	Continuing intonation

;	Small falling intonation
.	Falling intonation
=	Latching between utterances and words
> <	Noticeably quicker than surrounding talk
< >	Noticeably slower than surrounding talk
↑	Rising intonational shift
↓	Falling intonational shift
.hh	Audible in-breath
hh	Audible outbreath
yehhs	Laughter in word
(.)	Micropause (less than 0.2 seconds)
(0.5)	Time gap in tenths of a second
[yes]	Overlapping talk
[no]	
()	Unintelligible talk
(())	Information about embodied actions

3 "I'm Just Saying"

Multivocal Organizing in a Community Health Initiative

Annis Grover Golden and Nicolas Bencherki

There is a growing acknowledgement that organizations are not unitary entities and that they comprise a plurality of concerns and interests. This symphonic view of organizations has been referred as "plurivocal" or "multivocal" (e.g., Aggerholm, Asmuß, & Thomsen, 2012). The coexistence of multiple voices has mostly been viewed as a challenge, for instance, by multiplying ethical stances or taking strategic planning in divergent directions (Hautz, Seidl, & Whittington, 2017; van Oosterhout, Wempe, & Willigenburg, 2004). For community-based organizations (CBOs), which serve diverse populations, strive for inclusive decision-making processes, and deal with contradictory expectations from donors and other stakeholders, the challenges of multivocity may be even sharper (James, 2003; McAllum, 2014). In that sense, multiplicity among CBOs has been studied as so many tensions that impede their work and that must be resolved (Ganesh & McAllum, 2012; Sanders, 2012).

However, there is evidence that multiple voices are not anomalies in an otherwise univocal and smooth organizing process. On the contrary, organizations are constituted and are able to act, thanks to the way voices combine (Cooren, 2012; Cooren & Sandler, 2014). This reversal of multiplicity's part in organizing highlights that the symphony of voices is something that organizational members, as individuals, actively and reflexively *enact*, rather than simply arising from the sum of juxtaposed bodies with different interests, concerns, and opinions.

Building on these insights, our study looks in more detail at how multiple voices are uttered (including by a single person), how they are interactionally managed, and what organizing effects stem from the interactions. To do so, we follow a version of discourse analysis that considers language as a medium for interaction (Alvesson & Kärreman, 2000; Potter & Wetherell, 1987) to look at data from the Women's Health Project (WHP), a community-based participatory research project focused on health promotion in a small, racially, and ethnically diverse urban population center in New York State. The project's purpose was to identify effective strategies for encouraging underserved, minority women to obtain recommended reproductive health screenings (focusing on breast and cervical cancer) toward the goal

DOI: 10.4324/9780429297830-3

of eliminating documented disparities between African American and European American women's reproductive health. A key development was the spontaneous emergence of a group of community residents who encouraged their friends and neighbours to connect with the outreach efforts of the WHP's research team and its local partner organizations. This led the WHP to add to its intervention activities a "peer health advocate" initiative. Five local women who had displayed interest in WHP by attending community events and interacting with staff during outreach were hired by the Project and received training on outreach techniques and reproductive health information. The peer team then took the lead on community outreach, with the WHP capitalizing on their ability to shift between clinical and community voices. Thus, multivocity became a constitutive feature of the organization and its mission of increasing awareness of the need for obtaining preventive reproductive healthcare services and the available options for doing so in this community.

Drawing on recordings of team meetings that included the peer health advocates and the first author, who acted both as a researcher and Project Director, we look for the interactional details through which the women performed multivocity, and in so doing instantiated the WHP's liminal situation between fields of activity. First, we revisit scholarship on multivocity in organizational contexts, with special attention to non-profits. We argue that multiple voices are frequently seen as problematic issues to be managed, rather than, as some other research suggests, a driver of organizing and of organizational action. We elaborate a view of multivocity with more complexity than just the expression of conflicting individual preferences. Building on these insights, we describe our analytic approach to a recorded team meeting that typifies multivocal performances and issues. After presenting our analysis, we consider how thinking of multivocity as something people concretely do within their utterances may help extend current literature on voices in organizational settings and may provide practical insights on the workings of non-profits in marginalized communities.

Multiple Voices in Community-Based Organizations

Multiple voices coexisting in an organization have commonly been viewed as a complication when contrasted with simpler, univocal situations, with some authors describing organizations as political arenas where people wrangle to reconcile their diverging viewpoints (Crozier & Friedberg, 1980; Mintzberg, 1983). More specifically, the strategy literature deems that including more people in the planning process poses "risks and costs" (Hautz et al., 2017, p. 301), while business ethics scholars reluctantly realize that finding a single, unified theory to identify the "right" thing to do is illusory, and that instead multiple ethical voices must be listened to (van Oosterhout et al., 2004).

CBOs are particularly faced with the challenge of giving a voice to diverse individuals, since they often serve populations whose voices have been muted, such as disabled, poor, or otherwise marginalized people (Chaney & Fevre, 2001). Organizations have therefore had to encourage participation from those marginalized groups, including by innovative means such as artistic projects (Eynaud, Juan, & Mourey, 2018; Wang & Burris, 1997). Consistent with these goals, they also aspire to be inclusive organizations that extend decision-making to employees but also to beneficiaries and community members (Jäger & Kreutzer, 2011). Non-profits must therefore articulate multiple voices across organizational boundaries when it comes to their governance, as they are stewards to the combined interests of their beneficiaries, volunteers, donors, formal members, and directors (Lewis, 2005), in addition to coordinators of their workers' and beneficiaries' multiple identities (Meisenbach & Kramer, 2014). Moreover, some organizations must deal with multilingual contexts where the issue of brokering between voices becomes quite literal (Bencherki, Matte, & Pelletier, 2016).

An additional manner in which CBOs and non-profits must attend to multiple voices has to do with the necessity for them to establish partnerships with other organizations to fulfill their missions as well as their position between several fields of activity. Through working with other organizations, CBOs may form a new, collective identity that transcends any single organization (Koschmann, Kuhn, & Pfarrer, 2012). CBOs also have the duty to work for and with diverse people, including in terms of ethnicity (Henry & Pringle, 1996) and sexual identity (Bell, Özbilgin, Beauregard, & Sürgevil, 2011).

In the context of health promotion, one strategy preferred by CBOs in dealing with diverse populations, as well as government agencies, is to employ community health workers recruited from and trained among target populations to disseminate information, thus placing these people in a middle position, between the service providers and the community (Arvey & Fernandez, 2012; Balcazar et al., 2011). However, studies on community health workers have, for the moment, mostly been concerned with the *outcomes* of initiatives employing such workers, without much attention to *how* they communicatively manage their middle position.

Towards a View of Multiple Voices as Constitutive of Organizational Action

As an alternative to the "multiplicity as a challenge" perspective, some authors suggest that multiplicity is a constitutive feature of organizations, as well as of individuals, including organizational members (Bencherki, 2017; Cooren, 2006). This suggestion builds on Bakhtin's (1986) conception of polyphony, meaning that each utterance, text or communicative event already comprises multiple voices (Belova, King, & Sliwa, 2008;

Cooren & Sandler, 2014). A polyphonic lens recognizes that an organization's multiple voices do not fragment its alleged unity, but that they participate in constituting organizational reality. This could mean, for CBOs, that a multiplicity of voices might be more productively viewed as an asset for organizing and for people to accomplish their various goals. Indeed, from a communication perspective, apparently contradictory voices may be seen as "productive" or "collaborative tensions," as people interact to handle seemingly opposing imperatives (Lewis, Isbell, & Koschmann, 2010). In fact, in some organizations, members may even "cultivate" and reaffirm tensions that help them get on with their work (Matte & Cooren, 2015).

This cultivation is possible because tensions do not merely result from two opposing abstract forces; they are discursive performances, in which various expectations in terms of goals, values, or other principles materialize through speech and writing and are thus assessed against each other (Cooren Matte, Benoit-Barné, & Brummans, 2013). Whether these contradictory imperatives constitute a tension or not depends on *how* these demands are formulated initially, as well as *how* people invoke them again as relevant when they engage together in collective action. Thus, a CBO's strategy may stem from the way multiple voices are mingled, in order to shape a program of action that cannot be reduced to any single person's preference. Moreover, previous research suggests that organizational reality materializes through the integration of voices from multiple people, but also through the co-existence of voices in a single person's utterance (Cooren, Bencherki, Chaput, & Vásquez, 2015).

However, while the literature that bears upon multivocity in organizational settings has studied the potentially conflicting *suggestions* of different voices—voices can "suggest," "warn," or "guide" people to do something or against doing it (Cooren & Taylor, 1997)—it has offered us less in terms of extended discourse analyses of situated interactions in which not only discreet ideas or interests are expressed, but in which voices coalesce to display different genres of talk and to constitute and invoke discursive communities. Such an analysis, which we offer here, attends both to the suggestions that the voices make as well as the sequential way in which they are organized and the language they use. The same suggestion may be expressed in different ways by different voices, as is the case for the WHP. Indeed, similar "suggestions" concerning reproductive health—for instance, that women consult with their local health provider—must be expressed in different voices, each with their own vocabulary, tone, and other discursive features. For women in underserved communities to be persuaded to obtain recommended health services, then, health information must not be provided in a voice associated with the medical establishment, which African American women may be particularly mistrustful of (Holloway, 2011), but in a community voice. This entails challenges for the peer health advocates, as they work at bridging a communication disjuncture between community residents and local service providers. At the same time, they must also strive to preserve the WHP's credibility as a fledgling CBO, functioning within a community of organizations, and their own credibility as organizational members. To understand how the peers navigated these tensions through their communicative performances, we next provide further background on the case and our data collection, before turning to our analysis of the peers' talk in interaction.

Studying Multivocal Discourse

Case Setting

The WHP was initiated with funding from the National Institutes of Health as a community-based participatory research project in a smaller, racially, and ethnically diverse urban population center north of New York City. The project's immediate goal was to identify effective strategies for bridging a communicative disjuncture that local health and human service organizations had identified to the first author as existing between themselves and underserved, minority community residents. The ultimate goal was to increase the uptake of available reproductive health services, with a particular focus on lower income African American women, toward the end of reducing documented health disparities.

The Project's initial strategy for bringing together residents and CBOs consisted primarily of health education and resource fairs where women could meet with organization representatives in neighbourhood locations they were comfortable with. Of interest to us here is that, after approximately 18 months of community events organized by the research team in collaboration with CBOs, the WHP recruited women from the community as "peer health advocates," who took over some of the organization's community outreach activities and relayed information to their peers. The women who were recruited were identified because of their regular attendance at WHP events and their proactiveness in encouraging their fellow community members to interact with the research team and CBOs. While employing community health workers is a common strategy in health information dissemination initiatives, the WHP inverted the typical trajectory. Instead of first training individuals and then sending them off to the community, the project recruited women directly from the community, but focused on individuals who had already displayed a keen interest in reproductive health and proven their leadership among their peers; then it provided them with training on reproductive health information, offered by a well-established women's health organization, referred to here as Women's Health Services.

The first author audio recorded several team meetings in this phase of the project as part of documenting its workings as they developed over time. At the time, these recordings were not made with a specific research question in mind. Over time, however, the first author identified as a recurring issue how the peer health advocates communicatively constructed their roles as members of this organization who were also members of the community, a matter with both practical and theoretical implications. The team meeting we focus on here took place immediately after one of the training sessions.

The recordings were initially transcribed using a reduced transcription scheme. After selecting the segment, we focus on in our analysis, additional details were added, adapted from the transcription system suggested by Jefferson (2004), in the interest of providing readers with a clearer sense of the interaction.

Data Analysis Strategy

Given our interest in *how* peer health advocates express multiple voices, the analysis we present below is informed by the version of discourse analysis articulated by Potter and Wetherell (1987) and described by Alvesson and Karreman (2000) as viewing language as "a medium for interaction," and thus analyzing discourse in search of "what people do with language in specific social settings" (p. 1127). Wetherell and Potter (1988) underscore that individuals use discourse "constructively," meaning that "discourse has an action orientation: it has practical consequences" (p. 171). Consistent with a constitutive view of communication, this means that we do not only view discourse as an expression of opinions or cognitive states, but also as action, in the sense that what people say informs, suggests, warns, etc. other participants, thus in turn altering their own action (Cooren, 2010; 2015). Each discursive action's performance and each reaction to it is guided by prior turns of talk that cumulatively form the next turn's context, thus gradually constituting an organized social order that informs people's action (see Bencherki et al., 2016). Our analytical orientation to action is important as it clarifies that we are interested in the performative effect of talk, and that what words mean is witnessable in other participant's reaction to them.

Our approach to analyzing the peer health advocates' discourse is also guided by the insider/outsider team research approach to organizational inquiry described by Bartunek (2008). In this approach insiders are defined as "the individuals for whom the personally relevant social world is under study ... who hope to understand and act more effectively in the setting" (p. 4). Insiders are typically organizational practitioners, and outsiders are academic researchers, though Bartunek acknowledges the possibility of more complex combinations of statuses. Indeed, in our situation, the first author, Annis, has a dual status of "insider" who is also an "outsider" or academic researcher, as is typical in community-based participatory research. She is an insider for the purposes of this analysis by virtue of being the Project Director for the organizational entity we focus on, while at the same time, she is an outsider to the community of local residents and the community of local health and human service organizations by virtue of her status as a university professor. Nicolas, the relative "outsider," accepted an invitation to collaborate on this analysis of field data and theorizing about the results, given the project's congruence with his own methodological commitments and longstanding interest in CBOs.

The collaboration entailed a requirement on Annis's part to narrate to Nicolas the history of the Project and create ethnographic context for the communicational event we focus on here. This has provided a means for Annis to surface what might otherwise have remained taken for granted. The insider/outsider status of researchers thus enriches researcher reflexivity for both the insider and the outsider; moreover, given the focus of this particular analysis, the productive tensions between insider and outsider perspectives served as a sensitizing device insofar as the dual hats of the researchers mirror the dual hats of the "research participants" (i.e., the peer health advocates).

Our joint discussion concerning the Project's history and Annis' experience as its Director helped us construct an ethnographic narrative in which Annis' perceptions of the challenges were defined: she saw the "problems" of the WHP as twofold and interrelated. First, she identified a challenge with managing multivocity on the part of the peer health advocates that had to do with balancing their community-specific ways of understanding and talking about health information—an asset to them in interacting with other women in the community—with the need to convey information in a way that was nonetheless accurate. Second, a longer-range problem concerned the survival of this organizational entity given its liminal position between the community and health-related CBOs and its resource uncertainties. We focus here primarily on the former problem, though the success with which this problem is managed has implications for the latter, since it impacts the way in which the local community of CBOs views the WHP.

Following the definition of the relevant problems, Annis identified the segment of a team meeting we focus on here as being of particular interest in this regard. She chose the segment because it was typical of interactions involving peer health advocates while also capturing a key moment in the WHP's trajectory, as it consists of a debriefing session immediately following a training session the peers received from a healthcare provider partner organization.

As the two collaborators discussed this particular interaction, the notion of multivocity was found to provide a productive lens for viewing the communicative practices of the meeting participants. Working together, the co-authors' analysis of the meeting segment proceeded through a series of sessions characterized by tacking back and forth between the specifics of the performances of the actors in this particular social context, forms of discursive practices identified in the literature on discourse analysis, the broader ethnographic context of the communicational event, and implications for the "problems" identified above. Throughout this process, the second author's sensemaking frequently invited the first author to "open up" her experientially informed interpretations of the data, in an iterative process.

Managing Multivocity

The post-training debriefing session that we analyze here consists of discussion among the team members following a session that focused on contraceptive techniques and the relationship between pregnancy prevention and the prevention of sexually transmitted infections. The peers were asked by the Project Director to identify information that they were provided during a training session earlier in the day which they found particularly important and would like to pass along to other community residents. As they select information to discuss and articulate their understandings of the information provided by the trainers, the peers interactionally work through, with one another and with the Project Director (Annis) and the Field Coordinator, the central "facts" of the topics, and their significance, particularly within the context of their own community. Of relevance is the fact that Annis is a white, middle-aged university professor, and the Field Coordinator is an older African American woman, retired from a position managing a publicly funded reproductive healthcare clinic and currently an assistant pastor in a local church. The five peer health advocates are African American women between 35 and 55 years old who are, as noted earlier, from the local community. The session was audio recorded with the peers' consent.

The multivocity displayed in this event provides a window into an essential quality of this organizational entity and a fundamental challenge it faces: balancing the requirement for cultural competency in communicating with residents with the need to ensure that accurate health information is transmitted and that an organizational identity consistent with other, more established, community-based health and human service organizations' understandings of formal organizational membership is enacted.

Our analysis identified three modes in which the peer health advocates' discourse displayed and managed multivocity: *discursive positioning* in relation to present and absent others (Davies & Harré, 1990), *presentifying* contexts from outside the social context of the meeting (in the sense of Benoit-Barné & Cooren, 2009), and voicing multiple *discursive genres* (see Cornut, Giroux, & Langley, 2012). We identify instances of multivocity both within and between individual participants in the discussion, as the interaction among the peers unfolds, moderated by the Project Director. Given our space constraints here, we focus primarily on the peer health advocates, but we note that the Project Director also engages in these multivocal performances to balance her relational requirements with the other organizational members with organizational goals; that is, her recognition of the need to interact with community residents in a respectful, culturally competent manner, yet also convey accurate health information.

For each mode, we first describe the performance itself; we then illustrate it with discourse from the debriefing session; we explain how the specific discourse functions as an instance of this type of performance; and we discuss the effects the performance produces vis-à-vis productively managing tensions between multivocity and univocity. We present the modes in the order in which they are displayed in the group interaction.

Discursive Positioning in Relation to Present and Absent Others

One mode in which the peer health advocates' discourse displays and manages multivocity is *discursive positioning*. As defined by Davies and Harré (1990), this is "the discursive process whereby selves are located in conversations as observably and subjectively coherent participants in jointly produced story lines" (p. 48). They identify two forms of positioning: *interactive positioning,* in which "what one person says positions another," and *reflexive positioning,* in which "one positions oneself" (p. 48). As peer health advocates who are both members of the community that the project seeks to serve, and members of the project staff, they position themselves in relation to others both present and absent from the actual scene of the team meeting.

To provide some additional context for the segment of discourse that exemplifies this mode of multivocity, Annis, in her role as Project Director, had opened the group discussion by asking the peer health advocates what they had heard in that day's training session that they thought would be "most important to pass along to other women." The discussion then turned to the topic of birth control, with Shirley specifically focusing on information that had been provided about the effectiveness of the intrauterine device (IUD) but noting that the male partner would still "need the condom on anyhow, cuz to prevent sexual transmitted diseases." Annis takes this opportunity to remind the group of one of the key takeaways from the training, namely that "contraception and disease prevention are not one in the same, you know? That a condom will do both, ideally, um, but, just because you have – an IUD is a really effective form of birth control but it doesn't give you any protection against sexually transmitted diseases," a point that Shirley immediately aligns herself with by replying "None whatsoever." She then goes on to say:

1 *Shirley:* You know, some people feel like because they have them contraceptive
2   (.) uh (.) uh (.) uh (.) internally (.) that (.) uh (.) "oh <u>well</u> you know I
3   can't get pregnant" but they're not thinking about the risk.

Both forms of positioning identified by Davies and Harré are evident in this brief segment. With respect to reflexive positioning, Shirley positions herself as knowledgeable, specifically about the relationship between contraception and "risk" (of sexually transmitted infections). She makes a knowledge claim about sexual and reproductive health to the other members of the Project who are present in the field office for this discussion, who constitute the present others. She also reflexively positions herself as having knowledge of the other community residents, inferentially by virtue of being a community resident herself, and able to speak about what these absent others think and say. At the same time, she engages in interactive positioning, even though with absent others, positioning other community residents ("some people") as less knowledgeable than she is herself. Shirley literally speaks in both the voice of a trained peer health advocate and in the voice of the community as she drops into and then out of quoted speech, which is also performed in a different tonal registry.

These performances of discursive positioning produce powerfully significant effects vis-à-vis managing tensions between multivocity and univocity. While Shirley speaks in two voices, her discourse enacts univocity in relation to the organization's mission in the sense that she aligns with the single voice of the Project's overarching mission: to provide information related to reproductive health that community residents may be unaware of. Moreover, her multivocal discourse marks her dual status as a community resident and a Project member, yet this dual status is actually an essential aspect of the peer health advocate role within the Project and thus a performance of a unified organizational member role identity.

Presentifying the Community

A second mode in which the peer health advocates' discourse displayed and managed multivocity was through the discursive practice of presentification. Brummans and colleagues define this as

> the ongoing process of making something or someone present in time and space ... communication between agents allows 'us' or 'it' to be embodied or 'incarnated' in a certain way. [...] The incarnation that enables presentification occurs through the interplay between spoken and written language (conversations, speeches, document, memos, posters), nonverbal language (gestures, symbols), context (circumstances, previous interactions) and materialities (costumes, buildings, desks, computers).
>
> (Brummans et al., 2009, p. 57)

In the segment below, which immediately follows the segment discussed above in the group discussion, we see Shirley collaborating with another peer health advocate, Mary, to presentify, in the setting of the team meeting, institutions, roles, and modes of social interaction from outside of this setting, which are connected to their community life. This excerpt is lengthier, since the effect produced depends in part on Mary's repeated contributions. In this excerpt from the team meeting, we focus on Mary's contributions to the discussion and notice how she functions as a sort of chorus, affirming Shirley's contributions (we have highlighted Mary's contributions to make the pattern easier to see in this textual representation of their discursive interaction).

1	*Shirley:*	You know, some people feel like because they have them
2		contraceptive (.) uh (.) uh (.) uh (.) internally (.) that (.) uh (.) oh <u>well</u>
3		you know I can't get pregnant but they're not thinking about the risk.
4	*Annis:*	Right. [Right.
5	*Mary:*	[Yeah and] they need to think about the risk.
6	*Shirley:*	=Yeah because it's <u>really</u> something else these days.
7	*Mary:*	=Um-hum.
8	*Annis:*	Yeah. So if people were only gonna do <u>one</u> thing
9	*Shirley:*	That's not gonna work=
10	*Mary:*	It sure <u>ain't</u>.
11	*Shirley:*	You have to take both uh steps=
12	*Mary:*	Um-hum-hmm?
13	*Shirley:*	To protect yourself.
14	*Annis:*	Ri:ght. But if people were only gonna <u>u::se</u> one thing=
15	*Shirley:*	Just a condom, put on [a condom.
16	*Annis:*	[=Yeah.
17	*Shirley:*	Yes. And practice it.
18	*Mary:*	Yeah.
19	*Annis:*	It's like (.) it's so basic. And=
20	*Mary:*	=Mm hmm=
21	*Shirley:*	It <u>is</u>↑
22	*Annis:*	You know.
23	*Shirley:*	It's so simple to check it? ↑<u>You</u> put it on ↓your partner. You don't
24		need <u>him</u> to put it on. >↑You know how ↓to do that? <
25	*Mary:*	=Yeah. Yes.
26	*Shirley:*	↑Put it <u>on</u> ↓there. Make sure it's (.) not (.) broken?
27	*Mary:*	=Um-hum.
28	*Shirley:*	And then uh whatever (.) and if he wantsomemore then <u>take</u> that one
29		off and <u>put</u> another one on and check it ↑<u>too</u>
30	*Mary:*	Yeah. hhh
31	*Shirley:*	[I'm just ↑<u>saying</u>]

In effect, we see in this performance evidence that the peer health advocates, who are all members of the local community, support one another in their performance of the organizational member role (as part of the staff of the WHP) through communicative practices that are imported into this Project meeting setting from the community. More specifically, they deploy a "call-and-response" practice recognizable from African American churches, presentifying institutions and oral traditions from outside the immediate context of the team meeting. Shirley plays the role of the "leader," and Mary performs as an affirming audience member. It is notable that Annis' contributions, while a part of the discussion, are not a part of this flow, even when she is affirming Shirley's statements, thus marking her as a member of a different speech community. In addition, she performs another "pedagogical" role in this exchange, different from the other participants.

Pattillo-McCoy's (1998) analysis of African American church culture in a Chicago neighbourhood argues that the church provides a "cultural blueprint for civic life in the neighborhood," with "call-and-response interaction" identified as one part of a "cultural 'tool kit'" (p. 767) for social action (along with prayer and Christian imagery). Thus, this tool kit, or set of cultural practices, she maintains, informs social interactions outside of the physical boundaries of the church and church services, extending into secular contexts.

Functionally, Pattillo-McCoy explains, call-and-response "invoke[s] the collective orientation of Black Christianity" (p. 768). As such, she points out, it has organizing properties, constituting part of "*how* social action is constructed" (p. 768). Similarly, a study in another social context found that the use of call-and-response by teachers with their elementary school students was employed to encourage spontaneous and active participation in the collectivity, in contrast to the practice of requiring students to raise their hands and be called upon before they were permitted to speak (Haight, 1998). Within the context of the peer health advocates' interactions in this team meeting, we can see that through the call and response practice, multiple voices are joined, and univocity is affirmed, as one peer performs the role of supportive chorus to another peer's declarations. At the same time, individuals' voices and their right to be heard are affirmed through this discursive practice, as the leader role (the individual making a declaration) is shared among different group members, and other group members spontaneously jump in with affirmations (rather than requesting to be recognized). Thus, the very use of the practice, imported from a community context outside of the team meeting, but shared by the peers as members of that community, contributes to unity within the organization, and to the unity provided by their shared identities as peer health advocates, even as the practice itself requires the participation of multiple voices.

Voicing Multiple Discursive Genres

The label "genre" has mostly been applied to written organizational texts—
for example, strategic plans, annual reports (Cornut et al., 2012). However,
we can usefully borrow from this the notion of discourse that draws on
extra-organizational, institutional conventions and is deployed in specific
organizational social situations to orient interactants to specific organizational activities and aims. The notion of genre can then be usefully combined
with that of "voice" in the context of discourse on health-related matters.
In particular, we can borrow from Mishler's (1985) "voice of the lifeworld"
as performed by patients in medical encounters (when it is not suppressed),
and "voice of medicine" as performed by healthcare providers, which are in
turn derived from Habermas' (1984) Theory of Communicative Action. In
the communicational event we focus on here, we associate the voice of the
lifeworld with the everyday life of the members of this community rather
than patients per se; the voice of medicine is associated with expert knowledge of reproductive health. Thus, we hear two discursive genres: the voice
of the community (the language of everyday life in the neighbourhood) and
the voice of the clinic (the language of the expert trainers).

Returning to the excerpt above, we can hear Shirley slipping seamlessly
from a more generically clinical description of effective condom use (in
lines 15–26) to one that is contextualized within a more specific sexual
behaviour (in lines 28–29), which, it might be inferred, is drawn directly
from her own experience or/and indirectly from conversations with other
women and men in the community. Thus, we hear her transitioning from
one voice or discursive genre to another. At the same time, as she concludes
with "I'm just saying" we hear her acknowledging the shift and perhaps
the questionable appropriateness of deploying this lifeworld voice in the
organizational context of the team meeting. In their analysis of "I'm just
saying" as a metadiscursive expression in group discussions around controversial issues, Craig and Sanusi (2000) point out that "just" can function
as a hedge against an anticipated critique, as in *this is "just" my view*, and
others might take issue with it. Similarly, in this instance Shirley's "I'm
just saying" might be heard as indicating that others—for example, those
who speak in the voice of the clinic—might deem the genre she voices this
description in to be not fitted to the context (debriefing on a training session), but she is insisting on its accuracy: this is *just* the way it is. As Craig
and Sunusi point out, "just" can also be used in other ways than hedging;
for example, to provide emphasis (as in "just incredible"). This may be an
equally convincing interpretation of Shirley's intent in deploying this meta
discursive marker, particularly in this final position in her conversational
turn. Finally, "just saying" can be used to specify that the speaker's point
of view is located somewhere in the acceptable range on "an implied continuum of acceptable to unacceptable standpoints" (p. 438), perhaps "just" at
the boundary—in this case, a boundary between discursive genres.

We also notice that Shirley's description of using a condom is voiced in the second person "you," and while it is delivered in the voice of the expert, that is, the discursive genre of the clinic, in terms of its tone, it is also very plain language, thus fitting it to the neighbourhood world of the community. Thus, it can be heard as a rehearsal of her organizational role as peer health advocate in interacting with a member of the community.

Immediately after Shirley marks the conclusion of her turn with "I'm just saying," there is a definitive shift to the discursive genre of the clinic, with Patricia explicitly referencing the discourse of the trainers, Tina and Nancy, who are from a reproductive healthcare clinic (see below for a continuation of the transcript). Patricia reflexively positions herself as an expert in being able to not only reproduce the facts that were presented by the formally recognized experts but also to extrapolate from those facts a possible additional fact not explicitly addressed. This is a kind of scientific reasoning clearly in the discursive genre of the clinic, even though the clinical vocabulary is not entirely accurate. Shirley initially follows Patricia's lead in invoking the clinic with a version of a medical term for a part of the female reproductive anatomy. However, she quickly shifts back to the discursive genre of the community as she likens the nylon filament attached to the IUD to fishing line.

---

32 *Patricia:*   [(I have a question on) Shirley's um Shirley's thing. I wanted to ask Tina when um (.)
33   was it Tina or Nancy. I wanted to ask Nancy (.) even though (.) like she was saying using
34   the (.) um (.) the IUD string irritatin' the man (.) but also if it's irritatin' the ↑man it must
35   be irritatin' the woman by rubbing up against the wall of the <u>cervix</u>. (.) Don't you think?

36 *Lynette:*   =I would think. The string?

37 *Shirley:*   [Well not not scratchin' <u>her</u>. I mean I would say

38 *Patricia:*   [If it's scratching <u>her</u> (.) I mean

39 *Shirley:*   I mean (.) I'm just sayin' (.) your lebbia

40 *Patricia:*   [Yeah

41 *Shirley:*   [cuz the string's] too long and uh

42 *Patricia:*   =It could irritate [her <u>too</u> (.) yeah.

43 *Shirley:*   [and and uh it's like fish wire (.) I mean fish line. And <u>yeah</u> (.) <u>yeah</u> (.)
44   that's scratchin' [<u>you</u> ↑too.

45 *Patricia:*   [It could like (.) it could like cut her and cut him also.

46 *Shirley:*   That's right.

The effects produced by these discursive practices vis-à-vis producing and managing multivocity are threefold. First, speaking in the voice of the clinic helps to instantiate the organization's character as a health-related organization, and thus orients to the Project's overall aims and organizational identity. Second, speaking in the voice of the clinic also helps to set the speaker apart from other members of the community whom they are there to help and share helpful information with (thus, overlapping with the practice of discursive positioning). Conversely, speaking in the voice of the community establishes for the peer health advocates the cultural and linguistic competency that makes them credible messengers from the Project to the community residents, as well as to the community-based health and human service organizations the Project acts as a liaison to, and who value the Project and the peers precisely because of their ability to connect their organizations with community residents. Thus, as we pointed to earlier, in the context of the practice of discursive positioning, multivocity is a constitutive feature of both the unified mission and identity organization as a whole (as it strives to speak both with and for the members of the community and the local CBOs); and the unified definition and performance of the peer health advocate member role. We discuss this dynamic further below.

At the same time, this preoccupation with an outlier circumstance (i.e., the IUD needing adjustment after being inserted because of being improperly measured and creating discomfort during sexual intercourse) creates concern on the part of the Project Director about the fidelity with which the information about IUD's will be transmitted, which we see in her attempt to recontextualize and restate the "take-away" from the training session in lines 47–48 and 50. However, there is some resistance to her move and persistence in the "problem narrative" as demonstrated lines 51–56.

---

45 *Patricia:*   [It could like (.) it could like cut her and cut him also.

46 *Shirley:*   That's right.

47 *Annis:*   But they <u>can</u> adjust it. I mean when it's (.) I think the message was (.) if it's in
48   [properly=

49 *Mary:*   [yeah]

50 *Annis:*   =it's adjusted properly and the string is cut to the right length then it [works

51 *Lynette:*   [They need to]
52   think of something else to make that string out of.

53 Annis: Yeah.

54 *Shirley:*   Yeah. That's (.) that's <u>fish</u> line.

55 *Lynette:*   Fish line will cut you?

56 *Shirley:*   ↑<u>Shoot</u> ↓yeah.

57 *Louise:*   Well (.) have Women's Health Services had plenty (.) ah (.) a lot of complaints about it?

58 *Carrie:*   Well we don't know.

At the same time, it is also notable that in the final two turns here, two other peers bring a more "scientific" form of reasoning into the discussion, with Louise asking whether this problem is a common occurrence, and Carrie pointing out that the group was not provided with that information. These contributions implicitly ask the group to consider how much attention and concern the problem warrants and presumably how they should convey information about this form of contraception to other women in the community. While unresolved in the context of this team meeting, the exchange is indicative of the group's tolerance for multiple voices and viewpoints in the working through of how to make sense of the information provided in the training.

Discussion

In framing this chapter, we argued that multivocity is most often seen as a problem to be managed so that an organization can speak with a single voice. However, the fact is that, for many organizations, multivocity is actually an asset and even constitutive of organizational action. This is particularly the case for CBOs, which often work at the interface of several fields of activity and aspire to participatory decision-making, among other commitments. While this argument is not entirely novel, and how multivocity materializes in actual talk and contributes to organizing has been pointed to in prior research, we maintain that this research has provided less in terms of extended discourse analyses of situated and consequential interactions that demonstrate multivocity at the level of discursive communities and genres. In this sense, our discursive analysis advances contributions of two kinds. First, it extends current literature on multivocality in organizations by clarifying *how* multivocal organizing takes place within interactions. Second, keeping in mind Bartunek's (2008, p. 11) invitation to provide "a practical solution to identified problems," we discuss our findings' implications for the management of a CBO employing workers drawn from the focus community.

The Situated Performance of Multivocal Organizing

Our findings confirm that multivocity does not challenge otherwise unitary organizations; it is rather a feature of the way people talk and interact as they carry out their daily activities. The impression that multivocity is disruptive derives from the assumption that voices correspond to individuals expressing their preferences, interests, experiences, or trajectories, thus leading to the organization's "fragmentation" (Sullivan & McCarthy, 2008). However, our findings show multivocity also takes place through people's joint production of talk sequences. Through each of their utterances and how they arrange them, people also materialize different voices that are not only their own, but also those of the collectives they belong to, and make them available in the interaction for their joint scrutiny. This also means that whether those voices converge harmoniously or cause fragmentation depends on how they are materialized, picked up by others and incorporated in the unfolding of the interaction.

The perspective on voices that emerges from our analysis aligns with Bakhtin's (1986) dialogical theory. The Russian scholar viewed each utterance as already comprising multiple voices (Cooren & Sandler, 2014). In this sense, we extend recent work on organizational ventriloquism that has suggested that phenomena such as authority (Benoit-Barné & Cooren, 2009; Bourgoin et al., 2019) or ethics (Cooren, 2016; Matte & Bencherki, 2019) are interactionally accomplished as principles, duties, values, or rules express themselves through people's talk and action. Our contribution is original in the sense that we show that what is expressed is not only discreet ideas—a particular rule or interest, for instance—but also ways of talking that bring into the interaction the discursive communities they correspond to.

Our findings suggest that bringing into the interaction different voices and managing their relationship—or the productive tension between multivocity and univocity—is accomplished through at least three interactional processes, which map to the discursive practices identified in our analysis above. The first is *deploying alternative identities*. Empirically speaking, this was particularly visible when we looked at the way the peer health advocates performed *discursive positioning* and made different identity claims with respect to the way the interaction unfolded. We saw, for instance, that Shirley positioned herself as being knowledgeable both with respect to reproductive health issues and about community members, while also depicting others as being less knowledgeable than herself, for instance, through an imagined quoted speech episode. In doing so, Shirley is also claiming to embody the WHP's mission of articulating both identities and, thus, shows that she contributes to carrying out the organization's work. The understanding that some community members would benefit from additional reproductive health information is grounded in both Shirley's status as a member of that community and her status as a peer health advocate with knowledge and training different from other community members.

The second process we refer to as *transposing practices*, a particular form of presentification, the exemplar being the way the peers adapt the call-and-response interactional format, which they may use at church, but also in other community interactions, to the debriefing session. Consistent with Pattillo-McCoy's (1998) study of Church culture in African American communities, the use of the call-and-response format in the team meeting brings into the interaction an acknowledgement of prior organization—namely the structured relationships that these women already have. This organization allows them to jointly examine the new information they are faced with, for instance, by validating the main speaker's claims regarding how their community members would react to reproductive health information. It also separates community insiders from outsiders, in this case positioning Annis in the latter category, although at the same time she provides an essential contribution to the unified voice with which the project speaks to the community. Arguably, other forms of practices could be transposed and such transpositions have been described as sources of innovation (Boxenbaum & Battilana, 2005).

Finally, the third process consists in *melding voices*, in this case by merging community and clinical voices, which can be viewed as a practice of creating new discursive genres. In the same way, as metals are melded to create a new, stronger alloy, the work of peer health advocates is not only to switch *between* codes or discourses, or to translate terminology, but also to find ways of making different voices *co-present* within a single utterance. This is particularly apparent in the third part of our findings where Patricia initiates a conversation regarding whether an IUD's monofilament string may cause injury during intercourse. The conversation can be seen as an attempt to speak at once using clinical terminology and format (for instance by extrapolating from known facts) while also using community terminology and comparisons (by describing the string as a fish line).

Together, these three processes show that multivocal organizing proceeds through people's discursive performance of *who they are*, *what they do*, and *how they talk*. These three components are not abstract realities but must be observed in how people concretely engage in interaction.

Addressing the Practical Problem: Letting Voices Speak

The WHP itself, and later the peer health advocate initiative, was conceived as a practical solution to a problem voiced by local CBOs to the first author when she first began working in this community: connecting CBOs with underserved community residents (Matsaganis et al., 2014). However, the above analysis shows how multivocity in the context of the peer health advocate initiative can be both solution (to the problem of connecting CBOs and residents) and another problem—at once an asset and a potential liability for the organization.

From the Project Director's standpoint, the first problem was a localized interactional challenge of managing multivocity on the part of the peer health advocates to effectively share health information in the community's voice maintaining fidelity to the original sources. Said otherwise, the Project had to balance cultural competency with fidelity in the peers' interactions with the community residents. The second problem concerned the longer range survival of this liminal organizational enterprise (assuming that the community continued to find it valuable), and credibility with the local CBO stakeholder group (Golden, 2017). Our preceding analysis speaks most directly to the first problem, through its focus on a specific communicational event; however, the success with which the first problem is managed has implications for the latter one, since it impacts the way in which the local community of CBOs relates with the WHP and the peer health advocates.

The analysis shows how the peers discursively bridge between the world of the clinic and their neighbourhood world, enacting a delicate balance. They are most successful in the discursive performances that are at the margin, with elements of both the community and the clinic held in productive tension (e.g., Shirley's description of how to use a condom effectively; Mary's call-and-response affirmations). They are somewhat less successful in deploying the clinical discursive genre exclusively, not surprisingly given their comparatively limited experience with it. Conversely, we note—from the first author's additional field observations of team interactions—that the peers themselves recognize that employing a discursive genre that's too "street" (to use the language of the peers and their fellow residents) may run the risk of undermining their credibility with fellow residents as they enact the role of a community member who also has expert knowledge. From the Project Director's perspective, this can also undermine their credibility with the CBOs that the WHP is trying to connect with underserved residents. This is something that Shirley may be aware of when she qualifies a discursive performance that might be construed as shading over into "street" talk with "I'm just saying."

As noted in our findings, we can understand the dialog that follows Shirley's metadiscourse marker "I'm just saying," in which the peers discuss the potential problems of IUDs that have not been properly fitted, as a possible rehearsal of speaking in the voice of the clinic as fitted to their community. However, their rendition of the information they received and the sense they make of it does not, for the Project Director, map well onto the intentions of the expert trainers—as demonstrated by her attempt to steer the discussion away from the "problem narrative" and back toward the main takeaways as she understands them: the effectiveness of the IUD as a contraception method, though it provides no protection against sexually transmitted infections. Yet the transcript also shows that the peers are not uniform in their response. As our analysis earlier notes, two peers in the group attempt to temper the "problem narrative" with a more "scientific" assessment of the "evidence." The tensions between the multiple voices in this instance are not resolved within the context of this interaction, though it supports the view of the organization and the peers themselves as multivocal, with characteristics of the CBOs and community members they attempt to mediate between, and univocal in their commitment to this mediating role. We would further argue that univocity is not synonymous with harmony; there are disagreements, but the evidence suggests that they are managed. It is through this interactional management of multivocity that the polyphonic voice of the organization emerges.

Being able to reproduce health-related information with fidelity can be a significant issue for the WHP's credibility with its CBO partners, who are likely to take the conventional position that it is better to convey no information at all than inaccurate information. Thus, the "problem narrative" could be emblematic of a problem for the WHP. Alternatively, such a performance can be viewed by WHP members who speak fluently in the voice of the clinic (i.e., the Project Director and the Field Coordinator), as an opportunity to gain insight into the difficulties of community residents in translating health information delivered in the voice of the clinic—as well as presenting an opportunity for correction. If an organization member like the Project Director, who is *not* a community resident, and does not speak in that voice, does not allow for these in-between performances in which translation attempts may be imperfect, it will not be possible to see the *process* of translation. Conversely, if these community members are given a space in which to rehearse and check their understandings, an invaluable opportunity for refinement of multivocal organizing and mutual understanding can be opened up.

Conclusion

We conclude, reflexively, with a caution to both ourselves and to other community-engaged researchers. As the WHP's peer health advocate initiative progresses from a spontaneously emergent enterprise, originating as much from the community as from the academic research team that initiated this health promotion project, toward a more conventionally institutionalized mode (in the interests of its long-term survival), the initiative may find itself pushing up against the limits of multivocity. Our caution regards the need to keep sight of multivocity's value, lest in managing its potential problems, we manage it out of existence and sacrifice its benefits. We concede that multivocity can be challenging, but at the same time we note that the communicational event we've focused on here demonstrates that the peers themselves are already handling it with considerable skill, and there is value for "outsiders" in listening to people who speak in different voices to see how they are already dealing with it themselves. In the WHP, the first author's field experiences affirm that considerable allowance was made for the expression of non-professional talk within the context of closed team meetings, though a blending of genres was encouraged in interactions with community residents, and more "professional" talk was encouraged in interactions with CBOs. As the Project continues to evolve toward meeting the requirements of institutionalization, it will be important for the Project Director to encourage reflexivity on and tolerance for multivocity on the part of the peer health advocates and other organizational members they interact with. Organizing must leave room for multivocal expression; therefore, multivocity must be "managed" (i.e., intervened in) with caution so as to respect and value the multiple voices that CBOs ostensibly value.

As a final word, we note a push for medicalization and certification of the "community health worker" role (this being the role that the peer health advocates most closely correspond to) within the American healthcare system that is part of this study's setting. From a healthcare system standpoint, the issue of how the "bridging" services provided by community health workers can be paid for leads to the medicalization of the role so that it can be covered by health insurance plans. The peer health advocates' "outreach" activities cannot be billed for within the current system; it is not a bounded, commodifiable service like a clinical interaction. Nonetheless, we argue that it is a profoundly valuable service which embodies the value of multivocity and authentic connection to a *specific* community, rather than the more limited notion of valuing of the *idea* of a community, as represented in the more medicalized model of the community health worker. This leaves unresolved, however, the issue of resources to support such activities and the management of tensions in the long-term commitments to advocacy on the part of academics who aspire to help effect change in underserved communities.

Acknowledgement

Support for this research was provided by the National Institute on Minority Health and Health Disparities, National Institutes of Health to the first author (grant number P20MD003373). The content is solely the responsibility of the authors and does not necessarily represent the official views of the National Center on Minority Health and Health Disparities or the National Institutes of Health.

References

Aggerholm, H. K., Asmuß, B., & Thomsen, C. (2012). The role of recontextualization in the multivocal, ambiguous process of strategizing. *Journal of Management Inquiry*, *21*(4), 413–428. https://doi.org/10.1177/1056492611430852

Alvesson, M., & Kärreman, D. (2000). Varieties of discourse: On the study of organizations through discourse analysis. *Human Relations*, *53*(9), 1125–1149. https://doi.org/10.1177/0018726700539002

Arvey, S. R., & Fernandez, M. E. (2012). Identifying the core elements of effective community health worker programs: A research agenda. *American Journal of Public Health*, *102*(9), 1633–1637. https://doi.org/10.2105/AJPH.2012.300649

Bakhtin, M. M. (1986). *Speech genres and other late essays*. University of Texas Press.

Balcazar, H., Lee Rosenthal, E., Nell Brownstein, J., Rush, C. H., Matos, S., & Hernandez, L. (2011). Community health workers can be a public health force for change in the United States: Three actions for a new paradigm. *American Journal of Public Health*, *101*(12), 2199–2203. https://doi.org/10.2105/AJPH.2011.300386

Bartunek, J. M. (2008). Insider/outsider team research: The development of the approach and its meanings. In A. B. Bashni, N. Adler, S. A. Mohrman, W. A. Pasmore, & B. Stymne (Eds.), *Handbook of collaborative management research* (pp. 73–92). SAGE Publications. https://doi.org/10.4135/9781412976671.n4

Bell, M. P., Özbilgin, M. F., Beauregard, T. A., & Sürgevil, O. (2011). Voice, silence, and diversity in 21st century organizations: Strategies for inclusion of gay, lesbian, bisexual, and transgender employees. *Human Resource Management*, *50*(1), 131–146. https://doi.org/10.1002/hrm.20401

Belova, O., King, I., & Sliwa, M. (2008). Introduction: Polyphony and organization studies: Mikhail Bakhtin and beyond. *Organization Studies*, 29(4), 493–500. https://doi.org/10.1177/0170840608088696

Bencherki, N. (2017). A pre-individual perspective to organizational action. *Ephemera. Theory and Politics in Organization*, 17(4), 777–799.

Bencherki, N., Matte, F., & Pelletier, É. (2016). Rebuilding Babel: A constitutive approach to tongues-in-use. *Journal of Communication*, 66(5), 766–788. https://doi.org/10.1111/jcom.12250

Benoit-Barné, C., & Cooren, F. (2009). The accomplishment of authority through presentification: How authority is distributed among and negotiated by organizational members. *Management Communication Quarterly*, 23(1), 5–31. https://doi.org/10.1177/0893318909335414

Bourgoin, A., Bencherki, N., & Faraj, S. (2019). "And who are you?": A performative perspective on authority in organizations. *Academy of Management Journal*, 63(4), 1134–1165. https://doi.org/10.5465/amj.2017.1335

Boxenbaum, E., & Battilana, J. (2005). Importation as innovation: Transposing managerial practices across fields. *Strategic Organization*, 3(4), 355–383. https://doi.org/10.1177/1476127005058996

Brummans, B. H. J. M., Cooren, F., & Chaput, M. (2009). Discourse, communication and organizational ontology. In F. Bargiela-Chiappini (Ed.), *The handbook of business discourse* (pp. 53–65). Edinburgh University Press.

Chaney, P., & Fevre, R. (2001). Inclusive governance and "minority" groups: The role of the third sector in Wales. *Voluntas: International Journal of Voluntary and Nonprofit Organizations*, 12(2), 131–156. https://doi.org/10.1023/A:1011286602556

Cooren, F. (2006). The organizational world as a plenum of agencies. In F. Cooren, J. R. Taylor, & E. J. Van Every (Eds.), *Communication as organizing: Practical approaches to research into the dynamic of text and conversation* (pp. 81–100). Lawrence Erlbaum.

Cooren, F. (2010). *Action and agency in dialogue: Passion, ventriloquism and incarnation*. John Benjamins.

Cooren, F. (2012). Communication theory at the center: Ventriloquism and the communicative constitution of reality. *Journal of Communication*, 62(1), 1–20. https://doi.org/10.1111/j.1460-2466.2011.01622.x

Cooren, F. (2015). *Organizational discourse: Communication and constitution*. Polity.

Cooren, F. (2016). Ethics for dummies: Ventriloquism and responsibility. *Atlantic Journal of Communication*, 24(1), 17–30. https://doi.org/10.1080/15456870.2016.1113963

Cooren, F., Bencherki, N., Chaput, M., & Vásquez, C. (2015). The communicative constitution of strategy-making: Exploring fleeting moments of strategy. In D. Golsorkhi, L. Rouleau, D. Seidl, & E. Vaara (Eds.), *The Cambridge handbook of strategy as practice* (pp. 370–393). Cambridge University Press.

Cooren, F., Matte, F., Benoit-Barné, C., & Brummans, B. H. J. M. (2013). Communication as ventriloquism: A grounded-in-action approach to the study of organizational tensions. *Communication Monographs*, 80(3), 255–277. https://doi.org/10.1080/03637751.2013.788255

Cooren, F., & Sandler, S. (2014). Polyphony, ventriloquism, and constitution: In dialogue with Bakhtin. *Communication Theory*, 24(3), 225–244. https://doi.org/10.1111/comt.12041

Cooren, F., & Taylor, J. R. (1997). Organization as an effect of mediation: Redefining the link between organization and communication. *Communication Theory*, 7(3), 219–260. https://doi.org/10.1111/j.1468-2885.1997.tb00151.x

Cornut, F., Giroux, H., & Langley, A. (2012). The strategic plan as a genre. *Discourse & Communication*, 6(1), 21–54. https://doi.org/10.1177/1750481311432521

Craig, R. T., & Sanusi, A. L. (2000). "I'm just saying …": Discourse markers of standpoint continuity. *Argumentation*, 14(4), 425–445. https://doi.org/10.1023/A:1007880826834

Crozier, M., & Friedberg, E. (1980). *Actors and Systems: The Politics of Collective Action*. University of Chicago Press.

Davies, B., & Harré, R. (1990). Positioning: The discursive production of selves. *Journal for the Theory of Social Behaviour*, 20(1), 43–63. https://doi.org/10.1111/j.1468-5914.1990.tb00174.x

Eynaud, P., Juan, M., & Mourey, D. (2018). Participatory art as a social practice of commoning to reinvent the right to the city. *Voluntas: International Journal of Voluntary and Nonprofit Organizations*, 29(4), 621–636. https://doi.org/10.1007/s11266-018-0006-y

Ganesh, S., & McAllum, K. (2012). Volunteering and professionalization: Trends in tension? *Management Communication Quarterly*, 26(1), 152–158. https://doi.org/10.1177/0893318911423762

Golden, A. G. (2017, July 5). The Women's Health Project: A case study of the problematics of a liminal organization. Communication Constitutes Organization: The Practical and Social Relevance of CCO Thinking. European Group for Organizational Studies Pre-Conference Development Workshop, Copenhagen, Denmark.

Habermas, J. (1984). *The theory of communicative action*. Beacon Press.

Haight, W. L. (1998). "Gathering the spirit" at First Baptist Church: Spirituality as a protective factor in the lives of African American children. *Social Work*, 43(3), 213–221. https://doi.org/10.1093/sw/43.3.213

Hautz, J., Seidl, D., & Whittington, R. (2017). Open strategy: Dimensions, dilemmas, dynamics. *Long Range Planning*, 50(3), 298–309. https://doi.org/10.1016/j.lrp.2016.12.001

Henry, E., & Pringle, J. (1996). Making voices, being heard in Aotearoa/New Zealand. *Organization*, 3(4), 534–540. https://doi.org/10.1177/135050849634010

Holloway, K. F. C. (2011). *Private bodies, public texts: Race, gender, and a cultural bioethics*. Duke University Press.

Jäger, U. P., & Kreutzer, K. (2011). Strategy's negotiability, reasonability, and comprehensibility: A case study of how central strategists legitimize and realize strategies without formal authority. *Nonprofit and Voluntary Sector Quarterly*, 40(6), 1020–1047. https://doi.org/10.1177/0899764010378703

James, E. (2003). Commercialism and the mission of nonprofits. *Society*, 40(4), 29–35. https://doi.org/10.1007/s12115-003-1015-y

Jefferson, G. (2004). Glossary of transcript symbols with an introduction. In G. H. Lerner (Ed.), *Conversation analysis: Studies from the first generation* (pp. 13–31). John Benjamins.

Koschmann, M. A., Kuhn, T., & Pfarrer, M. D. (2012). A communicative framework of value in cross-sector partnerships. *Academy of Management Review*, 37(3), 332–354. https://doi.org/10.5465/amr.2010.0314

Lewis, L. (2005). The civil society sector: A review of critical issues and research agenda for organizational communication scholars. *Management Communication Quarterly, 19*(2), 238–267. https://doi.org/10.1177/0893318905279190

Lewis, L., Isbell, M. G., & Koschmann, M. (2010). Collaborative tensions: Practitioners' experiences of interorganizational relationships. *Communication Monographs, 77*(4), 460–479. https://doi.org/10.1080/03637751.2010.523605

Matsaganis, M. D., Golden, A. G., & Scott, M. E. (2014). Communication infrastructure theory and reproductive health disparities: Enhancing storytelling network integration by developing interstitial actors. *International Journal of Communication, 8*, 21.

Matte, F., & Bencherki, N. (2019). Materializing ethical matters of concern: Practicing ethics in a refugee camp. *International Journal of Communication, 13*, 5870–5889.

Matte, F., & Cooren, F. (2015). Learning as dialogue: An "on-the-go" approach to dealing with organizational tensions. In L. Filliettaz, & S. Billett (Eds.), *Francophone perspectives of learning through work: Conceptions, traditions and practices* (pp. 169–187). Springer.

McAllum, K. (2014). Meanings of organizational volunteering diverse volunteer pathways. *Management Communication Quarterly, 28*(1), 84–110. https://doi.org/10.1177/0893318913517237

Meisenbach, R. J., & Kramer, M. W. (2014). Exploring nested identities: Voluntary membership, social category identity, and identification in a community choir. *Management Communication Quarterly, 28*(2), 187–213. https://doi.org/10.1177/0893318914524059

Mintzberg, H. (1983). *Power in and around organizations*. Englewood Cliffs, NJ: Prentice-Hall.

Mishler, E. G. (1985). *The discourse of medicine: Dialectics of medical interviews*. Westport, CT: Praeger.

Pattillo-McCoy, M. (1998). Church culture as a strategy of action in the Black community. *American Sociological Review, 63*(6), 767–784. https://doi.org/10.2307/2657500

Potter, J., & Wetherell, M. (1987). *Discourse and social psychology: Beyond attitudes and behaviour*. London, England: SAGE Publications.

Sanders, M. (2012). Theorizing nonprofit organizations as contradictory enterprises: Understanding the inherent tensions of nonprofit marketization. *Management Communication Quarterly, 26*(1), 179–185.

Sullivan, P., & McCarthy, J. (2008). Managing the polyphonic sounds of organizational truths. *Organization Studies, 29*(4), 525–541. https://doi.org/10.1177/0170840608088702

van Oosterhout, J. (Hans), Wempe, B., & Willigenburg, T. van. (2004). Rethinking organizational ethics: A plea for pluralism. *Journal of Business Ethics, 55*(4), 385–393. https://doi.org/10.1007/s10551-004-1347-6

Wang, C., & Burris, M. A. (1997). Photovoice: Concept, methodology, and use for participatory needs assessment. *Health Education & Behavior, 24*(3), 369–387. https://doi.org/10.1177/109019819702400309

Wetherell, M., & Potter, J. (1988). Discourse analysis and the identification of interpretative repertoires. In *Analysing everyday explanation: A casebook of methods* (pp. 168–183). Thousand Oaks, CA: SAGE Publications.

4 Finding the Voice of a Protest

Negotiating Authority among the Multiplicity of Voices in a Pro-Refugee Demonstration

Salla-Maaria Laaksonen, Erna Bodström, and Camilla Haavisto

Introduction

The 2015–2016 European refugee crisis led to a surge of citizen activism across Europe. It had an impact on domestic politics, fuelling xenophobic political movements, and giving birth to social movements that support refugees and oppose government politics. One such movement was the *Right to Live (RTL)*, a pro-refugee sit-in demonstration (cf. Brown, Feigenbaum, Frencer, & McCurdy, 2018) held in Finland in several central locations in the city of Helsinki from February to September 2017. The RTL protest is an example of prominently local but still global citizen activism. Such forms of activism are local in the sense that they often tap into national political situations and debates, but remain global in their form: frequent sit-in demonstrations or urban "protest camps" organized by refugees/migrants across the globe during the 21st century (cf. Brown et al., 2018). Some of these demonstrations have been short-lived, independent, and narrow instances of "street politics," while others have been part of more centrally organized and wider pro-migration or anti-deportation movements (cf. Brown et al., 2018). As Feigenbaum, Frencel, and McCurdy (2013) show, the phenomenon of organizing protest camps is far from recent, but they have been an increasingly frequent organizational form of opposition over the past 50 years. As such, protest organizations are not just a passing tactic and should be investigated on their own terms. They can be a driving force in the organizing process and form a focal point in larger political movements (Feigenbaum et al., 2013, p. 2).

In Finland, however, the protest was the first of its kind in terms of its magnitude and visibility. In the beginning, it was intended to last only four days, and the organizers had no clear aims or statements, merely a general notion of unfair handling of asylum processes and deportations. Soon it became clear the demonstration was collecting crowds and raising interest. The activities started to consolidate, with an emerging need to organize and negotiate the purpose of the protest. Through this process of meetings and negotiations, the two main demands of the protest soon formed:

DOI: 10.4324/9780429297830-4

the ceasing of deportations of applicants who had been denied asylum, and the re-handling of the negative asylum decisions made by the Finnish Immigration Service, Migri, due to problems observed in the process. In this chapter, we investigate organizational voicing and related forms of authority by following the process of formulating the demands as well as other official communication by RTL.

From the perspective of organization studies and organizational voice, RTL demonstrated organizational multivocality tied to a multicultural, political setting: the protest team was organized around three somewhat separate ethnolinguistic groups: Iraqis, Finns, and Afghans, during a period of heated debate on migration and asylum. The idea of organizations as polyphonic sites in which the voices of their heterogeneous members are articulated has been widely addressed by scholars advocating a discursive approach to organizations (e.g., Hazen, 1993; Taylor & Van Every, 2000; Boje, 2001; Robichaud, Giroux, & Taylor, 2004; Cooren & Sandler, 2014). Following the conceptualization of organizations as communicative constitutions (CCO; Putnam, Nicotera, & McPhee, 2009; Cooren, Kuhn, Cornelissen, & Clark, 2011;), we are interested in the presence of various voices in RTL and the ways in which they become translated to a single organizational voice. At the same time, we explore the ways in which authority is negotiated in the process of formulating the voice of a polyphonic organization, which holds interests, experiences, and knowledge as well as beliefs and values from a variety of backgrounds (e.g., Hazen, 1993; Boje, 2001).

In our research context, we use the term "voicing" to refer to the process in which RTL aims to find and formulate a common, organizational voice to express its existence and demands to society—thus, to talk as RTL instead of its individual members or sub-groups. As we show in this chapter, several internal meetings, as well as the help of an external communication officer working pro bono, were needed in order for the activists to agree upon the precise phrasings for their main demands (also Haavisto, 2020). These demands also reached the form of a concrete text, both virtually and in printed leaflets, thus becoming a stabilized representation of the conversations that took place while they were crafted (Taylor & Van Every, 2000). As suggested by the CCO literature (e.g., Cooren et al., 2011), texts have agency in organizations, as they direct attention, orient interests, and discipline actors. Further, the process through which they are generated can be argued to be a process in which the organization is talked and written into existence, as its members position their interests to the collective in a process of *authoring the organization* (Taylor & Van Every, 2000) and generating a common voice (e.g., Vasquez et al., 2018; Langley & Lusiani, 2015 for strategy texts).

Using interviews, ethnographic field notes and textual data such as public statements and other external messages communicated by RTL, we examine the interplay between the different voices of the protest during its over seven-month-long life cycle and investigate how they come to constitute a single organizational voice of RTL. More specifically, we ask how the organization was authored in and through the communicative process of forming the demonstration demands and external statements. How were the grassroot-level voices translated to form the voice of the multicultural and polyphonic protest organization?

Next, we explain our theoretical starting points for studying social movement organizations (SMOs) as communicatively constituted organizations (CCO), in which authority is a communicative accomplishment that exists not only in talk but also in various forms of text. Then we present our case and data in more detail before moving on to our analysis, which starts by discussing how existence of authority is denied in RTL, but still becomes visible through organizational practices. Then, we discuss two processes of voicing and authoring the RTL organization: the process of forming the protest demands and the virtual voicing of the organization using social media. Our findings highlight how different forms of authority, viewed as a dynamic, communicational, and relational property of organizational relationships (Benoit-Barné & Fox, 2017), are intertwined with the processes of voicing the multivocal organization.

Social Movement Organizations as Discursive Sites of Polyphony

The scholarship on new social movements has focused on the movements born after the mid-1960s, with postmaterialistic goals, and a focus on human rights issues or representation of marginalized groups (McAdam, Tarrow, & Tilly, 2001). Such movements often pursue social goals instead of directly political ones, although the definition of "being political" has also changed over recent decades (Fenton, 2016). As organizations, new social movements are often single-issue based, local, and relatively disorganized (Byrne, 1997). They are seen to foster forms of direct democracy, which includes an aim toward democratic forms of organizing (Polletta, 2002; Fenton, 2016). Such forms include ideas of distributed leadership and the practice of listening to all voices in the collective. Some scholars highlight the social network nature of SMOs: instead of hierarchies, they are based on mutual, organic connections among their members (e.g., Tilly, 1978; Diani, 1995; Rao, Morrill, & Zald, 2000; Krinsky & Crossley, 2014). It can be assumed that an organization that emerges from such premises would retain and also show some aspects of organizational multivocality; the ideals of democracy and mutual connectedness contribute to the endeavour to retain visible heterogeneous voices that represent the diverse starting point of the organization.

The organizational scholarship that sees organizations as being CCO views organizations as essentially polyphonic entities, which emerge from the communicative interactions among their members, the organizational actors (e.g., Taylor & Van Every, 2000; Robichaud et al., 2004; Cooren,

Brummans, & Charrieras, 2008). These organizational actors can be both human and non-human, such as technologies, documents, or spaces (Putnam et al., 2009; Cooren et al., 2011). In particular, CCO theorizing emphasizes the interplay between the two modalities of communication, text and conversations, which together establish, sustain and dissolve the organization in recursive processes of articulation (Taylor & Van Every, 2000; Cooren et al., 2011). Organizing as a communicative process involves constant translations between conversations and texts that describe, represent, and to some extent petrify those conversations (Taylor, Cooren, Giroux, & Robichaud 1996; Taylor & Cooren, 1997; Taylor & Van Every, 2000; Putnam et al., 2009). This means texts, or earlier conversations, can be used to incorporate other voices into the ongoing conversation, or to lend plausibility to the given utterance. For example, Benoit-Barné and Cooren (2009) show how principles and posted notes are mobilized to invoke authority in conversations, or Robichaud et al. (2004) describe how a mayor of the city summons other actors and previous conversations to constitute a collective voice of the city as he addresses citizens in a consultation meeting.

CCO scholars emphasize the constitutive power of communication; power is practiced through meaning production, as different issues are produced, framed, constructed, and deconstructed (e.g., Deetz & Mumby, 1990; Cooren, 2004; Cooren et al., 2011). By emphasizing the role of communication in organizing, the CCO approach challenges the classical theoretical approaches to organizations that see communication merely as a means of transmitting information, inside an existing container known as the organization. By acknowledging the constitutive role of communication, CCO also helps us understand the constructivist, social side of the organization (Kuhn, 2008, p. 1230)—communication is not only a means of transmitting information *within* an organization, but a fundamental force that calls organizations into existence. By emphasizing the complexity and processual nature of organizations, the CCO approach offers new theoretical tools for understanding the ways in which organizations come into being as precarious entities, and how different forms of coordination and power are embedded in communication flows in organizational settings (Dobusch & Schoeneborn, 2015). In this section, our focus lies on the meaning production and situated conversations that took place around the collective, multi-author process of producing a discursive representation of the RTL organization, and its demands: a text that sought to describe the premises and mission of RTL.

The Communicative Constitution of Authority

Studying authority and power in non-hierarchical organizations brings attention to the ways in which authority is performed and established in organizational action and communicative practices. It can be assumed that in a polyphonic organization, many competing voices exist, and that these voices are strategically used for authority (Cooren & Sandler, 2014). New social movement studies often emphasize the autonomy of these movements and the individuals within them, as well as the forms of new radical politics that they enable (Fenton, 2016). Fenton (2016), however, also suggests that these approaches fail to consider the broader relations of power and state politics. In a similar vein, the studies that emphasize the communicative constitution of organizations have been criticized for their lack of consideration for the manifestations of power in the process of organizing (e.g., Reed, 2010; Novak, 2016). Taylor and Van Every (2014) argue that while the notion of authority is concurrently present in organizational life, few studies explicitly focus on it. Following the premises of CCO, if organizations are considered to be entities constituted in communication, authority can also be studied as a communicative accomplishment (see Benoit-Barné & Cooren, 2009; Taylor & Van Every, 2014).

The discussion on authority connects with studies on leadership, but the concepts are not synonymous. Traditionally, authority refers to the power or right to give orders and make decisions, often possessed by leaders who occupy a position of power in the organizational system (Benoit-Barné & Fox, 2017). In SMO studies, the classical notion posits that leaders are essential for SMOs (e.g., Michels, 1969), as they are the actors who make movements strive over time and accomplish action. However, some more recent works on digital activism highlight the diminishing importance of leadership in the new networked forms of social action (e.g., Bennett & Segerberg, 2012). Despite the fact that both of these contradictory perspectives still exist, a few authors (e.g., Barker, Johnson, & Lavalette, 2001; Sutherland, Land, & Böhm, 2014) have claimed that both authority and leadership are underexamined areas in SMO studies. In particular, Sutherland et al. (2014) note that the theorizing of leadership in capitalist organizations is inadequate to understand the construction of leadership in horizontal, often anarchist SMOs. It has been suggested that the identification of authority in social movements calls for an investigation of the processes taking place, such as communication. As Krinsky and Crossley (2014, p. 2) remind us:

> people designated as leaders in a community are not necessarily the real leaders; the organizer has to find the real leaders by finding out who the people are to whom others talk and listen, and from whom others seek help and advice.

Thus, while an organization might seem leaderless, it is not necessary *leadershipless* (Sutherland et al., 2014). Instead of direct control and command chains, leadership takes more subtle forms such as the management of meaning and a discursive definition of reality (Smircich & Morgan, 1982). The urge for democratic, flat organizations in SMOs might, hence, expose the movement to organic leadership structures. Fyke and Sayegh (2001), for example, suggest that if an organization aims to refuse leadership positions, it becomes exposed to the risk of re-creating informal hierarchies rooted in existing, social power relations.

Organizational communication studies have explored authority beyond formal authority positions as a process of communication. From this perspective, authority is the capacity to make decisions and create meanings, but also a performance in interaction or a dynamic, negotiated communicative process of *coorientation* (Benoit-Barné & Fox, 2017). In this study, we follow the proposition of Taylor and Van Every (2014) and connect the question of authority to the communicative constitution or organization; we see authority as something that is negotiated through communication in the interrelations between the different agents in an organization. In their seminal book, Taylor and Van Every (2000) connect authority to the emerging thirdness of the organization: authority is established by speakers as they make the organization present in the discourse in order to act as its agents. For this to be possible, the organization must be collectively *authored*, assembled by people and mediated by text (Taylor & Van Every, 2014, p. 27–28). In line with this thinking, Benoit-Barné and Cooren (2009) talk about *presentification*, the practice of making various sources of authority present in organizational interaction. According to them, authority exists between entitlement (status, structure) and negotiation: locally and situationally accomplished authority is enacted as organizational members mobilize things and beings, such as ideas, other individuals or documents, texts, in micro-level interactions. Authority is, hence, strongly connected to things that are "not physically present, but influence the unfolding of the situation" (Benoit-Barné & Cooren, 2009, p. 10; also Cooren et al., 2008; Cooren & Sandler, 2014). Most importantly, these things imbue authority when connected to the authored organizational "it."

Texts and Authority

In connection to authority and authoring, a particular focus in the CCO literature has been on texts, an important mediating object in the constitutive process (see Taylor & Van Every, 2000). As Timothy Kuhn (2008, p. 1323, emphasis in original) formulates: "In constitutive terms communication is defined as *a process in which contextualized actors use symbols and make interpretations to coordinate, and control both their own and others' activity and knowledge, which are simultaneously mediated, and productive of, 'texts'*." Thus, organizations exist through language use, but also in various manifestations of language in communicative events and interactions (Taylor & Van Every, 2000), according to Kuhn (2008) either as concrete texts, such as contracts, documents, and websites; or more abstract figurative texts, such as principles, values and tacit knowledge (Cooren, 2004).

Kuhn (2008, p. 1234) lists three central characteristics for concrete and figurative texts. First, they have relative permanence, meaning that the foundation on which the actors base their interpretations endures beyond the immediate time and setting of the conversations; text is seen as permanent and solid. Second, texts are not unitary or monolithic entities but rather networks of meaning built through intertextuality and symbols (Corman et al., 2002; Kuhn, 2008). In these networks, meanings can be activated by situational framing or by other texts. Third, the meanings attached to texts may be conflicting in practice because texts are reappropriated and recontextualized across practice sites. Nevertheless, texts perform various functions in organizations: they work as abstracted representations of the intentions or their creators, and later work as common objects that frame and coorientate conversations, direct attention, and discipline actors (Taylor & Van Every, 2000; Kuhn, 2008, p. 1236; Fayard & Metiu, 2013). Thus, on the one hand, texts are reliable and efficient devices that fix meanings, but on the other, they are contingent and open to several potential interpretations (Vasquez et al., 2016).

Further, Kuhn (2008) argues that certain types of texts exhibit more agency than others. In particular, he highlights the idea of an "authoritative text" produced as a representation of the official organization (cf. Cooren et al., 2011). Kuhn (2008, p. 1236) writes "As cooriented conversations and texts become imbricated and validated by interactants, an abstract text is produced that represents the firm as a whole" and encourages "actors to subordinate personal interests to the collective good" (Kuhn, 2008, p. 1236). The resulting authoritative text is a conception of the organization, depicting and specifying its structure, activities and outcomes, legitimacy, and power relations in the firm's practice (Kuhn, 2008). An authoritative text functions as a reference point that represents, mediates, directs attention, disciplines, and links people and practices. In addition, it is a necessary component of coorientation within the organization and can, therefore, be a site of struggles over meaning, thus acting as a focal point for the constitution of authority.

With a focus on organizational voicing and authoring—the process through which RTL activists aimed to form a collective, organizational voice for RTL—this study aims to track the birth of such an authoritative text, both figuratively and concretely, by tracing how authority became embedded in the textual representations of the negotiated voice of the organization in the RTL demonstration.

Data and Method

Our empirical case is an SMO, the Right to Live, a pro-refugee sit-in demonstration (cf. Brown et al., 2018) organized in Finland between February and September 2017 to criticize the asylum processes and deportations of asylum seekers. A demonstration camp, occupied around the clock, was situated in the core of the city, first outside Kiasma, the Museum of Contemporary Art, then at the Helsinki Railway Square for the majority of the time (over four months), then again outside Kiasma, and finally on The Three Smiths' square, all very central and visible locations at the heart of the city. The demonstration team consisted of three somewhat separate ethnolinguistic groups: Afghans, Iraqis, and Finns. This made RTL a multicultural and polyphonic organization formed by people with differing cultural backgrounds and multiple languages, English often being the sole common language, if any: although the shared language of the demonstration was English, not all team members could speak it. The Afghan group was composed of people fluent in the Dari language, the Iraqi group of people fluent in Arabic, and the Finnish group mainly of people fluent in Finnish. However, the groups were internally diverse and polyethnic. The Afghan group consisted of a variety of ethnicities, including Pashtun, Tajik, and Hazara. The Iraqi group included ethnic Arabs and Kurds. The Finnish group also included some people not fluent in Finnish; settled immigrants in Finland.

Our data were collected during a participatory ethnography conducted as part of the demonstration. Access to the protest organization was possible because one of the authors had already been an active member of RTL since it began in February 2017. Having gained a trustworthy position within the organization, this author easily obtained research permission from the collective. The researcher's position as both activist and researcher (Couture, 2017), not activist researcher (Hale, 2001; Speed, 2006), made it possible to negotiate and re-negotiate ethical issues with the activists. This meant, in practice, being open and reflexive about one's own "ethical boundaries": about how to negotiate the changing roles between an academic and an activist (Couture, 2017) and keep academic and activist work clearly separate. While the activist position entails the aim of making a direct difference to society by working with the studied communities and engaging in public debates, the academic position follows critical scholarly traditions and aims for rigorous, transparent, and data-driven work.

The dataset included in-depth interviews ($N = 18$), field notes, photographs taken at the site ($N = 40$), and external communication material produced by RTL. The ethnographic data were collected between May and July 2017. Field notes of 23 single-spaced pages were written onsite at the demonstration as well as during circa 60 hours of observation in the meetings related to the demonstration. The meetings were attended by and open to all the active members of the demonstration. The topics covered ranged from very practical issues such as maintaining the demonstration to more strategic ones such as the future and scope of the activities. The photographs depicted everyday life and events at the demonstration, the demonstration site, and the participants.

Eighteen semi-structured interviews of the organizers and supporters of the RTL demonstration were conducted in May–August 2017. The interview questions covered the interviewees' own paths to becoming an active member of the demonstration, their own activities and tasks during the demonstration, their views on leadership and decision-making in the demonstration, and their experiences of and narratives about the communication practices of the demonstration. Six of the interviewed organizers were part of the Iraqi group, three of the Afghan group, and five of the Finnish group. Five of the interviewees were supporters of the demonstration (a term used by the interviewees). The informants were selected on the basis of their roles in the demonstration, and the level of their activity observed during the ethnography. We wanted to interview informants who played key roles in the strategic and intellectual work as well as others who were on site but played a less prominent role in terms of brainstorming and decision-making. The interviews lasted from 20 minutes to 1 hour and were all transcribed verbatim. In the case of the Iraqi and Afghan protesters the interviews were conducted in English, but with Finnish protesters and supporters interviews were conducted in Finnish. The authors translated all the quotations from the Finnish language interviews into English.

Finally, social media material and press releases published by the RTL demonstration organization (published under the brand StopDeportations) were collected. This dataset included 78 blog posts and 2,857 tweets posted in May–Dec 2017. The longer time period was chosen for the communication material in order to track the activities of the organization after the demonstration ended. This dataset, however, was only used for reference purposes to chart out the timeline; no in-depth textual analyses were conducted using the data.

Our main research questions aimed to determine how the organization was authored in and through the communicative process of forming the demonstration demands and external statements. How were the grassroot-level voices translated into the voice of the multicultural and polyphonic protest organization? In this context, as an analytical definition, we identify voice in a two-fold way. Through voice, individuals and collectives can have a de facto possibility to articulate meaningful demands in the organizational context, with an aim to influence processes such as routines, codes of conduct, and communication practices. This can be done in print, through speech and/or by gestures, mediated or not, and it acquires active listening by several parties. At the same time, voice functions as a metaphor for the authored organization, assembled by the members through text and conversation (Taylor & Van Every, 2000). On this more publicly visible level, the voice of the organization matters for how the organization is seen, related to, and interacted with. These two identifications are intertwined, yet together relevant for the study of a polyphonic organization.

To answer these questions, we used the interview transcripts as our primary data, but also used field observations, field notes, and the external communication material of the RTL as support data. The first author conducted an inductive analysis of the interview material using Atlas.TI. The first round of open, thematic coding yielded 37 codes describing the interview content. The next round of analysis focused on passages that concerned authority and forming the organization's voice. First, we concentrated on the passages with explicit discussions on decision-making and leadership in the demonstration, and the interviewees' stories about organizing and responsibilities (coded as *hierarchies*, *decision making*, and *participation*). Second, we analyzed the interviewees' stories and views on the process of formulating the official demands and their descriptions of the external communication practices of RTL (coded as *demands*, *external messages*, and *social media dissemination*). Such focus allowed us to explore how the activists described the practices through which RTL spoke as an organization, as well as the decisions and negotiations behind the communication outcomes. During the final round of analysis, we re-read these sections of the material and compared them to the realized practices visible in the field notes and RTL's public communication and discussed our notions together and agreed on three central perspectives: first, the presence of hidden forms of authority related to cultural and practical issues in RTL; and second and third, their interplay with the two central voicing processes of the protest organization: formulating demands and communicating online about the protest.

Results

The Hidden Voice: The Story of No Leader

Our investigation reveals an emerging protest organization that negotiates authority in a context in which those with authority persistently deny it. In their discourse and organizational routines, the interviewees fostered a concept of a leaderless organization (cf. Sutherland et al., 2014). When directly asked, the interviewees generally described the organization as democratic and flat. Our ethnographic notes confirmed this characteristic, as they did not record any discussions on a specific leader of the demonstration. Rather, the negotiations, in meetings, for example, revolved around practical issues, such as the division of work, or who would make tea or wash the dishes. Within the organization, *leaderlessness* seems to have been taken for granted, already—perhaps wordlessly—agreed upon. Thus, the concept of a leader seems to be an issue brought in from the outside (in the form of the interviewer) rather than emerging from the inside. Some interviewees did mention the existence of a core team and referred to certain leader figures, but at the same time stated that no clearly demarcated groups exercised leadership. Almost all the interviewees denied the existence of leaders, but said that their group had *representatives* or *specific duties*:

There is not a leader, but there are representatives ... because in demo there's hundreds of people so, everybody cannot talk in the media, everybody cannot, (go in the) meetings so that is why there is need to be some, specific person to, represent .... And we all are working togetherly.

(Afghani protester)

I think there is no leader in the demo. 'Cause every person he, know his job, in the demo, and we cannot continue without him... So, we are just one family, trying to, fix this misery in Finland.

(Iraqi protester)

Despite the overarching narrative of a leaderless demonstration, status positions emerged, as the practical role divisions still inadvertently created status and even leader roles. On the one hand, they reflected the existing hierarchies of the asylum seekers' cultures and communities; on the other, specific skills, such as language skills and local knowhow, built status positions. Thus, authority became visible in connection to practices and spaces: in meeting practices and when greeting camp visitors, but also in the more mundane activities of fetching water or occupying the kitchen tent. In all the subgroups, hierarchies were formed organically through different levels of participation, which were constantly renegotiated in action:

... for me, it's been to some extent unclear what the decision-making system actually is and who has influence over what. There is, on the one hand, a lovely anarchistic side where everybody's voice is equal, or that's what it looks like, but in the asylum seeker community, among the Afghan and Iraqi, there are some characters who have a lot of power by nature, those who the members of their group listen to and follow, and what they say carries more weight.

(Finnish supporter)

The different authoritative roles also became visible during the participatory observation. For example, one of the members of the Iraqi community called an emergency meeting after being away for a week. The justification was that he needed to get back on top of things after being gone, and others complied with this—which indicates a significant status in the demonstration organization. The field notes from that meeting support the interpretation: he mainly led the discussion in the meeting and was also the one who mainly spoke for his own community, while the floor was shared more evenly between the members of the other two communities. This was not a question of language skills, since the Iraqi group had several other members with proficient English skills, but it shows he was generally a person of status in the demonstration and specifically within his own community. However, neither he himself nor anyone else aimed to give him a leader status. It seemed more a matter of necessity: somebody had to call the meeting, raise the matters to be discussed, and lead the discussion. In the meeting, other people were also allowed to bring new matters to the table.

Within the demonstration organization, however, there were differing views on protest ownership, which also was reflected in voicing practices. An overarching principle advocated particularly by the Finns was that the demonstration was organized, and decisions were made by and for the asylum seekers, and that they should represent the face of the demonstration outside (see Haavisto, 2020). There was an aim, for example, to push the asylum seekers to talk to any journalists who visited the camp. This ideal can perhaps be traced back all the way to the sans-papiers movement, a series of protests organized and led by migrants, for migrants starting from France in 1990s (Freedman, 2008). However, what is interesting is that the emphasis on this issue seemed to come from the Finnish organizers more than from the Iraqis and Afghans: whereas the latter emphasized the equality and flatness of the organization, the former further focused on the active role of the Iraqis and Afghans. While these aspirations connect to authority, they are more related to practices of representation and public image of the protest.

However, a few interviewees mentioned that despite this principle, the Finns ended up acting as the main communicators on the ground, since they had a shared language with most visitors. The ethnographic notes indicate how this was visible in both daily interactions, for instance, at the tea tent, and in more strategic communication, such as during negotiations with the city. Further, according to one of the interviewees, the Finns often led the talk in meetings and were also asked to do the same by other subgroups, who liked to follow the structured meeting style adopted from the somewhat institutionalized practices of progressive movements (cf. Polletta, 2002). At the same time, this setting, combined with cultural differences, seemed to generate tensions in the decision-making process, as some members regarded the advice given by the Finns as orders— which might also be related to personal communication styles. Thus, it seems that although the idea of a democratic, flat organization existed as an ideal, the organizers of the demonstration ended up taking different roles for practical reasons, whether it was washing the dishes or trying to maintain the bigger political picture of asylum seekers' situation in Finland. These roles then overlapped with status within the demonstration organization. Hence, authority was not necessarily embodied by a person; it was performed and acquired in interaction (Benoit-Barné & Cooren, 2009; Taylor & Van Every, 2014), in connection with the epistemic authority positions of the Finns (Benoit-Barné & Fox, 2017). In addition, as we will discuss next, practical authority was also reflected in the process of voicing the organization.

The Negotiated Voice of the RTL: Formulating Demands

According to the Finns we interviewed, the protest was not very organized or goal-oriented at first, a matter over which they expressed frustration. Thus, they initiated a process to formulate clear demands for the demonstration and to find a shared voice. The demands were prepared in a series of meetings, accompanied by heated Facebook discussions, and a workshop held by an NGO worker. There were first four, then two main demands, which were later followed by several sub-demands and releases targeted at specific organizations. The main objective was to start communicating externally as clearly as possible and to disseminate the message. On another level, however, the activists and their allies aimed for politically realistic demands. The process of formulating the demands was connected to the questions of dissemination and effectiveness (*How to get the message out there?*), but as we will show, it is also related to the process of negotiating RTL's organizational identity (*What are we here for?*).

> A few people from the Iraqi team and the Afghan team wrote [the statements], because they were allowed to form them themselves. So there were multiple items, in my mind, at the time when ... [an NGO] held training for us where we went through the demands and then made a timeline of what would happen. What can happen, what is realistic, what can happen when, what needs a new government ...
>
> (Finnish supporter)

Natalie Fenton (2016) maintains that in social movement, participation itself is often seen as the main purpose and outcome of the political protest rather than the actual policy impact. This was clearly different in the case of RTL: the demands were formulated with a clear political purpose and concrete means to achieve the goals were planned. The interview data show that this was mostly a concern of the Finns, who considered the more general statements acknowledging the difficult situation of refugees too vague. Finally, the protesters agreed upon four main issues to object to: the random, unjustified negative decisions made by the immigration services; the compulsory return policy for refugees in Finland and the violent treatment during the process of deportation; the removal of asylum seekers—especially families—with negative decisions from the refugee centers; and the cutting of their financial aid. While everybody eventually agreed with the demands, the interviews clearly show that the process by which they were formulated was not easy:

> [It was not easy to come to these demands] because we had to talk about it for a very long time...and, a few of the Afghan organisers...we were talking about it (over a week), writing drafts after drafts after drafts after drafts and we came out with one, that we all had to agree on.
>
> (Afghan protester)

Formulating external messages forced the group to discuss their goals and, at the same time, revealed cultural tensions and communicative practices of authority. Again, the practical skills intervened with the process: the professional skills and merits of the Finns were involved in these negotiations and even mobilized as arguments. In the following statement, an Iraqi protester explains how the Finns invoked their professionalism as an object of authority in a conversation while planning the demands:

> R: Yeah. It was really hard and we got many troubles because of that. Some people from the Finnish they, said, we got some, problems between us inside. Because some of them they advised "No we should, put these demands. I know about this 'cause that's my professional thing"…But finally everything's good and we have the demands.
>
> (Iraqi protester)

Indeed, the interview data demonstrates the vital role of the Finnish volunteers and organizers, particularly because of their knowledge of the Finnish political and administrative system, and also because the Iraqi and Afghan participants were distracted by the constant threat of deportation during the process. The refugees agreed that the formulation of the protest's demands and the lobbying efforts would have been impossible without the help of Finnish volunteers. But in addition to their local knowhow, the Finns also brought in a discourse of efficacy, in regard to both realistic goals and the process of formulating the actual messages. A Finnish supporter explains how the group became increasingly smaller and how no longer everybody approved all the changes:

> We organized meetings with the asylum seekers, meetings in which we tried to formulate them together, because that was the only possible starting point. But then what often happened was that it was difficult to move forward, and the groups got smaller, and then in the end the actual writing might have been done by the Finns only. The main content was there, but the contextualization and how things were presented was pretty much left to the supporters and activists, because of language skills and contextual understanding.
>
> (Finnish supporter)

Texts can indeed be sites of struggles over meaning, as the CCO literature reminds us (Taylor & Van Every, 2000; Cooren, 2004; Kuhn, 2008): not everybody in RTL agreed with or settled for the demands. A set of additional claims were made by the Afghan community, who did not get all they wanted to say into the final version. To preserve multivocality, they formulated their own demands that were then published via the official virtual channels. The original demands were, although practical, quite generic because they aimed to represent all asylum seekers in Finland—not only those from Iraq and Afghanistan. Therefore, although partially overlapping with the general demands, the additional demands of the Afghans aimed to address the specific situation in Afghanistan and that of Afghan asylum seekers.

The process of formulating the demands was the first tangible organizational task in which the members engaged. Despite the problematic process and the lack of consensus in the writing phase, the interviewees regarded the demand statements as the textual reference point for the whole protest. The claims became a stabilized text, the principles of the demonstration that made the organization present by acting on its behalf. Because they were formulated through a seemingly democratic process, they began to embody the "family" of the demonstration and hence carry polyphonic authority. By this we mean that through their cooriented formulation, the demands were, somewhat paradoxically, considered to represent all voices, even though it was acknowledged that all voices were not always present or equal in the process:

> … no I haven't heard anyone being particularly against them, so they are clear in that sense, that they have risen from joint consciousness and from all the conversations and the main problems.
>
> (Finnish supporter)

Thus, as the form of the demands was formulated and accepted, the original disagreements, long meetings, and negotiations were forgotten and replaced by a shared satisfaction over the communally produced voice of the organization. Thus, the demands were not only stabilized but also a *stabilizing* element for the protest. The demand statements and the tangible flyers on which they were printed became objects that made the organization present: the written claims and statements began to act as textual agents performing on behalf of the organization, both within and outside it. They became a text through which bystanders could be approached, a text by which the politicians could be contacted, and a text that made the organization present not only in the public sphere but also as an entity for the protesters themselves. Hence, it was a tangible text that built agency for the protest, and, following the theorizing of Timothy Kuhn (2008), an authoritative text that represented the organization as a whole and encouraged its members to work for the collective good.

The Public Voice: Virtual Communication Practices

Once the demands were formulated, they also boosted the external communications of the demonstration, particularly on social media. Official organizational channels were founded for strategic external communication and for virtual lobbying. Both official Facebook and Twitter accounts were used for communicating to Finnish citizens, raising awareness about

Figure 4.1 A tweet from the official account showing a visual message that points to the practices of the Immigration Authority, which was accused of working with refugee quotas: "On the flip board of Migri this would be me."

the refugee situation and reaching virality (see Figure 4.1). Direct communication and tagging were used to influence Finnish decision-makers and authorities. To some extent, the lobbying also used the activists' personal accounts, in the case of the Finnish supporters in particular. Both the refugees and the Finns expressed a feeling of responsibility to disseminate information about the demonstration:

> I try to post information all the time and have conversations — I think it's important to use social media to build the community, to share information, influence opinions, and also that the communication officers tell those who are not active that this is happening!
>
> (Finnish supporter)

As mentioned in the quotation above, a dedicated group of people started to work as communication officers due to their previous experience in media communications and copyediting texts. Their work included formulating the messages sent by the demonstration: social media posts, press releases, and statements. In addition, they acted as contact persons for the media and sometimes other actors, such as the city of Helsinki. Our interview data also indicate that they tried to urge all members to communicate using their own channels.

To some extent, forms of virtual communication allowed all members of the demonstration to voice RTL: anybody with the necessary technical and language skills could post about the event and its demands using various channels and dedicated hashtags. However, in this kind of diverse organization, linguistic and communicative skills vary as greatly as the organizational members themselves, from multilingual to illiterate people. Some protesters, especially those from Afghanistan, were indeed multilingual, speaking, for example, Pashto and Dari, although not necessarily English. Therefore, the demonstration members used several unofficial channels, many of which were targeted toward a specific language or cultural group. For example, separate Facebook groups existed for the Arabic and Dari speakers. A Finnish-English support group was founded for local supporters, i.e., people who were not part of the most active core group of supporters but who wanted to offer practical support such as providing coal, food, or clothing. All these groups were used to communicate about the progress of the demonstration and more generally about the refugee situation in Finland. Some channels not directly related to RTL were also used, such as the ones mentioned by an Afghani protester in the following:

> We have some, ... social media by Facebook, and, by Twitter ... with the name of ... Demonstration of Refugee in Helsinki. And we explain about that, and we have some, other, A Voice of Refugees, we have that page, and, one is Home of Refugees ... And we have, active members (...) about our situation and, every day they, which news, which thing that happening in our home country, and they put it on that group.
>
> (Afghani protester)

To some extent, the virtual communication channels of the protest organization offered space for true polyphony: all members of the demonstration were allowed and encouraged to communicate in their own channels and groups—in the various languages represented in the demonstration. Nevertheless, professionalism and skills again generated authority and a position from which to speak for the organization, or concretely *in* the organization's voice and profile as afforded by the social media tools. The following quotation from a protester shows how online communication was rather left to the "professionals":

> Yeah, I use Facebook, but sometimes when I have (shift night), at morning...But it's not all the time. There is, some guys they are, professional with these things.
>
> (Iraqi protester)

In this regard, the practicalities were intertwined with the voicing practices, as the people who organically started acting as communication officers also administered the RTL accounts. Particularly for the general public in Finland, the voice of the demonstration was heard through the official channels of RTL and through media coverage, mostly in Finnish, English, or sometimes Swedish. This is a practice that was undoubtedly effective for the political goals, but also limited the scope of people able to participate in the voicing of the protests, and to some extent separated the official voice from the democratic idea of the grassroot-level voices of the organization (see Gerbaudo, 2017).

Discussion and Conclusion

Our data illuminate how the multicultural starting point of the RTL demonstration generated explicit discussions about authority and the voice of the organization: Who should talk on behalf of the demonstration? What is our main message? Who can decide it? While the activists cherished the idea of multicultural polyphony, it seems they regarded it essential to filter the multiplicity of voices into univocality in order to create a recognized entity and to communicate strategically and effectively. The Finnish supporters in particular advocated such practices. Our data highlight how authority became visible through practical tasks and skills, as well as through the existing cultural hierarchies in the asylum seekers' communities, and further, how these forms of authority were reflected in the processes of voicing the organization. Most importantly, both processes of voicing we examined were markedly communicational processes, where skills from meeting practices, negotiation skills, copy-writing, and social media skills were essential. We suggest that the mediated society and current communication-heavy forms of doing a protest (Bennett & Segerberg, 2012; Gerbaudo, 2017) are lifting the importance of communication skills, which then become interwoven with questions of authority.

In line with the arguments presented in previous research on no-leader SMOs (Smircich & Morgan, 1982; Fyke & Sayegh, 2001; Sutherland et al., 2014), when leadership positions were refused, hierarchies and positions of authority formed roots in the existing power relations—in the case of RTL, in connection with both traditional/cultural power and practices/merits. The interview data and field notes both show how the practical roles taken up by the protesters inadvertently created status positions and even leader roles in the demonstration organization. Such roles were related, first, to the everyday tasks in the demonstration, but also to more professional tasks that required existing skills and knowledge. Practical authority also affected the processes of voicing the organization to bystanders and officials, in which language skills played a considerable role. Thus, authority in the protest organization was, to some extent, based on meritocracy. Second, the existing cultural hierarchies, particularly in the Iraqi and Afghan groups, led to some persons being regarded as "naturally" more powerful than others. In both cases, the emerging status positions or leadership roles were not decided upon or appointed by the protest organization; they became visible through practices and practicalities. Further, the Finns' ideas of conducting a protest "correctly" following the practices that were generally accepted in progressive SMOs (Polletta, 2002) were adopted by the RTL organization and helped increase the authority of the Finnish supporters—further accentuated because of their knowledge of the local administrative system and language. At the same time, they relentlessly maintained the idea of a demonstration that was owned and represented by the asylum seekers themselves (Haavisto, 2020).

As a part of the "correct" ways of doing a protest, Finns also initiated the process to form the official demands for RTL, a process that highlighted the tensions between the actors and their voices inside the organization. In the light of our data, the negotiations emerged as a process in which authority was negotiated in communication and action (Benoit-Barné & Cooren, 2009; Taylor & Van Every, 2014). Essentially, it was a process of forming a text, but it also appeared as a negotiation about the organization and its purpose—of authoring the organization (Taylor & Van Every, 2000). In an organization in which no authority seemingly or allegedly existed, the centripetal process of voicing carved out existing authority positions and hierarchies. They connected first, to the question of who were invited to the meetings where the demands are made—not all our interviewees were—and second, to the skills and the professionalism of the Finnish supporters in particular. Various forms of capital (Bourdieu, 1991) became embedded in the demands through the process: the social and cultural capital the Finns possessed through their knowhow and language skills and the symbolic capital the asylum seekers possessed, particularly certain traditionally prestigious figures in the community. Hence, the existing forms of authority—meritocracy, traditional—intertwined with communicative authority in the process of authoring the organization.

Another form of voicing RTL was using social media for communication and lobbying. Online, the cultural diversity and polyvocality of the organization, was given more space, as the social media dissemination was allowed to be fragmented, multilingual, and multivocal. Unofficial social media groups were founded to fit all purposes with names not directly connected to the RTL protest. From the perspective of voicing and authoring the organization, however, they were separate from the official channels supporting the voice of RTL, which were mostly administered by communication officers. Other groups remained as micro-stories that participated in the constitution of the organization (Taylor & Van Every, 2014), but they were not fully incorporated to the authored organizational voice, nor worked to stand for the organization like the demands did. This practice allows the organization to maintain its multivocality on one hand, but also to meet the requirements of effectively communicating a protest on the other.

Simultaneously, the demands, produced in a democratic process of meetings and online conversations, became a stabilized textual representation of the organization, an authoritative text (cf. Kuhn, 2008), in which organizational goals were formulated and through which the organization was made present—regardless of the stories the interviewees told about a problematic process. This is indicative of the power and authority possessed by texts as discussed by Kuhn (2008): They are permanent and solid and carry the ability to direct attention and discipline actors. We argue that the negotiations that led to the demands played an essential role in building authority for the demands—something that even the official social media messages were lacking. As an end result of the process, the demands made the organization present by acting on its behalf in various, subsequent interactions; they made it possible for actors to speak on behalf of the organization (Taylor & Cooren, 1997). Hence, through the demands, the *organization* emerged from the collective; the state of entitative being was found (Robichaud et al., 2004; Nicotera, 2013). The demands perhaps did not perform the political claims they stated, but they did perform the organization into existence (Taylor & Cooren, 1997; Cooren et al., 2008); in this sense, they were not statements of fact, but acts of speech with consequences (Austin, 1962). It seems that in a multivocal organization, the ability of texts to incorporate polyphony and retain some of the contingency of meanings present in the process of their creation allow them to serve as coorientating devices in the organization. Despite the difficult process of their realization, they are considered to include all the voices of the organization, perhaps empowered by the aura of a democratic process.

References

Austin, J. L. (1962). *How to do things with words*. Oxford: Clarendon Press/Oxford University Press.

Barker, C., Johnson, A., & Lavalette, M. (2001). Leadership matters: An introduction. In Barker, C., Johnson, A., & Lavalette, M. (Eds.), *Leadership and social movements* (pp. 1–23). Manchester: Manchester University Press.

Bennett, W. L., & Segerberg, A. (2012). The logic of connective action: Digital media and the personalization of contentious politics. *Information, Communication & Society, 15*(5), 739–768.

Benoit-Barné, C., & Cooren, F. (2009). The accomplishment of authority through presentification: How authority is distributed among and negotiated by organizational members. *Management Communication Quarterly, 23*(1), 5–31.

Benoit-Barné, C., & Fox, S. (2017). Authority. In Scott, C. & Lewis, L. (Eds.), *The international encyclopedia of organizational communication* (pp. 1–13). Hoboken, NJ: John Wiley & Sons, Inc. https://doi.org/10.1002/9781118955567.wbieoc011

Boje, D. M. (2001). *Narrative methods for organizational communication research*. London: SAGE.

Bourdieu, P. (1991). *Language and symbolic power*. Cambridge, MA: Harvard University Press.

Brown, G., Feigenbaum, A., Frencer F., & McCurdy P. (2018). Introduction: Past tents, present tents: On the importance of studying protest camps. In Brown et al. (Eds.), *Protest camps in international context: Spaces, infrastructures and media of resistance*. Bristol: Policy Press.

Byrne, D. (1997). *Social movements in Britain*. London: Routledge.

Cooren, F. (2004). Textual agency: How texts do things in organizational settings. *Organization, 11*(3), 373–393. https://doi.org/10.1177/1350508404041998

Cooren, F., Brummans, B., & Damien C. (2008). The coproduction of organizational presence: A Study of Mdecins Sans Frontires in action. *Human Relations*, 61(10), 1339–1370. https://doi.org/10.1177/0018726708095707.

Cooren, F., Kuhn, T., Cornelissen, J., & Clark, T. (2011). Communication, organizing, and organization. *Organization Studies*, 32(9), 1149–1170.

Cooren, F., & Sandler, S. (2014). Polyphony, ventriloquism, and constitution: In dialogue with Bakhtin. *Communication Theory*, 24(3), 225–244.

Corman, S. R., Kuhn, T., Mcphee, R. D., & Dooley, K. J. (2002). Studying complex discursive systems centering resonance analysis of communication. *Human Communication Research*, 28(2), 157–206. https://doi.org/10.1093/hcr/28.2.157

Couture, S. (2017). Activist scholarship: The complicated entanglements of activism and research work. *Canadian Journal of Communication*, 42(1), 143–147.

Deetz, S., & Mumby, D. K. (1990). Power, discourse, and the workplace: Reclaiming the critical tradition. *Annals of the International Communication Association*, 13(1), 18–47. https://doi.org/10.1080/23808985.1990.11678743

Diani, M. (1995). *Green networks*. Edinburgh: Edinburgh University Press.

Dobusch, L., & Schoeneborn, D. (2015). Fluidity, identity, and organizationality: The communicative constitution of anonymous. *Journal of Management Studies*, 52(8), 1005–1035.

Fayard, A.-L., & Metiu, A. (2013). *The power of writing in organizations: From letters to online interactions*. New York and London: Routledge.

Feigenbaum, A., Frenzel, F., & McCurdy, P. (2013). *Protest camps*. London: ZedBooks.

Fenton, N. (2016). *Digital, political, radical*. Cambridge: Polity.

Freedman, J. (2008). *Immigration and insecurity in France*. London: Routledge.

Fyke, K., & Sayegh, G. (2001). Anarchism and the struggle to move forward. *Perspectives on Anarchist Theory*, 5(2), 30–38.

Gerbaudo, P. (2017). Social media teams as digital vanguards. *Information Communication and Society*, 20(2), 185–202. http://doi.org/10.1080/13691 18X.2016.1161817

Haavisto, C. (2020). Impossible activism and the right to be understood: Communication perspectives on the emergent refugee rights movement in Finland. In Hellström, A., Norocel C., & Bak Jorgensen, M. (Eds.), *Welfare and culture: Attitudes of immigration, party political transmutations and civil society engagement*. New York: Springer International Publishing.

Hale, C. R. (2001). What is activist research? *Items (Social Science Research Council)*, 2(1–2), 13–15.

Hazen, M. A. (1993). Towards polyphonic organization. *Journal of Organizational Change Management*, 6(5), 15–26. http://doi.org/10.1108/09534819310072747

Krinsky, J., & Crossley, N. (2014). Social movements and social networks: Introduction. *Social Movement Studies*, 13(1), 1–21. http://doi.org/10.1080/147 42837.2013.862787

Kuhn, T. (2008). A communicative theory of the firm: Developing an alternative perspective on intra-organizational power and stakeholder relationships. *Academy of Management Review*, 29(8–9), 1227–1254.

Langley, A., & Lusiani, M. (2015). Strategic planning as practice. In *Cambridge handbook of strategy as practice* (pp. 547–563). Cambridge: Cambridge University Press. https://doi.org/10.1017/cbo9781139681032.032.

McAdam, D., Tarrow, S., & Tilly, C. (2001). *Dynamics of contention*. Cambridge: Cambridge University Press.

Michels, R. (1969). *Political parties: A sociological study of the oligarchical tendencies of modern democracy*. New York: Transaction Publishers.

Nicotera, A. M. (2013). Organizations as entitative beings: Some ontological implications of communicative constitution. In Cooren, F. & Robichaud, D. (Eds.), *Organization and organizing : Materiality, agency, and discourse* (pp. 66–89). London: Routledge.

Novak, D. R. (2016). Democratic work at an organization-society boundary: Sociomateriality and the communicative instantiation. *Management Communication Quarterly*, 30(2), 218–244. http://doi.org/10.1177/0893318915622455

Polletta, F. (2002). *Freedom is an endless meeting: Democracy in American social movements*. Chicago: University of Chicago Press.

Putnam, L., Nicotera, A., & McPhee, R. (2009). Introduction: Communication constitutes organization. In Putnam, L. & Nicotera, A. (Eds.), *Building theories of organization: The constitutive role of communication* (pp. 1–19). New York, NY: Routledge.

Rao, H., Morrill, C., & Zald, M. (2000). Power plays: How social movements and collective action create new organizational forms. *Research in Organizational Behavior*, 22, 237–281.

Reed, M. I. (2010). Is communication constitutive of organization? *Management Communication Quarterly*, 24(1), 151–157. https://doi.org/10.1177/0893318909351583

Robichaud, D., Giroux, H., & Taylor, J. R. (2004). The metaconversation: The recursive property of language as a key to organizing. *The Academy of Management Review*, 29(4), 617. http://doi.org/10.2307/20159074

Smircich, L., & Morgan, G. (1982). Leadership: The management of meaning. *Journal of Applied Behavioural Studies*, 18(3), 257–73.

Speed, S. (2006). At the crossroads of human rights and anthropology: Toward a critically engaged activist research. *American Anthropologist*, 108(1), 66–76.

Sutherland, N., Land, C., & Böhm, S. (2014). Anti-leaders(hip) in social movement organizations: The case of autonomous grassroots groups. *Organization*, 21(6), 759–781.

Taylor, J., & Cooren, F. (1997). What makes communication "organizational"?: How the many voices of a collectivity become the one voice of an organization. *Journal of Pragmatics*, 27(4), 409–438.

Taylor, J., Cooren, F., Giroux, N., & Robichaud, D. (1996). The communicational basis of organization: Between the conversation and the text. *Communication Theory*, 6(1), 1–39.

Taylor, J., & Van Every, E. (2000). *The emergent organization: Communication as its site and surface*. New York: Taylor & Francis.

Taylor, J., & Van Every, E. (2014). *When organization fails: Why authority matters*. New York: Routledge.

Tilly, C. (1978). *From mobilization to revolution*. Reading, MA: Addison-Wesley.

Vásquez, C., Bencherki, N., Cooren, F., & Sergi, V. (2018). From 'matters of concern' to 'matters of authority': Studying the performativity of strategy from a communicative constitution of organization (CCO) approach. *Long Range Planning*, *51*(3), 417–435. https://doi.org/10.1016/j.lrp.2017.01.001

Vásquez, C., Schoeneborn, D., & Sergi, V. (2016). Summoning the spirits: Organizational texts and the (dis)ordering properties of communication. *Human Relations*, *69*(3), 629–659. https://doi.org/10.1177/0018726715589422

5 Amplifying Voices

Hip-Hop as a Mode of Engagement for Community Organizing in the Context of the Black Lives Matter Movement

Clément Decault

Introduction

February 26, 2012. Neighborhood watch volunteer George Zimmerman fatally shot 17 years old, Trayvon Martin in Sanford, Florida. Minutes before Martin's death, Zimmerman called 911 to alert the Sanford Police Department of a "real suspicious guy [...] walking around, looking about" in his neighborhood ("Transcript of George Zimmerman's Call to the Police," n.d.). Notwithstanding the dispatcher's instruction not to follow Martin, Zimmerman decided to go forward and confront the young Black man. Police officers arrived shortly after Zimmerman's lethal shot at Martin's chest, while several witnesses called 911 to notify authorities of the ongoing altercation in the meantime. Later, the police accepted Zimmerman's account of the confrontation despite his implication in the murder and released him after a few hours of custody and questioning. Based on Florida's Stand Your Ground statute, police considered that there was no evidence to refute Zimmerman's claim of having acted in self-defence.[1]

July 13, 2013. George Zimmerman is acquitted by the Florida state court in the killing of unarmed teenager Trayvon Martin. The jury returned a verdict of not guilty of both second-degree murder and manslaughter despite controversies surrounding the investigation. Shortly after the acquitment, the story started to come out through the news media and social media. Within weeks, protesters gathered in several cities to denounce this injustice and to demand Zimmerman's arrest. The event ignited a public discussion on institutional racism[2] and social justice throughout the United States, with social media becoming a key space of disclosure for similar incidents occurring elsewhere in the country. In fact, the mediatization of the killings of several Black men and women by white police officers in the months that followed Zimmerman's acquittal came to increase tensions and to intensify the anger amongst Black communities over police brutality against Black Americans. While anti-Black police violence and, more broadly, anti-Blackness at the hands of the state and its institutions are well-entrenched in the American society; today's specific modes of recording and mediatization helped mobilize citizens throughout the country.

DOI: 10.4324/9780429297830-5

Uprisings in both Ferguson, Missouri, following Michael Brown's killing in August 2014 and Baltimore, Maryland, following Freddie Gray's murder in April 2015 by police officers showed protesters' ability to gather and organize, strategically taking the street to denounce injustices. These lethal incidents led to series of protests involving thousands of civilians in cities around the country to condemn police brutality as well as the legal system's failure to hold killers accountable and its inability to deliver justice equally for all people.

According to Keeanga-Yamattha Taylor (2016), the tragic and highly mediatized murders of several Black men and women by police or vigilante officers—which followed Zimmerman's acquittal—acted as a catalyst, capturing people's attention and drawing them "out from their isolation into a collective force with the power to transform social conditions" (p. 153). People from different parts of the country mobilized by joining already existing or newly born grassroots organizations, bringing into being new forms of leadership, new tactics, and new modes of organizing. "For reasons that may never be clear, Brown's death was a breaking point for the African Americans of Ferguson—but also for hundreds of thousands of Black people across the United States" (*ibid.*). Among them, activists who expose, denounce, and fight the persistence of racism and structural inequalities in the United States.

In this chapter, I will discuss how communication means have contributed to community organization and organizing in the context of the Black Lives Matter movement. By looking at how social activism is shaped by hip-hop artists involved in the Black Lives Matter movement, I will argue that artists are key actors in the organization of the social movement. My research shows how hip-hop can serve as a mode of engagement for mobilizing and organizing communities through creative and expressive processes initiated and sustained by the artists. Following Yarimar Bonilla's and Jonathan Rosa's (2015) statement that "[s]ocial movements have long used media and technology to disseminate, escalate and enlarge the scope of their struggles," I suggest that in its articulation to activism in the context of the Black Lives Matter movement, hip-hop plays that role, thus contributing to its organizing. By grounding their social activism into empowering and educational strategies, artists contribute to the building of relationships with, within, and between communities through hip-hop. Thus, studying hip-hop in its articulation to activism sheds light on how both hip-hop and activism are shaped by social forces, and brings into focus "how significantly technology and economics contribute to the development of cultural forms" (Rose, 1994, p. 23). As Andreana Clay (2006) argues, "youth of color use hip hop not only as a place to escape, identify, and create meaning with other youth, but also to organize to fight structural oppression and to develop a political consciousness" (p. 118). When grounded in activism, hip-hop today can serve as a way to mobilize local and global communities towards political organizing and social change.

Coming to Voice

Communication and networking are central to the Black Lives Matter movement, with the Internet and social media making mobilization against injustices easier for grassroots organizations, local activists, and community members alike. First introduced by Patrisse Cullors in response of Alicia Garza's "A Love Letter to Black People" post on Facebook in the wake of Zimmerman's acquitment, the hashtag #BlackLivesMatter became one of the "rallying cr[ies] for the movement" on social media, starting as a slogan for activists to later become "a global phenomenon" (Freelon, McIlwain, & Clark, 2016, pp. 33–34). Despite some overlap between #BlackLivesMatter and organizations or activists mobilized on the ground, the Black Lives Matter movement is "much bigger than any one organization" as Deray McKesson reminds us (*ibid.*, p. 9). In fact, the movement "encompasses all who publicly declare that Black lives matter and devote their time and energy accordingly," argues McKesson. The social movement then emerges as a global network of collective forms of political organization and action, disrupting traditional forms of hierarchical community organization (Castells, 2015; Gilroy, 1991).

As an autonomous and developing network, the Black Lives Matter movement can, thus, be understood as being developed and shaped by the participation of a plurality of "voices." As Nick Couldry (2010) stresses, the concept of "voice" has less to do with the sound of a person speaking than with "the expression of opinion or, more broadly, the expression of a distinctive perspective on the world that needs to be acknowledged" (p. 2). "Voices" are political, "especially in contexts where long entrenched inequalities of representation need to be addressed" as they express and reveal singular, situated, and often excluded or erased perspectives on the world (*ibid.*). In the context of the Black Lives Matter movement, it appears imperative to acknowledge how localized and systemic power dynamics determine who gets to speak and whose voices get to be heard. In fact, for people living oppression and injustices, finding one's voice goes beyond solely giving an account of oneself or one's place into the world. As Black feminist author bell hooks (1989) asserts, "coming to voice" or "moving from silence into speech" is a revolutionary gesture. It is a political act "that challenges politics of domination" that would render nameless and voiceless people engaged in liberation struggles (*ibid.*, p. 8). Speaking, in this context, becomes "becomes both a way to engage in active self-transformation and a rite of passage where one moves from being object to being subject" (*ibid.*, p. 12). While Black Lives Matter can be understood as a movement developing and being shaped by a plurality of "voices," it also demonstrates an effort to collectively come to voice and to make possible the construction of local subjectivities and identities with a global consciousness about power relations (Lipsitz, 1994).

Today, technology is strategic to the development of social movements and to the circulation of information about what is happening in communities organizing to fight against oppression and injustices. In the context of the Black Lives Matter movement, the Internet and social media have also shown to be strategic in the circulation of protesters and their supporters' own narratives without having to rely on mainstream news outlets. According to Yarimar Bonilla and Jonathan Rosa (2015), today's increased use and availability of digital technologies "has provided marginalized and racialized populations with new tools for documenting incidents of state-sanctioned violence and contesting media representations of racialized bodies and marginalized communities" (p. 5). In many of the cases that followed Trayvon Martin's, they argue, "the use of mobile technology to record and circulate footage of events has played a key role in prompting public outcry" (*ibid.*). In effect, Zimmerman's recorded call to 911—as well as a witness' call to 911 recording Zimmerman's shot at Martin; a witness's video recording of New York City police officers' brutality use of a chokehold in the murder of Eric Garner; dash cam footages of both Sandra Bland brutal traffic stop arrest by Texas State Trooper Brian Encinia and Samuel DuBose fatal shooting by University of Cincinnati police officer Raymond Tensing also during a traffic stop arrest—all offered documents, records, and archives of the incidents and played a far-reaching role in rendering them public, visible, and undeniable. However, and as this research discusses, although technology and social media are pivotal and necessary to the circulation of information and the organization of the Black Lives Matter movement, people showing up and taking the streets are still fundamental to make it a movement (Kweli, in Maté, 2014). While digital technologies offer populations new tools for organizing, there "ain't nothing to tweet about" without people organizing on the ground, whether in the form of spontaneous protests or activist actions (*ibid.*).

Setting aside debates between techno-optimists and skeptics, Jeffrey S. Juris (2012) argues nevertheless that "new media influence how movements organize" while "places, bodies, face-to-face networks, social histories, and the messiness of offline politics continue to matter" (p. 260). Media technologies have always played a role in the shaping of social networking and social movements, as well as on how they organize. According to Juris (2012), the important question is "how new media matter; how particular new media tools affect emerging forms, patterns, and structures of organization; and how virtual and physical forms of protest and communication are mutually constitutive" (p. 260). In the following sections, I will discuss how hip-hop activists have played an important role in the organizing process of the Black Lives Matter movement through a series of organizational practices that tended to blur distinctions between Internet and "on-the-ground" community activism. As part of the movement, artists feel indebted to the people leading the movement on the ground with whom they tie meaningful relationships. Accordingly, artists acknowledge bearing a responsibility to raise their own voice, whether it is to call out an injustice or to support and amplify those of whom are risking their lives fighting for social change.

Hip-Hop and Organizing the Black Lives Matter Movement

Emerging in New York City in the early 70s, hip-hop helped create a democratic space by authorizing certain "voices" to participate in open conversations and creative minds to share stories and points of view about daily experiences of the social and political world. According to Imany Perry (2004), hip-hop opened up a "discursive space provided within the artistic and cultural community" (p. 5). If similar spaces of participation already existed in different forms, with the birth of hip-hop, Tricia Rose (1994) claims, these spaces have gone public. In the world of hip-hop, "holy and well-behaved gestures sit next to the rough and funky," as it allows for a wide range of expressions and positions "even within the music of one artist." Open discourse renders visible a world of complexity and contradictions, with each artist providing but one orientation within a diverse community "to be understood within the context of that community" (Rose, 1994, p. 6). However, while hip-hop emerged as a democratic space "in which expression is more important than the monitoring of the acceptable," it is not inherently liberatory (*ibid.*). In fact, there is no inherent link, no necessary connection between hip-hop and critical thought or speech. "Because each local neighborhood or city has its own particular history and story," Patricia Hill Collins and Sirma Bilge (2016) argue, "hip-hop takes different forms and advances distinctive issues" (p. 118). "There is no hip-hop leader or archetypal form of hip-hop," they add.

As a musical form or genre, hip-hop has taken many shapes since its emergence. As of late 1980s, various industries started to grow interest in hip-hop and see opportunities for commercialization. Markets quickly became pivotal to hip-hop's production, circulation, and consumption in the forms of magazines, radio stations and programs, record companies and labels, clothing styles, and labels or food advertising since the 1970s (Dimitriadis, 2004). As such, market dynamics have been decisive yet not deterministic in the popularity of hip-hop as well as in the shaping of ideas, images, and symbols that it channelled, although it is important to recognize how hip-hop—as any musical form—does not take place outside of capitalist commercial constraints (Rose, 1994). In other words, "hip hop's moment(s) of incorporation are a shift in the already existing relationship hip hop has always had to the commodity system," as Rose argues, with consumption being intrinsically tied to modes of creation, dialogue, and, more broadly, communication (p. 40) According to George Lipsitz (1994), whatever role ideas, images, and symbols serve in the profit-making calculations of the music industry, "these expressions also serve as exemplars of post-colonial culture with direct relevance to the rise of new social movements emerging in response to the imperative of global capital and its attendant austerity and oppression" (p. 27).

But then, if hip-hop is not a liberation music, how does it provide ways to critically explore and think about socio-political struggles? The analysis that follows will show how hip-hop artists involved within the Black Lives Matter movement work towards providing critical understanding and exploration of complex power dynamics that structure their art form, as well as mobilizing communities and their members through critical education and mentorship.

Methodology

From a methodological perspective, I examine artists' activism "in the making" by focusing on its articulation in discourse. Indebted to Stuart Hall, I use the concept of articulation to refer to "the form of connection that can make a unity of two different elements, under certain conditions," a connection that is by no means necessary or essential, and which is made possible through and within discourse (Grossberg, 1986, p. 53). I approach discourse as "a group of statements which provide a language for talking about... a particular knowledge about a topic" (Hall, 1992, p. 201). Analyzing patterns of regularities and singularities, which circulate through the artists' discourse, allows a problematization of different social and citizen-lead modes of activism through art. Taking into account the singularity of each statement, based on ideas, projects, and possibilities they articulate (Allor & Gagnon, 1994), I study the modes of inquiry and conscientization put forth by five hip-hop artists, as well as the forms of situated knowledge that is produced through their activist practices and through discourse.

Considering the strategic role of the Internet in the organization of the Black Lives Matter movement and in the circulation of alternative "voices," this research focuses on hip-hop artists' online presence and visibility. Today, the Internet has become essential to the promotion and organization of artistic work, as well as to activist networking and actions. In this regard, it is necessary to take into consideration online contributions to a networked social movement, in order to examine how activism is made by those involved in it. The five artists whose activist work is at the heart of this research—and whose description will be integrated below along with research results—were selected for this research based on their considerable online presence: their online activities display long-term and continuous engagement in activism, as well as numerous contributions to a diverse array of media outlets between February 26, 2012[3] and April 2017. They all come from different backgrounds and regions of the United States and make use of distinct strategies for organizing communities in relation to context. Nonetheless, differences crossing and shaping various activist practices provide with significant material to interrogate multiple yet singular conditions of articulations of social activism to artistic practices.

Due to heterogeneity in contributions with respect to the artists' discrete online presences,[4] it proved to be impossible to carry out a standardized model of material collection and analysis. However, as my research goal is to explore and analyze complex articulations of activism made by hip-hop artists through different modes of participation, it appears important to take a close look at these different modes for exploring their diverse underlying conditions of articulation. Hence, on the basis of an archive gathering artists' statements in journal papers, blog posts, written and recorded interviews, testimonies, public talks, and contributions to panels and round table conferences, I analyze how issues are being addressed from the artists situated points of view. By doing so, I expose patterns of regularities and singularities arising from a discourse analysis of activists' statements who, despite their multiple shapes and formats, are constitutive articulations of the social movement and contribute to its organizing.

Analysis

Modes of Social Engagement

Aisha Fukushima is an international singer, public speaker, and educator from Seattle, Washington, and Yokohama, Japan. She founded "RAPtivism," short for "rap activism," in 2009, a project which now spans nearly twenty countries and four continents. It aims to establish connections and develop collaborations between socially engaged activists and artists. Inspired by hip-hop artists who informed her passion for music and cultural activism, Fukushima considers that artists can inspire people on international stages, teaching people "about the power of music as means of communicating and connecting people" (The People's Minister of Information JR, 2015). She points out the importance of the "power of culture and the role that culture has played in many social movements over time" (Averhart, 2017). Naming the civil rights movement and the Arab Spring as movements where "music has [...] been a huge catalyst in getting a message out and in amplifying the youth voices," (*ibid.*) she quotes journalist and famous author on hip-hop Jeff Chang by stating that "cultural change is often the dress rehearsal for political change" (5th element, 2013).

Tef Poe is a rapper, musician, and activist from St. Louis, Missouri. He is one of the co-founders of the Hands Up United organization, defined as "a collective of politically engaged minds building towards the liberation of oppressed Black, Brown and poor people through education, art, civil disobedience, advocacy and agriculture" (HandsUpUnited, n.d.). To him,

> [i]t's important to have [rappers] as your frame of reference when viewing Ferguson['s protests] from a bird's-eye view, because this is honestly the only way you'll begin to understand the logic that caused us to fight back. Tupac Shakur was a bandanna-wearing, marijuana-smoking,

middle-finger-flipping, book-reading, politically engaged young Black man with anger issues. Our closest example of a push for revolution in America during our lifetime for the most part came from his war cry. The current movement reflects people like him to the fullest—black males with their shirts off, tattoos all over their flesh and bandannas on their faces, covering their mouths from tear gas.

(Poe, 2014).

According to artists like Fukushima and Tef Poe, hip-hop acts as a catalyst for the development of a culture through which a plurality of voices collectively mobilizes. Hip-hop sets the scene for social and political change; it is a context builder for "bottom-up" change towards which activists work in their communities (World Citizen Artists, 2015). Such a change can take place worldwide, considering how hip-hop culture can become the common basis from which a conversation could start, thus "desegregating different spaces and altering perceptions" despite contextual singularities (Fukushima, 2012). Here, hip-hop becomes a way for people to blend and to participate in the creation of a culture based on "a common love of the art," as Fukushima argues (TEDx Talks, 2012). While Fukushima collaborates with artistic and activist communities in Denmark, Senegal, South Africa, Japan, and France, to name a few, she's been able to develop relationships with refugees, victims of gang violence or police brutality. Tef Poe, on the other hand, mainly collaborates with communities and members of St. Louis, Missouri, where he resides, while still tying key relationship with artists and activists throughout the country.

FM Supreme, also known as Jessica Disu, is an artist, activist, educator, and "humanitarian rap artist" from the West Side of Chicago, where she is involved as a leader and a mentor to youth. From her perspective, "imagination is greater than knowledge" (Zimmerman, 2016). She argues that it is important to nurture youth's imagination and creativity, because living in impoverished and oppressed communities "limits your view of reality and the limits of what possibilities could be" (*ibid.*). Yet, FM Supreme states that "[t]he grass isn't greener on the other side. The grass is greener where we water it" (Reid-Cleveland, 2016).

According to Jasiri X, hip-hop is the key to encouraging today's youth. Jasiri X is a hip-hop artist and activist from Pittsburgh, Pennsylvania. He has been involved in national civil rights movements since 2006. He delivers keynote addresses and speaks on scholarly panels at colleges and universities, and he is the head and creative director of *1Hood Media*, an organization he cofounded in 2011. He is now mentoring youth and organizing workshops where he works to "cultivate and guide the talents that lay dormant inside a seemingly uncultivated mind thereby" (Jasiri X, n.d.). Mixing artistic and pedagogical objectives, he argues that hip-hop is an educational tool, "influencing young artists to make better decisions in their individual lives and inspiring them towards personal responsibility in the culture of their communities" (ibid.). He asserts that "[a]rt should move culture and thought forward, it should represent progress. It should be used in a positive manner to uplift and unify our communities" (ibid.). Jasiri X relies on hip-hop to communicate with young people and motivate them on a more intimate level. He confesses that "Hip-Hop artists introduced [him] to a variety of concepts and gave [him] the encouragement to pursue an education beyond what [he] learned in school" (Bajer, 2016). From a similar approach, Aisha Fukushima sees hip-hop as "one of those ways that we start to learn more about ourselves and feel more empowered in ourselves to make decisions that access our potential" (KSFS Radio, 2013). She emphasizes that arts can act as a means for Black individuals of educating themselves. Her conceptualization of such a task as a process, rather than an end, stems from a holistic understanding of "social problems" that cross and shape Black people's lives and experiences today.

> I don't think that there is just one way to solve everything. […] I think that the arts, and particularly coming from a raptivism perspective, have a really powerful role in that. […] When I'm working doing hip hop clubs or doing performance lectures, whether I'm in Japan or I'm in Oakland at the Freedom School or I'm in San Francisco teaching middle-schoolers: I see the process being very important. It's not only about the message 'Are you fighting the power? Are you saying this?', it's about the process, it's a healing process. It's a creative process in light of all the destruction that you're surrounded by, we are creating something, even out of 'nothing.' The resource we have in our mind, to shine that jewel.
>
> (*ibid.*)

Both Jasiri X and Aisha Fukushima's strategies work towards creating and circulating narratives and collective understanding through hip-hop from situated points of view, in order to disrupt racist historical narratives through unacknowledged and forgotten "voices." These voices, thus, provide a language for talking about situated experiences of power, individually and collectively shaped in relation to structural and institutional constraints.

According to Talib Kweli, a Brooklyn-based rapper who has been in the rap business for more than 20 years, "[e]ducation is key, but westernized education alone will not save [black people]. [18 years-old] Mike Brown [who's been shot by Darren Wilson, an officer from the Ferguson Police Department] was scheduled to attend Vatterott College this fall, that didn't save him" (Kweli, 2014b). Thus, education should also take place beyond and away from schools, and hip-hop activists could act as mentors in the process of educating in a historical and political context where systemic inequalities, injustices, and oppression affect Black youth and threaten their lives. Here, activists' educational work takes the form of what Paulo

Freire calls "a practice of freedom": freedom from an educational system that fails to take into account the incompletion of human knowledge, and most of all, as Aisha Fukushima argues,

> because the school system and a lot of different systems haven't taken into account the richness of [black] communities and the wealth of [their] history and [their] resilience. That's a thing that is forcibly forgotten in our narratives and in our collective understanding."
>
> (KSFS Radio, 2013)

Critical Education

The discussion that precedes shows how hip-hop activists are key actors of social change with the goal to inspire communities both at an individual and collective level. Despite variations related to different strategies, their engagement aims at creating and implanting meetings, discussions, and social bonds amongst community members and between different communities. For example, Jasiri X and his organization 1Hood work with local artists to help them develop their creativity and personal skills; FM Supreme promotes her art to the youth, aiming at offering them new sources of inspiration; Tef Poe and Talib Kweli document activism on the ground, opening alternative spaces of representation for Black communities; and Aisha Fukushima raises awareness about transformative social action amongst community members while encouraging the building of new relationships and collaborations between them. As such, all artists intent on creating, developing, and improving social links between community members and members from different communities. Their actions aim at extending citizen participation to the benefit of communities and their members. Through hip-hop, activists engage in diversifying citizen's participation and facilitating the acts of "coming to voice" or "moving from silence into speech" (hooks, 1989). For this reason, they are actors of individual and collective empowerment and resistance through the acts of creating and sharing. They mentor a dynamic and relational process of "coming to voice" by bringing together both individuals' capacity for action and communities' ability to integrate its members' contributions. According to Williams Ninacs (2008), a community's ability to develop its members' capacities for action is critical to its members' empowerment as much as its collective empowerment. In fact, individual empowerment and community empowerment are intertwined and mutually constitutive. Hip-hop activists push for positive changes by reinforcing community members' skills, confidence, imagination, and role as part of a social group in and through creative processes of critical thinking and learning. Consequently, they are part of "an intentional, ongoing process centered in the local community, involving mutual respect, critical reflection, caring and group participation, through which people lacking an equal share of valued resources gain greater access to and control over those resources" (Cornell Empowerment Group, 1989, p. 2, in Melkote, 2000).

Although artists find inspiration in other social movement modes of action and organization, included the civil rights movement legacy, Talib Kweli argues that "the strategies that were employed [during the civil rights period] don't necessarily work today. Information travels so much faster, and people's ideas of race, class and diversification are completely different" (Kweli, 2014a). However, it appears that their strategies towards individual and collective empowerment through education resonate with those used by other oppressed communities in their fights for emancipation and autonomy. As Paulo Freire (2005 [1970]) discusses it in his Pedagogy of the Oppressed, education played a central role in empowering impoverished and illiterate workers from Northern Brazil in the 1960s. Taking stance from his own involvement with revolutionary organizers and educators, Freire theorizes an approach to education and organizing. In response to the top-down "banking" approach of education, "in which the scope for action allowed to the students extends only as far as receiving, filing and storing the deposits," Freire develops a pedagogy aimed at developing a critical consciousness and understanding of systems of oppression in order to transform them. By doing so, he posits "problem-posing education" as a liberating and empowering instrument in the context of struggles for liberation, bringing forward its role in organizing oppressed populations. While banking theory and practice tends to offer a mythicized and abstract explanation of human relations and to inhibit students' creativity, problem-posing theory and practice "take the people's historicity as their starting point" (Freire, 2005 [1970], p. 84). It bases itself on creativity "and stimulates true reflection and action upon reality, thereby responding to the vocation of persons as beings who are authentic only when engaged in inquiry and creative transformation" (ibid.). In practice, "problem-posing education" entails the disclosure of injustices and the awakening of critical consciousness towards oppressive situations based on lived experiences. Such an approach to education lays ground for social change as long as it provides students with ways "to critically explore and engage in decolonial horizons that break silences, disrupt dominant narratives, and create a transformation consciousness" (Cervantes & Saldaña, 2015, p. 86).

As Freire (2005 [1970]) argues, "[t]here is no such thing as a neutral educational process" (p. 34). Education is a political act. Stemming from Freire's work, bell hooks (1994) points out that school curriculums and teaching practices tend to regard Black children as objects rather than subjects. By emphasizing the perspective of "great white men," curriculums tend to perpetuate the politics of racism, sexism, heterosexism, and other oppressive dynamics of power, imbued in "banking" education, hooks argues. Aisha Fukushima shares the same perspective and suggests taking into account the incompletion of human knowledge in order to challenge the Eurocentric understanding of history that mutes and renders invisible Black history. Her educational work as a teaching artist promotes education as an instrument of social change through cultural action and liberation, with collective experiences and histories being central to the learning process. In the same way, Jasiri X considers that critical education is possible through hip-hop. Numerous artists have influenced his life and his work, pointing him towards different books and alternative sources of education, naming different artists, books, and concepts in their rhymes. Through his own practices and actions, Jasiri X encourages youth to seek knowledge outside of a standard classroom setting and to pursue an education beyond what is taught in schools. In this way, artists' articulation of hip-hop consists of an epistemological intervention into the dominant historical narrative that crosses and shapes banking theory and practices of education. In that context, hip-hop opens up a discursive space by which dominant narratives can be contested for the epistemic violence they generate and the "voices" they mute, exclude, or erase (Couldry, 2010; Spivak, 1988).

Leadership

Although they aren't official spokespersons for a social movement, artists still play a key role in the organization of the Black Lives Matter movement. As artists allow for the expression of voices through education and mentorship, they open up a discursive space within which heterogenous individual voices can be articulated while contributing to building some sort of unity through art. Artists play a leading role in the organizing process of the Black Lives Matter movement by merging individual and situated voices—including theirs—to the ongoing discussion on social justice held throughout the United States. Whether in classrooms, during workshops, or as part of organizations, they promote and facilitate a process of "coming to voice" (hooks, 1989) by creating a context for expression. For instance, Aisha Fukushima believes that her art project helps to build bridges between communities and across cultures, emphasizing how musical forms have helped in "bringing people together, in desegregating different spaces and altering perceptions" in the past of the United States (Fukushima, 2012). While bringing together individual and situated voices, artists work to establish connections between communities and community members around shared issues and concerns about the social world. This point is central to understand how multivocality takes part to the organizing process through the artists' voices, as their voices are not just another voice: they become an articulation of different voices. As such, artists must constantly manage tensions between univocality and multivocality, thus playing a key role in the shaping of a shared political and empowering consciousness.

Tef Poe considers that in order for social change to come, "then the musicians and artists of our world will serve as beacons of light" (Poe, 2012). This form of leadership forged around participative projects with, amongst, and between communities and is identified as "mentorship" by Jasiri X and FM Supreme. Jasiri X builds on his experience and the anti-violent approach promoted by his organization (*1Hood*) in order to act "as a mentor in the process" of educating, inspiring, and stimulating youth creativity though hip-hop (Jasiri X, n.d.). Aside from his musical practice, Jasiri X collaborates with public schools with the intention of raising youth's awareness of arts practice and how it benefits for community unity and solidarity (Transformative Culture Project, 2015). Confident that education "is supposed to help you find your purpose in life, and a lot of time school don't do that at all," his mentorship aims at developing talents and cultivating youth love towards themselves and their communities (Re-Active, 2016). His work as a mentor thus seeks to build and provide a favourable framework for community organizing by guiding and supporting youth through their creative projects. Through her mentoring, FM Supreme aims at developing youth imagination and creative abilities. Influenced by her own mentors, she helps youth create positive images and representations of themselves: "Reframing the media, becoming their own media. Changing the narrative through music" (CreativeMornings HQ, 2014). She embodies a new form of participative leadership at the individual level through her religious engagement, thus guiding, accompanying, and inspiring youth through music in similar manner to other historical engagements (Craddock-Willis, 1989).

Artists' mentorship appears to articulate and take shape around their pedagogical work, undertook with and for other citizens. As Jasiri X emphasizes how inadequate schools can be to inspire youth, FM Supreme suggests that cultivating their imagination through art helps to counter dominant narratives of oppression. Through her *Raptivism* project, Aisha Fukushima emphasizes creativity both in and outside of the classroom, providing tools to re-imagine the world and think critically. Endeavours towards emancipation thus show to stem from local concerns, as artists seek for and carry out local modes of action. As such, artists act according to beliefs and values based on a practical reading of the world, rather than abstract ideological, philosophical, or political tenets. According to Ève Lamoureux's (2009) historical analysis of "political art," such an observation gives evidence of the ontological change which occurred between "*avant-gardist*" and "*postmodern*" expressions of socially engaged art. While "*avant-gardist*" artists—guided by a double *Aufklärung* and German Romanticism legacy—acted as guides through emancipation, gifted with the ability to read and unveil the fundamental political conditions to implement change, those whom Lamoureux (2009) calls "*postmodern*" artists arose from deep conjunctural and cultural, social, institutional, and political mutations. Facing the historical failure of ideas of progress and emancipation, *avant-gardist* suffer from the "crisis of modernity" and what Jean-François Lyotard (1979) famously called the collapse of "grand narrative" (*la fin des métarécits*). According to Lyotard, a loss of faith in metanarratives and universalizing theories has reconfigured human relations to science and art since World War II, creating an ontological radical change as to how artists then oriented by the general interest of society henceforth came to embody a "freed" *postmodern* subject.

While *avant-gardist* artists authority stemmed from their privilege access to truth and the essence of things, *postmodern* artists' work interrogates how reality is shaped and calls into question societies founding principles based on situated and locally informed experiences. Postmodern art allows for the multiple, the heterogeneous, and the singular to surface, thus opening up a space within which normative, universalist, and homogenizing points of reference could become challenged (Lamoureux, 2009). Socially engaged postmodern artists thereby play an important role in provoking thoughts and sparking off public debate from the complexity of their standpoint, rendering visible plural, heterogeneous, and individualized relations to their experiences of reality. As such, they provide a language for talking about a particular knowledge, about a topic (Hall, 1992). Unlike *avant-gardists* artists whose work tends to deliver an explicit message, Lamoureux stresses, *postmodern* artists opt for new forms of art action, loaded with an immediate and practical purpose. Tef Poe explains this clearly when he stresses the accountability of his work to the people he stands with: "So I feel like it's my job to say what Pookie and Ray Ray would say if they was up there" (Poe & Yates, 2014). In other words, his work must benefit the people risking their lives on the frontline, for his capacity to support his community with and through his art determines the significance of his actions. As they deliver a message through their writings, artists must remain transparent and accountable if they claim to be part of a movement. Talib Kweli considers that the relationship between artists and their fans, in this context, is one of reciprocity. As artists get their inspiration from situated and everyday lived experiences of power by various communities and their members, they are indebted to these communities.

At some point, my analysis blurs Lamoureux's dichotomization of "political art" history and the duality it establishes. In fact, FM Supreme displays diverse forms of what Lamoureux associates to *avant-gardism*: "I just got to spread the words, spread the message" (The Black Youth Project, 2012). This form of representation, channelled through an explicit message, however, remains oriented towards communities and their everyday experiences of power and oppression, aiming at providing them with tools to understand violence and foster peace in Chicago's toughest neighbourhoods. FM Supreme reaches out to youth through her talks and raps with the purpose of serving and amplifying the voices of young people, promoting peace building techniques, inspiring, and empowering youth through her art. Therefore, her work pushes for an effective change in violent and oppressive narratives that shape the youth view of reality and the limits of what possibilities can be (Zimmerman, 2016). Her work stems from practical needs of disrupting narratives of oppression and disempowerment through strategic action rather than from abstract universals of peace and non-violence.

Artists are not some perceptive individuals with the ability to read and unveil the fundamental political conditions in order to implement change. Rather, they adapt and adjust their activist strategies in relation to communities' needs, within—rather than with or alongside—which they fight for social change and work at defining fundamental political conditions required for social a change to happen. Artists then act as cultural actors, contributing to unifying and amplifying "voices" and situated experiences of power through the building of relationships with, within, and between communities. Quoting Aisha Fukushima, "worldwide hip-hop culture represents a platform for collective consciousness and global citizenship," that can, as my analysis shows, organize and blossom through activism (5th element, 2013). The platform allows the articulations of heterogeneous and situated perspectives and knowledge to occur and to materialize in texts and artistic performances. Lamoureux's conceptualization of *postmodern* art turns out being challenged by the emphasis that the artists put on the "message," using it as a means of sharing experiences without lecturing or speaking in the name of communities. Rather, they use their art and words to create collaborations and sharing life experiences, thus allowing connection and identification between communities and their members while participating in constructing local identities with a global consciousness in that process (Gilroy, 1991; Lipsitz, 1994).

Conclusion

Highlighting how education has been strategic to the development of political fights and social movements, Patricia Hill Collins and Sirma Bilge (2016) claim that a critical understanding of social inequalities and their consequences on people's lives is key to individual and collective empowerment. In the context of the Black Lives Matter movement, as this chapter has shown, hip-hop can serve as a way to engage in the process of critical education and understanding of complex dynamics of power. Artists whose work is at the heart of this chapter use hip-hop as means for communication and connecting communities and their members, encouraging the expression of a variety of perspectives and experiences of the social and political world. As such, artists cultivate citizen participation, creativity, and skills as parts of organizations, in classrooms, through public speaking and programs that support communities to develop their resources for collective action. They act as mentors in the process of organizing communities and promoting social change, while working to create and implement democratic spaces authorizing various "voices" (Couldry, 2010) to participate in open conversations through artistic practices. Despite variations related to the different strategies they employ, artists' engagement aims at diversifying citizen participation and facilitating acts of "coming into voice" (hooks, 1989) as well as at building some sort of unity through art.

Within the Black Lives Matter movement, inputs from the hip-hop activists offer some significant insights to critically reconceptualize notions such as social engagement, education, and leadership. As artists' social engagement and organizing strategies are shaped by conjunctural social forces, artists develop and adjust modes of community organizing in relation with communities. They play a leading role for the expression of multiple individual voices and, more importantly, for the organizing process by which these voices can be articulated to the ongoing discussion on social justice held throughout the United States. They rely on art as an educational tool in order to inspire community members and promote social change within and between communities amongst which they work. As such, they lay ground for individual and collective empowerment by initiating and participating to creative processes of critical thinking and learning. Through hip-hop, they engage in community building by developing community members' skills, confidence, imagination, and role as part of a social group.

In response to highly mediatized events of institutional racism and lethal violence, hip-hop artists' activism plays an important role in the mobilization and organization of communities throughout the United States. While their activism predates the killings of Trayvon Martin, Michael Brown, and Freddie Gray—around which the Black Lives Matter movement developed—their role is strategic to the formation and growth of the social movement. Despite variations related to different strategies in use, they actively contribute and engage in bringing into light and revealing experiences of the social world, situated knowledge and stories. Alongside athletes, writers, filmmakers, and producers regularly using their platform to raise their "voices," artists bring forward singular perspectives on the world, ultimately providing a language for talking and thinking—not only about but also—with and to specific members of oppressed communities experiencing the ongoing violence of colonial power (Alcoff, 1991). In the particular socio-historical and political conjuncture of the United States today, and in its articulation to activism, hip-hop becomes a means for affirming the humanity of Black people and fighting cultural and historical narratives of oppression.

Notes

1 For a more detailed account of the shooting, see Marc Lamont Hill (2016), *Nobody. Casualties of America's War on the Vulnerable, from Ferguson to Flint and Beyond*. New York, NY: Atria Books.
2 According to Keeanga-Yamattha Taylor (2016), institutional racism, or structural racism, "can be defined as the policies, programs, and practices of public and private institutions that result in greater rates of poverty, dispossession, criminalization, illness, and ultimately mortality of African Americans. [...] Institutional racism remains the best way to understand how Black deprivation continues in a country as rich and resource-filled as the United States" (p. 8).

3 February 26, 2012 is the day George Zimmerman killed Trayvon Martin, as well as the day public reaction started to take place and circulate.
4 If some artists have access to an online newspaper platform (Tef Poe) or use blogs to promote their online contributions (Jasiri X), others mainly use the Internet as a platform to promote their art (Aisha Fukushima). While Talib Kweli benefit from a wide media coverage due to his fame, FM Supreme and Aisha Fukushima are more particularly popular amongst local news media outlets and activist groups.

References

5th element. (2013, July 29). RAPtivism Interview with Aisha Fukushima. Retrieved from 5th element.jp—Music+politics+youth website: http://5th-element.jp/issue/july-2013/article/raptivism-interview-with-aisha-fukushima-in-english

Alcoff, Linda. (1991). The problem of speaking for others. *Cultural Critique*, (20), 5–32.

Allor, Martin, & Gagnon, Michelle. (1994). *L'état de culture: Généalogie discursive des politiques culturelles québécoises* (Vol. 1). Groupe de recherche sur la citoyenneté culturelle.

Averhart, Sandra. (2017, March 22). To Celebrate Women's History Month UWF Welcomes Raptivist Aisha Fukushima. Retrieved from http://wuwf.org/post/celebrate-womens-history-month-uwf-welcomes-raptivist-aisha-fukushima

Bajer, Erica. (2016, September 26). Five Questions with WPSC Keynote Jasiri X. Retrieved from The Brock News, a news source for Brock University website: https://brocku.ca/brock-news/2016/09/five-questions-with-wpcs-keynote-jasiri-x/

Bonilla, Yarimar, & Rosa, Jonathan. (2015). #Ferguson: Digital protest, hashtag ethnography, and the racial politics of social media in the United States. *American Ethnologist*, 42(1), 4–17.

Castells, Manuel. (2015). *Networks of outrage and hope: Social movements in the internet age*. Cambridge, UK; Malden, MA: Polity.

Cervantes, Marco Antonio, & Saldaña, Lilian Patricia. (2015). Hip hop and nueva canción as decolonial pedagogies of epistemic justice. *Decolonization: Indigeneity, education & society*, 4(1). 84–108. Retrieved from http://decolonization.org/index.php/des/article/view/22167/18473

Clay, Andreana. (2006). "All i need is one mic": Mobilizing youth for social change in the post-civil rights era. *Social Justice*, 33(2 (104)), 105–121.

Clay, Andreana. (2012). *The hip-hop generation fights back: Youth, activism and post-civil rights politics*. New York, NY: NYU Press.

Couldry, Nick. (2010). *Why voice matters: Culture and politics after neoliberalism*. Los Angeles, CA; London: SAGE.

Craddock-Willis, Andre. (1989). Rap music and the black musical tradition: A critical assessment. *Radical America*, 23(4), 29–37.

CreativeMornings HQ. (2014). *FM Supreme: Jessica Disu*. Retrieved from https://www.youtube.com/watch?v=SzefOXdYTvg

Dimitriadis, Greg. (2004). *Performing identity, performing culture: Hip hop as text, pedagogy, and lived practice*. New York, NY: Lang.

Freelon, Deen, McIlwain, Charlton D., & Clark, Meredith D. (2016). *Beyond the Hashtags: #Ferguson, #Blacklivesmatter, and the Online Struggle for Offline Justice* (SSRN Scholarly Paper No. ID 2747066). Retrieved from Social Science Research Network website: https://papers.ssrn.com/abstract=2747066

Freire, Paulo. (2005 [1970]). *Pedagogy of the oppressed.* New York, NY: The Continuum International Publishing Group Inc.

Fukushima, Aisha. (2012, October). *RAPtivism: BLACKANESE POWER.* Presented at the Mixed Roots Conference, Osaka University. Retrieved from https://www.youtube.com/watch?v=wr_LgWTyeeU

Gilroy, Paul. (1991). *"There ain't no black in the union jack": The cultural politics of race and nation.* Chicago, IL: University of Chicago Press.

Grossberg, Lawrence. (1986). On postmodernism and articulation an interview with Stuart Hall. *Journal of Communication Inquiry, 10*(2), 45–60.

Hall, Stuart. (1992). The west and the Rest: Discourse and power. In S. Hall & B. Gieben (Eds.), *Formations of Modernity* (pp. 184–227). Cambridge; Malden, MA: Polity Press.

HandsUpUnited. (n.d.). Practice. Retrieved June 18, 2016, from Hands Up United website: http://www.handsupunited.org/practice/

Hill Collins, Patricia., & Bilge, Sirma. (2016). *Intersectionality.* Cambridge, UK; Malden, MA: Polity Press.

Hill, Marc Lamont. (2016). *Nobody: Casualties of America's War on the vulnerable, from Ferguson to flint and beyond.* New York, NY: Atria Books.

hooks, bell. (1989) *Talking back: Thinking feminist, thinking black.* Boston, MA: South End Press.

hooks, bell. (1994). *Teaching to transgress: Education as the practice of freedom.* New York, NY: Routledge.

Jasiri X. (n.d.). Jasiri X Artist Statement. Retrieved from Jasiri X – Freeing Minds One Rhyme at a Time website: http://jasirix.com/?page_id=1419

Juris, Jeffrey S. (2012). Reflections on #Occupy Everywhere: Social media, public space, and emerging logics of aggregation: Reflections on #Occupy Everywhere. *American Ethnologist, 39*(2), 259–279.

KSFS Radio. (2013). *M. Payton Interviews Aisha Fukushima on KSFS Radio.* Retrieved from https://www.youtube.com/watch?v=TnAXKkDymX4&t

Kweli, Talib. (2014a, May 9). Hip-Hop Activist Talib Kweli on Ferguson: "There Needs to Be an All-Out Revolution" to Change Racism. Retrieved from Billboard website: http://www.billboard.com/articles/6243701/talib-kweli-ferguson

Kweli, Talib. (2014b, August 23). The Point That Went Missing. Retrieved from Medium website: https://medium.com/@TalibKweli/the-point-that-went-missing-ddd041896d5b#.g0bs5yahg

Lamoureux, Ève. (2009). *Art et Politique: Nouvelles Formes d'engagement Artistique au Québec.* Montréal: Éditions Écosociété.

Lipsitz, George. (1994). *Dangerous crossroads: Popular music, postmodernism, and the poetics of place.* London; New York, NY: Verso.

Lyotard, Jean-François. (1979). *La Condition Postmoderne: Rapport Sur le Savoir.* Paris: Éditions de Minuit.

Maté, Aaron. (2014, August 22). "Black Life Is Treated with Short Worth": Talib Kweli & Rosa Clemente on Michael Brown Shooting. Retrieved from Democracy Now! website: http://www.democracynow.org/blog/2014/8/22/black_life_is_treated_with_short

Melkote, Srinivas R. (2000). Reinventing Development Support Communication to Account for Power and Control in Development. In K. G. Wilkins (Ed.), *Redeveloping communication for social change: theory, practice, and power* (pp. 39–54). Lanham, MD: Rowman & Littlefield Publishers.

Ninacs, William A. (2008). *Empowerment et Intervention: Développement de la Capacité d'agir et de la Solidarité*. Québec: Les Presses de l'Université Laval.

Perry, Imani. (2004). *Prophets of the hood: Politics and poetics in hip-hop*. Durham, NC: Duke University Press.

Re-Active. (2016). *News & Politics – Re-Active EP.#15: Jasiri X: Hip-Hop and the Movement* [Re-Active]. Retrieved from https://www.youtube.com/watch?time_continue=7&v=RCComGkLQYo

Reid-Cleveland, Keith. (2016, September 12). Chicago Rapper FM Supreme Talks Hip Hop, Black Lives Matter and Benefits of Travel. Retrieved from The Black Youth Project website: https://blackyouthproject.com/chicago-rapper-fm-su-preme-talks-hip-hop-black-lives-matter-and-benefits-of-travel/

Rose, Tricia. (1994). *Black noise: Rap music and black culture in contemporary America*. Middletown, CT: Wesleyan University Press.

Spivak, Gayatri Chakravorty. (1988). Can the subaltern speak? In L. Grossberg (Ed.), *Marxism and the interpretation of culture* (Macmillan Education, pp. 66–111). Basingstoke: Springer.

Taylor, Keeanga-Yamahtta. (2016). *From #BlackLivesMatter to black liberation*. Chicago, IL: Haymarket Books.

TEDx Talks. (2012, August). *Hip Hop Lives—Raptivism Around the World: Aisha Fukushima at TEDxSitka*. Presented at the Sitka, AK. Retrieved from https://www.youtube.com/watch?v=A2dXNtpV6_0

Tef Poe. (2012, May 31). Destructive Ignorance in St. Louis and South Florida and the Unfulfilled Potential of Trayvon Martin and George Zimmerman. *Riverfront Times*. Retrieved from https://www.riverfronttimes.com/musicblog/2012/05/31/destructive-ignorance-in-st-louis-and-south-florida-and-the-unfulfilled-potential-of-trayvon-martin-and-george-zimmerman

Tef Poe. (2014, September 24). Hip-Hop Is Failing Us. *Riverfront Times*. Retrieved from https://www.riverfronttimes.com/musicblog/2014/09/24/hip-hop-is-failing-us

Tef Poe, & Ashley Yates. (2014, October). *Ferguson Youth Take over Clergy/Cornel West event #FergusonOctober*. Retrieved from https://www.youtube.com/watch?v=w1SGVSGUF5I&feature=youtu.be

The Black Youth Project. (2012). The *Pledge: FM Supreme*. Retrieved from https://www.youtube.com/watch?v=H9BVTN3L5T8

The People's Minister of Information JR. (2015, September 2). Aisha Fukushima takes over the planet. Retrieved from San Francisco Bay View website: http://sfbayview.com/2015/09/aisha-fukushima-takes-over-the-planet/

Transcript of George Zimmerman's Call to the Police. (n.d.). Retrieved September 28, 2019, from http://www.documentcloud.org/documents/326700-full-tran-script-zimmerman.html

Transformative Culture Project. (2015). Jasiri X's "America's Most Wanted: Hip Hop, Media and Mass Incarceration." Retrieved from https://www.youtube.com/watch?v=8k6r4sQ7PAM

World Citizen Artists. (2015). Aisha Fukushima: World Day of Elimination of Racial Discrimination. Retrieved from https://www.youtube.com/watch?v=LDFh2XhXUlI

Zimmerman, Peter. (2016, July 28). Activist Jessica Disu: "The culture of policing in our country needs a radical transformation." Retrieved from WGN Radio—720 AM website: http://wgnradio.com/2016/07/28/activist-jessica-disu-the-culture-of-policing-in-our-country-needs-a-radical-transformation/

6 Taking a Relational Approach to Rhetoric and Discourse

(Re)Considering the Voices of Recycling and Sustainability

erin daina mcclellan and Kat Davis

Introduction

Recycling is often discussed as an individual effort, impactful in mitigating waste only when it is officially mandated in policy and collectively embraced as a way of living in everyday life. Because successful recycling policy requires consistent practices of recycling to be adopted and engaged in everyday life, (re)considering how many different voices influence our understandings of recycling is an important first step to being able to successfully engage in a shared discourse of sustainable living among an inevitably diverse group of humans. While both official policies and everyday practices affect how we understand recycling, we argue that it is only when formal university, city, and state policies reasonably co-exist *in relation to* the more mundane expressions of recycling as a value-laden practice that a larger discourse of sustainability can be constituted as both collectively shared and individually engaged. A multivocal rhetoric of recycling is often connected to the univocal message that recycling is a positive and impactful practice that unequivocally contributes to and ideal *and* achievable understanding of sustainable living. (Re)considering this relationship as more complex requires us to more closely examine how specific rhetorics of recycling are related to a larger shared discourse of sustainability in ways that are not always easily recognizable.

When we focus primarily on what specific rhetorical experiences with recycling share with a well-aligned discourse of sustainability, we often fail to notice the underlying tensions that prevent such a discourse from easily guiding the way we *actually* live in everyday life. Thus, rather than discussing how underlying tensions between specific rhetorics of recycling and a larger shared discourse of sustainability cause rifts in understanding, we embrace these moments of discontinuity as a way to invite critical engagement with ideal discourses, like that of sustainability, and celebrate the diverse, often conflicting, voices that constitute them. These voices are diverse in the way they understand and practice recycling, but also in the amount of influence they hold in relation to their position. We, thus, specifically focus on the integration of vernacular, mundane, and everyday

DOI: 10.4324/9780429297830-6

rhetorics of recycling that explicitly and implicitly communicated about how recycling was meaningful in this research but also the formal, official, and authoritarian voices about what recycling is and should be in relation to a large-scale event like the one we chose to focus on in this chapter.

Rather than seeking to simplify this complexity, we argue it is important to preserve it such that we can better understand how the embedded tensions between vernacular sense-making and official policy produce (im) possibilities for sharing larger discourses that guide our decision-making about pivotal issues like sustainable living. We used rhetorical field methods to study the rhetorics of recycling "in action" from the planning stage through the post-event coverage of a large-scale concert event on a U.S. mountain west university campus. By examining the various rhetorics of recycling that emerged in relation to a larger discourse of sustainability that situated such moments, we were further able to examine both rhetoric and discourse as complex and thus uniquely meaningful. We see the various rhetorics about recycling to be impactful precisely because they are complexly intertwined with a larger framing discourse of sustainable living.

The remainder of this chapter will thus focus on how the more explicit aim of examining *various* voices engage in rhetorics of recycling. By doing so, we can better understand vernacular sense-making about recycling *and* the official policies it speaks to in more complex ways. We first review a relational approach to rhetoric and discourse, attending to both points of discontinuity and rhetorics of incongruity among official and vernacular rhetorics engaged at this specific two-day event. We then consider how various rhetorics of recycling related to the event intersect with a larger discourse of sustainability in meaningful ways. Our analysis focuses on how points of discontinuity present across multiple voices engaged in the three stages of the event constituted various incongruities that invite us to (re) consider the univocal ideal of sustainability in more complex ways.

Rhetoric and Discourse: A Relational Approach

Before we begin discussing the study in more detail, we will first explain both why we see the relationship between rhetoric and discourse to be significant and how we see the role of voices that are engaged in a study to be a significantly meaningful part of its analysis. One way the rhetorics we examined were distinctly different emerged in relation to official and vernacular use. While both official and vernacular texts have been the focus of various rhetorical analyses, the relation between the two is less often examined. Since official policies must guide everyday practices in habitual ways for the policy to be effective, we find it is useful to also consider the diverse, and often competing, voices that constitute the role and/or impact of everyday practices. We further see these vernacular voices to be always in relation to larger norms and ideals that everyday practices are embedded within. Thus, larger discourses provide insight into the otherwise taken for granted ways that these norms and ideals are understood and experienced in everyday life. For this project, rhetorics of recycling were identified, engaged, and understood in relation to larger considerations of how recycling is important, valued, and impactful as appeared in a larger discourse of sustainability or sustainable living.

While this may seem obvious, a relational focus is neither often directly addressed in rhetorical analysis nor in discourse studies. While a specific slice of a larger discourse is often critically examined and discussed, we rarely discuss the implication(s) of such a discussion for the larger discourse(s) to which they contribute. It is thus our intention to devote the remainder of this essay to analyzing how specific components of the rhetoric of recycling at this two-day concert event demonstrate both what we know about recycling *and* the ways that such a rhetoric informs our understanding of sustainability as a larger, idealized way of living. Focusing on how specific points of discontinuity reveal broader perspectives by incongruity, we aim to illustrate how invisible complexities often appear and disrupt the oft-peddled univocal narrative of recycling as a uniformly "good" practice.

While it is conceptually straightforward to consider recycling as supportive of the goals advanced by a discourse of sustainability, a critical examination of such a rhetoric as a complex sense-making mechanism engaged in everyday life and captured in official policy reveals something else: a rhetoric of recycling analyzed in relation to a discourse of sustainability does *not* always promote the romanticized notion of living in harmony with the earth. There are real obstacles to how rhetorics of recycling are (re)presented in everyday life, and it became clear in our examination that specific tensions in how rhetorics of recycling were engaged throughout the planning, support, and evaluation of this event revealed three points of discontinuity that helped us to (re)consider sustainability through more than one perspective.

Vernacular Practices and Official Policy

Vernacular rhetoric, while often grounded in the work of Dante, who saw such rhetoric to be that of the common people, was further clarified by Hauser (1999). By articulating rhetoric as "the symbolic inducement of social cooperation" (p. 14), it was possible to examine the "vox populi" [voice of the people] (p. 24) in a more concentrated manner. This focus on the vernacular became tightly connected to both the ideas of discourse and publics. But what is most important for our study is how the very vernacular voices that Hauser writes about remain in relation to the various discursive ideals and norms that are presented in more official capacities. When (re)considering this relation, we face "perhaps the most obvious difficulty [that] stems from grounding 'the public' in *shared interests* ... An emphasis on interests necessarily accentuates these differences between peoples and groups" (p. 30). In other words, "discursive practices provide the evidentiary base for studying and interpreting the constitution of social will"

(p. 13). So, thus, we argue, vernacular practices of rhetoric must always be (re)considered in relation to the more official policies that discursively constitute the "reality" in which such vernacular understandings emerge.

Official policies and government mandates are often drafted and enacted without wide swaths of public knowledge or buy-in. This is not to insinuate coercive, deceitful, or ill-intentioned practices but rather draw attention to how many people are not aware of the public policies that mandate how they "should" live in their communities. Given the well-documented ways that climate change is affecting communities across the globe in various measures, we find the shared discourses surrounding environmental policy-making and enactment particularly worthy of closer examination. For this reason, we have chosen to focus on the discourse of sustainability as it is manifest in various rhetorics of recycling engaged by a specific group of stakeholders who participated in a two-day large-scale concert event at a western U.S. university.

By seeking to understand recycling in an everyday context, not just through official policy about recycling practices and processes, we examined rhetorics of recycling in their various forms because they revealed how different voices produced different understandings of the value of recycling for often very different reasons. While regionally recognized for their conservation efforts, our city and region host some of the biggest swaths of protected and unpopulated public lands, making issues of waste mitigation and land preservation particularly relevant to a broad public. The culture of conservation and preservation might seem to be inherently folded into the area's urban policies and practices, but this is not always the case. While voices of conservation are prominent and audible in an easily recognizable discourse of sustainability that is circulated by politicians and policy alike, such voices are responded to and/or ignored in ways that complicate the alignment between vernacular community practices and more amorphous formal policies, especially those at the national or regional levels. For example, while advocates for protecting public land perhaps easily share the central values of conservation that a discourse of sustainability embraces, they do not always agree that recycling is central to conservation efforts that both support. These differences may seem nuanced at first glance, but they often expose larger tensions that effect decision-making and disrupt opportunities to work together toward aspirational aims, like living sustainably. Thus, when everyday practices like recycling are not engaged across people who otherwise espouse a shared commitment to a unifying discourse of sustainability, it is important to stop to examine these points of discontinuity.

Points of Discontinuity, Perspectives by Incongruity, and Constituting (Im)possibility

Kenneth Burke (1969) wrote that part of a critic's job was to analyze text in search of "perspectives by incongruity." In other words, it is a salient part of a rhetorical critic's job to ask not just what the text *says* but also what it *does not say.* Burke's call for critics to ask, "what is *not* present in the work?" and/or "what has been ignored, or remains unseen, in what has been presented?" helps us to (re)consider how we come to know what is (im)possible in the world. In other words, by putting together the very perspectives that we often evaluate as "incongruent" might actually allow for a different understanding of both perspectives separately. Similarly, Michel Foucault (1969) claimed that points of discursive discontinuity (rather than continuity) better reveal what is most salient to society because such revelations encourage societal tensions to be examined in more personally relevant ways than large-scale explanations of such tensions that rely upon abstractions and reference socially distant consequences.

Both Burke's discussion of perspectives by incongruity and Foucault's proposal to identify and analyze points of discontinuity advocate for locating and naming tensions that appear across rhetoric and/or discourse. While Burke claims that identifying and naming embedded tensions within a rhetoric or across rhetorics allow us to understand practices we might otherwise not consider or see as consequential, Foucault argues that it is necessary to live into society's inevitable points of tension, not erase them from existence or smooth over its cracks to present an illusion of strength. Together, these theoretical perspectives encourage us to consider specific rhetorics *in relation* to what we understand to be (im)possible as constituted through larger discourses about often abstract and complex topics like sustainability. Specifically, the tensions that revealed themselves through analyzing rhetorics of recycling across various voices, from different perspectives, and with different audiences provided a framework that guided our analysis of how rhetorics of recycling engaged in relation to a specific two-day event were always in relation to understandings of the (im) possibilities of living sustainably embraced by a larger and more widely recognized discourse of sustainability.

(Re)considering Rhetorics of Recycling

Exploring the mundane rhythms of public life as most significant in the liminal space where official and vernacular rhetoric interact provides a unique opportunity to examine rhetoric as both individually engaged and collectively experienced. Analyzing how historical documents, public statements, and performances of resistance or support of any localized rhetoric interact can help us better understand how observable interactions, verbal reflections, and contextual interpretations are significant to understanding how people come to understand and use what they know in everyday life. Embracing Burke's call, it is particularly important to locate the points of discontinuities in these rhetorics as a way to (re)consider what we might otherwise take for granted about both recycling and sustainable living. By examining *both* official policies related to recycling in our city *and* the ways that rhetorics of recycling were engaged during this two-day event, we were able to identify specific ways that tensions appeared when determining what was (im)possible about recycling efforts, waste management practices, and coordination among otherwise disparate parties working to support the event. Specifically, points of discontinuity emerged around "looking good," being "successful," and "making a difference." Voices diverged across various rhetorics of recycling in ways that were not always publicly visible, imploring us to (re)consider how Kenneth Burke's call to diligently ask what is *not* being discussed and whose voices are *not* being heard to be useful in rhetorical analysis and discourse analysis alike.

Environmental Rhetoric and Green Discourse

A broader reading of environmental rhetoric as a body of scholarship argues that the "common topics and commonplaces" of environmental rhetoric, like recycling, "allows audiences culturally relevant access to potentially complicated ideas" (Ross, 2013, p. 92). As such, rhetoric must be (re)considered to help us account for the varying audiences and rhetorical situations it constitutes such that a "shared understanding" among stakeholders can be imagined. While Ross focuses on the ways meaning can—and should— better utilize rhetorical tools to be successful, we would reflect that such a focus on continuity and congruity simultaneously fails to account for the points of weakness and tension that Burke and Foucault remind us are also integral for rhetoric and/or discourse to constitute new meaning and/or influence. Indeed, Kirby and Lora-Wainwright (2015) claim that a discourse of sustainability has (un)successfully infiltrated "green policy" in Japan, reflecting that "Scrutinising [sic] how nations like Japan exploit (and speak about, and justify) these loopholes adds a relatively underexamined register of analysis that can provide insights into political motives, cultural dispositions and internal pressures of great significance" (p. 46).

Kirby and Lora-Wainwright (2015) further explain that "airing the voices of those actually involved in processing operations to help convey the murky ethical contours of e-waste conversion as lived in highly sensitive smuggling and scavenging communities" can be highly relevant to revealing whether these policies are having the effect that their creators intend (p. 46). In other words, without critical examination of points of *dis*continuity, there are important embedded aspects of an otherwise univocal rhetoric that fails to identify embedded perspectives by incongruity. Therefore, identifying a rhetoric's tensions does not mean that the rhetoric is faulty, but rather stronger, because it addresses its foundational cracks as it is built, making relationally relevant decisions rather than imagining each new phase of building as a separate event.

Examining a collection of diverse voices (often (re)presented in separate but related "texts") provides a very different account for how a rhetoric hangs together (or pushes apart) ideas that require some level of congruity to live communally. Human social life requires living amongst multiple and competing voices about what is and what should be. Studies of rhetoric have long posited that what we are able to imagine as possible is inevitably connected to our past and present experiences and understandings of the world in which we live. Thus, a relational orientation to the study of rhetoric calls forth a more comprehensive examination of voices across texts that engages both historically and presently to invite a more robust discussion of what can—and should—happen next. Such an approach is particularly useful to consider as complex examinations of rhetoric attempt to analyze cultural, political, and social-justice-related points of discontinuity and/ or perspectives by incongruity. By preserving the sanctity of complexity in a world that seems to call forth oversimplification as a way to deal with an increasingly complex relational orientation to the world, we hope to invite other analyses to look "beneath the surface" of seemingly univocal explanations of complex phenomena. This can help us have a stronger and more effective way of moving forward together toward a shared vision of the future, with a shared collective moral consciousness, and with a shared commitment to live together rather than apart.

A Colossal Concert, a Legion of Volunteers, and a Band of Skeptics

In late summer, a concert of unprecedented proportion headed a mid-sized university campus in the mountain west with predicted numbers of attendees to exceed 80,000 people over two days. The university stadium set to host the event prepared for months to secure full-time and temporary staff to support the event. Because it was a university-hosted event, a campus-based sustainability team was also invited to collaborate with stadium staff to develop a pilot recycling program, specifically aimed at collecting the no-longer-recyclable plastic water bottles that would be discarded in mass numbers during the two-day event. While a university-owned and operated building, the stadium has been granted "auxiliary status," meaning that it is exempt from standard university facility requirements, including those governing recycling practices. The two-day concert event was held at a university facility, staffed with non-university employees and volunteers, and found itself at the center of a request to pilot a recycling program coordinated among the university's sustainability team, university facilities staff, temporary contract employees, and city employees. The entire effort was subject to university, city, state, and federal policies addressing both waste mitigation and recycling.

Thus, the pilot became a particularly noteworthy opportunity for the sustainability team to be able to work with university stadium staff, privately contracted waste services employees, and city employees supporting metropolitan recycling efforts who might not have otherwise been incentivized to work toward a more permanent plastics-only collection program adoption. Given our ability to capture various rhetorics of recycling across various stages of planning, implementation, and reflection about the two-day event, we realized that this allowed us to (re)consider a very visible account of the recycling program as overwhelmingly "successful." While perhaps an accurate assessment, such an account simultaneously reflected a limited, and simple, understanding of recycling at the event as only about the final amount of material saved from the landfill. Thus, analyzing a more robust collection of rhetorics of recycling revealed disagreements about how recycling could—and should—be practiced and/or prioritized, differences in prioritizing waste mitigation policy over other procedural norms, and overall, complicated the presentation of the recycling program as successful based solely upon the measurable amount of recyclable material collected at the culmination of the event.

While we have no interest in downplaying the significance of this measure, we also recognize the very important tensions that such a measure fails to account for when it informs a larger discourse of sustainability (if we just recycle "more" we can be "more" sustainable). By revealing the complexities that are otherwise not immediately apparent in such a discourse of sustainability, we are also able to discuss the usefulness of (re)considering incongruence and resistance to such a univocal discourse. In other words, by making the tensions about recycling more visible, we can better attend to them as in need of negotiation rather than cover them up in attempt to appear unified. This can strengthen the impact of discourse in guiding our decision-making over time rather than weaken it from the inside-out. By embracing the diverse ways that various rhetorics of recycling impact our understandings of "sustainability," we are more likely to collectively pursue sustainable living as real possibility for shared living. Since sustainability requires *collective* coordination to be impactful, (re)considering how points of discontinuity arise within and across rhetorics of recycling can help our abstract ideals like those espoused in a discourse of sustainability to better shape how we engage in everyday practices like recycling in more visible ways.

The Problem with Plastic

The opportunity to create this pilot program came at a time when recycling itself had become politically charged by a series of event. In January 2018, in an act commonly referred to as building a "green wall," China stopped taking plastics #3 through #7 to be recycled. This required a global shift in waste management practices as China was receiving almost half of the world's plastic imports, including all plastic exports from the United States (Parker & Elliot, 2018). While recycling practices were unequivocally supported as "good" for the environment during the time prior to 2018, they were largely touted as such because they remove waste from our local communities. The practice of collecting and sending plastics to a different community in China, however, can hardly be considered part of a sustainable plan for waste mitigation long-term. After the erection of the "green wall," communities like ours were not ready to forego their recycling programs entirely but they were abruptly forced to address the complexity of recycling in a way that they had not had to prior to the ban.

In response to China's "green wall" ban, our city, in partnership with its privately contracted waste hauler, developed a plan to continue to divert recyclable plastics from the landfill and recover non-recyclable plastics for an energy conversion project. This plan altered messaging about recycling that was sent to all city residents. Most notably, the waste provider for the city announced it would no longer accept all plastics (specifically, no water bottles). This change in messaging about recycling (re)constituted how people understood recycling, making it (im)possible in different ways, specifically complicating how residents understood the role of recycling plastics. The city's new mandate changed both *what* was considered recyclable and *how* recycling was possible.

A third-party contractor emerged during this time, promoting its waste-to-energy program capable of converting plastics into diesel fuel. It gained a corporate sponsor in Hefty, who provided special orange "energy bags" required to hold specially designated plastics, which were then referred to as "orange bag recyclables." While hoping to be a solution to the sudden "green wall" problem, the messaging of "what goes where" accompanied by a free roll of orange bags was not broadly successful in reconstituting how city residents understood and practiced recycling. The city's slogan— "when in doubt, throw it out" along with its accompanying "curb it" website that identifies no less than 82 separate categories of materials that can/not be recycled do little to clarify the new expected practices. Since clean streams of recycling material are required to successfully mitigate waste, the ability to recycle as much material as possible is predicated on first *understanding* how it works. Thus, while the discourse of sustainability continues to clearly embrace recycling as an impactful practice in living more sustainably, the rhetorics of recycling have grown increasingly more complex.

While a discourse of sustainability is often uniformly supportive of recycling, federal, state, and city entities do not always clearly support recycling practices, making accountability a moving target. While the EPA clearly states that mandates about recycling are a state responsibility, our state moves that responsibility to municipalities, stating that recycling is "an optional service provided at the discretion of local governments or by private recycling companies" because the state does not "mandate waste diversion goals" but rather "supports and encourages pollution prevention and recycling...through public education and outreach activities." While policy increasingly shifts responsibility to individual consumers of waste material, businesses, and producers of waste material remain relatively unaccountable for engaging in waste prevention practices. Similarly, mass marketing has shifted to sell the idea of living sustainably as part of a collective city brand, ultimately making it a place where like-minded people want to live together. While appealing to a broad audience, and specifically to a younger generation of people who are noticeably more vocal about protecting the environment, such marketing practices reify the message that recycling is an individual choice, albeit one that can—and should—be practiced as part of a sustainable lifestyle. Amidst this backdrop, however, rhetorics of recycling emerged as part of the everyday life that we experienced related to this two-day event.

Rhetorical Field Methods and Analytic Frames

Utilizing rhetorical field methods[1] as a guide, we collected and analyzed a cadre of voices who engaged in various rhetorics about the concert's pilot recycling program. Specifically, one of the authors took field notes and engaged in both formal and informal interactions with stakeholders throughout the planning, implementation, and reflection stages of the event. Stakeholders included facilities staff, city employees, temporary employment staff, and a team of volunteers referred to here as the "sustainability team." With a shared motivation to positively impact waste mitigation practices (and policies), these stakeholders were often spread across roles that involved only part of the recycling efforts needed for the pilot program to work. Thus, the cadre of environmentally focused volunteers that comprised the sustainability team was pivotal to the success of the program. The team regularly and unglamorously sorted through trash as part of their commitment to mitigating waste at other large events to ensure that collected recyclable materials could be successfully processed in "clean" streams without contamination by non-recyclable materials. This dedicated work diverts large amounts of waste from the landfill each year. The sustainability team at this event was a committed and experienced team of volunteers working under the leadership of university staff who was charged with creating a collaborative pilot recycling program for large events.

Across these various stakeholders, there was both a shared commitment to the pilot recycling program yet a clear difference in individual stakeholder motivations for doing so. Thus, examining rhetoric beyond its univocal (re)presentations can reveal how a shared discourse is constituted in its individual points of tension and discontinuity. Such incongruences remind us that complexity is revealed during organic moments of meaning making more than in repeated parts of pre-existing discourse. It, therefore, makes good sense to examine potentially divergent rhetorics as they "live" in the world together rather than analyze only selected individual texts in contextually isolated moments. Given the sometimes equally complex context of this two-day event, we chose to approach the rhetorics of recycling related to this event during three distinct phases: *pre-event planning*, *event support practices*, and *post-event coverage*.

While each phase engaged slightly different rhetorical artifacts, we specifically focused on how rhetorics of recycling both aligned with and diverged from each other in bodily, material, symbolic, and linguistic form. Rhetorics of recycling were identified during the pre-event planning in field notes and e-mails that reflected detailed accounts of formal meetings, during the support event phase in written descriptions of interactions with event participants and material environments, and during post-event coverage through social media posts and news reports after its culmination. By using these phases to help us identify rhetorics of recycling, we were further able to analyze how such rhetorics engaged a larger discourse of sustainability in the ways they aligned and diverged.

Pre-event Planning

The pre-event planning phase of the two-day concert began when a member of the sustainability volunteer team was asked to coordinate with campus facilities staff to outline what might be needed for a pilot recycling program to work at the event. This was a big opportunity given the facility hosting the concert, like several other campus buildings that serve the larger community, was exempt from standard campus policies on recycling. Thus, there was hope that a successful pilot recycling program could provide a new protocol for recycling in otherwise exempt buildings, making a significant impact over time by ultimately diverting a large amount of waste from the landfill. We will refer to this phase of the event as "pre-event planning" due to its formal discussions, email exchanges, and decision-making processes about what resources to allocate to recycling efforts, what training and process expectations to include and/or exclude at the event, and evaluative measures for assessing the event after it had concluded.

While stakeholders in the pre-planning event phase all engaged in rhetorics of recycling, they did not all engage in like-minded discussions about how recycling could (or even should) be implemented at the event. All stakeholders, however, were invested in planning a "successful" pilot recycling program in some way. It was, thus, not surprising that the sustainability team initiated coordinating stakeholder planning to envision and implement a pilot program to divert non-recyclable plastic waste and other recyclable material from this large-scale concert event and begin thinking about how to impact mitigating waste at the stadium beyond these two-days.

One of the most insightful parts of the pre-event planning phase occurred when stakeholders attempted to collaborate about the allocation and assignment of resources to the recycling effort. This was particularly poignant in the various meetings and e-mails brainstorming the (im)possibilities for the program. We collected field notes and reviewed emails to reveal how rhetorics of recycling were engaged among facilities stakeholders as the sustainability team formally submitted their recommendations for a successful pilot program:

Sustainability Team Recommendation	Facilities Stakeholder Response
Target audience to encourage collecting recycling through visible announcements, fan guide, etc.	"This isn't the kind of crowd that is going to recycle"
Plastics-only collection containers, aluminum-only collection containers, and trash containers should be together	"There isn't enough room to provide recycling containers with every trash can"
Clear plastic bags should be used to hold bottles to increase likelihood of no contamination after the event	"These can be provided" (Note: bags ran out and had to use another building's materials during the event)
One 40-yard plastics-only dumpster and one 40-yard aluminum-only dumpster should be provided for recycling collection	"There is not enough room in the back of the complex to hold five additional 40-yard dumpsters that have already been ordered for trash" (adding to the original two 40-yard dumpsters that the stadium regularly uses). One 8-yard recycling dumpster in the stadium is accessible on site; additional recycling to be deposited in another building's dumpsters.
Custodial staff should be trained on how to handle recyclables: • Plastics stay tied in bag and are deposited in plastics-only dumpster • Aluminum deposited into aluminum-only dumpster loose	"The third-party company hired for custodial services at the events [a 'temp agency'] does not provide event-specific training to its workers." To ensure recycling is done correctly, the volunteer team will have to do it themselves.
#1 plastic cups could be collected and recycled as well (zero waste goal)	"We do not know what type of cups will be ordered"
All recycling dumpsters should be *not* accessible to the public to ensure lack of contamination (which would send the entire dumpster to the landfill)	"Recycling dumpsters accessible in the stadium parking lot need to stay visible because it will make the university look bad to remove them"
Beer Garden should have recycling cans behind the bar since they are required to pour all liquids into cups	"The beer garden will be too busy to be focus on sorting materials"
A shift of volunteers should be employed after the event is over to collect recycling from stadium seating	"The third party workers hired to clean the stadium seats quickly will not allow volunteers a chance to collect recyclables"

While these responses collectively reveal various degrees of willingness and unwillingness to prioritize allocating resources to the pilot, its ultimate success was most commonly connected to its measurable deterrence of waste. This significant amount of recycled material would not have been possible, however, if the sustainability team had accepted the responses of facilities stakeholders to their original requests for resources and program support. In other words, it was only through a series of interventions and changes to the plans as they would have been if they would have accepted all of the resistance captured in the stakeholder response table above. Much of this original resistance became relatively invisible over the next two phases of the event, especially after all stakeholders received broad-based acclaim for their successful recycling efforts after the event was over. While the voices participating in the pre-event planning phase of the concert engaged in rhetorics of recycling that often appeared incongruous, this discontinuity was much less apparent when the discourse of sustainability was reflected in coverage of the event that celebrated their coordination as a unified effort. A similar divide continued as recycling practices were engaged in relation to an ever-changing understanding of the (im)possibility of recycling efforts and support resources.

Event Support Practices

In many ways, the most poignant aspects of a rhetoric of recycling at this event were embedded in the displays and practices of recycling during the event itself. This was often the case even more than the language capturing sense-making about it. For example, despite the refusal to meet the sustainability team's requests for additional recycling containers, plastic-only containers and aluminum-only containers made it onto the concourse. Although in many places throughout the stadium there was only a trash container *or* one type of recycling container, rather than all appropriate containers, as requested. Trash receptacles were not consistently paired with "Aluminum Only" and "Plastic Bottles Only" containers, and the signs requested to help people self-sort were made with very small font. Beer garden employees were not provided with back-of-the-house recycling bins but instead provided cardboard boxes lined with the appropriate aluminum-only and plastic-only liners and handwritten labels above each. Similar containers were fashioned at the pour station entrances, where concert-goers were required to pour the contents of their bottles or cans into a designated plastic cup.

Dumpsters were utilized in ways that facilities and city employee stakeholders indicated would not originally be possible. The amount of produced trash versus recyclable material predicted by the same stakeholders proved highly inaccurate. And stadium staff eventually agreed to forego paying their usual temporary workers to "quickly" clean the stadium after each event, instead paying $2,500 to various non-profits who provided volunteers to clean the stadium after concert-goers had departed. But like the lack of foresight in ordering recyclable plastic cups for liquids (rather than the non-recyclable ones that were ordered), waste mitigation efforts were hindered due to a lack of volunteer training about how to sort materials to ensure clean streams for recycling.

Although this phase presented a variety of tensions between what was said and what was done, much of what was done was highly impactful.

For example, even though facilities staff told the sustainability team that there was no room to add recycling containers behind bar, bartenders gladly sorted recyclable material into makeshift boxes and containers with sharpie-labeled titles to remind them what should be sorted where. Similarly, sustainability team members successfully moved trash and recycling receptacles and dumpsters alike to ensure clean streams of material could be maintained. So while the event's recycling support practices were often spur of the moment, ad hoc, innovative, and unplanned, they were also the practices that were overwhelmingly supported by concert attendees and event employees alike, with post-event coverage specifically highlighting much of these organic efforts to increase recycling.

Post-event Coverage

After the event, the sustainability team used the detailed recordings of their efforts to demonstrate the success of the pilot program, especially in terms of the statistical difference that their recycling program made in terms of metric tons diverted from the landfill. What was not as clear in that reporting, however, was how the success was only possible because they worked around many of the stakeholder resource and systemic limitations that emerged during the pre-event planning stage. Likely the most errant claim made by stakeholders prior to the event was that the type of people attending a country music event would not (want to) sort their trash from their recyclables. However, when given the opportunity to self-sort, concert-goers overwhelmingly succeeded. There was almost no contamination caused by placing the wrong type of material in a labeled container when an aluminum-only container was placed next to a trash receptacle. When an aluminum-only and/or plastic-only container was placed on the concourse without a trash receptacle present, however, there was significantly higher contamination. And while this concern was clearly articulated by the sustainability team during the pre-event planning stage, the benefit of pointing out that the plastic-only containers were the most highly contaminated when placed alone in any area of the stadium *after* the event was that such a recommendation could not be ignored in the same way if the pilot program is to be adopted in the future.

Perhaps one of the most notable successes was that two full 40-yard dumpsters filled with recyclables were successfully processed after the event. What was not as visible was that the large trash-only dumpsters were not emptied between events as stakeholders had planned and at the end of the two-day event, three 40-yard dumpsters reserved exclusively for trash remained completely unused. In other words, stakeholder experts on events clearly underestimated the amount of recycled materials that would be collected and overestimated the amount of trash that would be produced.

Beyond these successes reported by the sustainability team, there were additionally two prominently featured collections of coverage that represented how non-stakeholders viewed the event's recycling efforts. First,

comment sections connected to local news coverage about the pilot recycling program's success represented a variety of types of posters but an
overwhelming praise for the recycling efforts of the program. Second, various social media platforms connected to the vent illustrated varied levels
of gratitude expressed by both concert-goers and event employees after the
culmination of the event. One compelling story of the pilot recycling effort
was shared on the social media pages of local news channels, resulting in
numerous comments expressing appreciation for the recycling volunteers,
with posts stating things like what "an awesome job" was done and that the
volunteers were the "real rock stars." And another group of comments advocated for more action beyond the successes of the pilot program, expressing frustration about how much waste was produced, calling for not just
increased recycling efforts but a focus on waste reduction. Concert-goes and
event employees consistently thanked volunteers for their efforts throughout
the concert and frequently asked how they themselves could get involved
in similar efforts in the future. These expressions demonstrated that recycling was not just an individual practice but a shared effort that was both
engaged collectively and appreciated widely. In this way, the habits of most
concert-goers were seen to align with recycling as a part of participating in
large-scale events, while the perceptions of most facilities staff was that this
practice was premised on individual choice and ideology. This discontinuity
in both understanding and performing recycling was prominently revealed
in the coverage of the event across various media channels and postings; it
was particularly apparent in the lack of resistance to these expressions of
gratitude and celebration of recycling efforts that were posted publicly.

Interestingly, the goal of "looking good" that facilities stakeholders drew
attention to during the pre-event planning phase was accomplished in the
post-event media coverage. However, given the dumpster was moved to the
back of the building for better access and protection of a clean stream of
materials, the need for the dumpster to stay where it was in the front park-
ing lot for "good PR" proved to be much less compelling when post-even
media coverage focused more on the volume of material successfully recycled rather than the "presence" of a visible recyclable materials dumpster.
Thus, incongruity in what "good PR" entails helps us to (re)consider how
collaborative practices often result in a reported univocal narrative that
does not always account for the various divergent voices that led to any
widespread perception of "success."

This impactful waste mitigation at the event was the result of complex
collaborations among a variety of stakeholders, who while collectively
incentivized to engage in rhetorics of recycling as a way to implement a successful pilot recycling program, did not always align in their expectations
and efforts to support that pilot in its implementation. The sustainability
team was credited with emptying and consolidating recycling bags during
and after the events; sorting commingled recyclables and contaminants into
clean streams of aluminum and plastic bottles; and taking loads of clean

recyclables to the appropriate dumpsters. In this way, the post-event coverage of the event displayed rhetorics of recycling as individually supported and the values embedded in a larger discourse of sustainability as recognizable across them all. While the post-event coverage clearly demonstrates the success of the pilot recycling program as a waste mitigation effort, discontinuity was apparent most notably between the content of rhetorics of recycling found in the pre-event planning phase and the post-event coverage. The incongruities that were produced in the tensions about what was (im)possible in such a pilot program were not always visible nor would they have necessarily been accessible to non-stakeholders. This warrants a further (re)consideration about the need to make more visible these tensions, not to point out weakness but to embrace complexity.

Using Discontinuity and Incongruity to Analyze Rhetorics of Recycling and a Discourse of Sustainability

Analysis of this two-day event implores us to (re)consider how a discourse of sustainability is constituted through various and often competing rhetorics of recycling engaged by various voices, for very different purposes, and targeted for diverse audiences. After looking across the vernacular and official forms of rhetoric, the performative and discursive displays of recycling that emerged, and the material and symbolic representations of recycling as a practice of sustainable living, we found three particular tensions—or discontinuities—that emerged around how recycling does (and does not) serve as a central part of a discourse of sustainable living. Such an analysis helps us (re)consider how our city's recycling efforts (un)successfully work to promote larger understandings of "sustainability" not just as a future goal but as a value guiding our everyday practices. By illustrating how official rhetorics of recycling (like those found in policy) can set socio-cultural expectations that are (not) always apparent in everyday recycling practices, we aim to reveal how challenges to idealized (re)presentations of sustainable living can often shift those expectations in important ways. As we will demonstrate further in our analysis, identifying prominent tension points among different rhetorics of recycling can serve to interrupt an otherwise continuous understanding of recycling as unequivocally "good." We see the resulting incongruities produced by these points of discontinuity to invite us to (re)consider both the ideal notion of living sustainably *and* the practices of recycling as we actually encounter them in everyday life.

Recycling as a Shared Commitment, Collective Moral Consciousness, and Common Vision of the Future

Multiple voices appear across these themes that call to question the utility of promoting a singular, univocal discourse of sustainability over the benefits of coming to understand such a discourse's multivocal contributions in more detail. The latter, we argue, is imperative for working toward a truly collaborative effort to live more sustainably together. To expect people to reject their individuality if they are to meaningfully contribute to living together sustainably is preposterous. Thus, it is equally preposterous to expect collective ideals like those embedded in a discourse of sustainability to be enacted by every individual in the same way. For this reason, successful large-scale efforts, like recycling, require both the opportunity for various rhetorics about them to emerge *and* the opportunity for the points of discontinuity among them to be constantly up for discussion; this is the way that rhetorics of recycling, for example, can change the embedded values and/or ideals of a discourse of sustainability to reflect that habits and expectations of those who engage them over time. The three specific incongruities we identified in rhetorics of recycling at this event addressed (1) a shared commitment, (2) a collective moral consciousness, and (3) a common vision of the future. These three incongruities will be further discussed in relation to the tensions and points of discontinuity manifest within them.

Shared Commitment

First, rhetorics of recycling surrounding this event clearly portrayed recycling as a *shared commitment* to living that treats recycling as a contribution to improving our local communities and the health of our environment. Various policy-related documents and news coverage about recycling reflected that recycling, while often addressed as an individual activity, was discussed as impactful when it was collectively engaged. This was most apparent at the event when the 25 volunteers who comprised the university's sustainability team met with event stakeholders to plan how to mitigate waste, strategized about how to increase waste mitigation during the event, and ultimately increased the amount of clean stream recyclable material on a significant scale over two days. These volunteers did more than just sort through trash; they performed recycling both individually and together in a way that openly and actively encouraged others to join them. This was most apparent in informal expressions of gratitude expressed during and after the event along with posted comments on social media actively supporting the effort. Comments like "thank you for your hard work" and "*this* is the culture of [where we live]," implicitly and explicitly supported these efforts to engage in waste reduction strategies. In this way, these expressions (re) present an interest in shifting expectations for other large-scale events to have similar possibilities for recycling.

By challenging the stadium staff's initial claim that "this isn't the kind of crowd that is going to recycle," the volunteers disrupted the narrative that some types of people recycle, and others do not. This (re)presentation of discontinuity demonstrates the complexity that is visible when expectations based on past experiences are confronted with practices that directly counter accounts of "the way it is"; this is the way that change begins. It is worth noting that first city-mandated recycling program began in the United States only 40 years ago (Goodyear, 2018). Thus, the discontinuity amongst these rhetorics also reveals an embedded tension between recycling as something individuals "want" to do and something that is a "normal" way of living together. Perspectives by incongruity, thus, invite us to consider how information seeking can change so drastically over time, fundamentally altering the way we understand the world *and* act in relation to others in it. From looking up information in encyclopedias to "google-ing" anything you might want to know wherever you are on your smart phone, what we do as "habit" fundamentally become collective practices that change the way we live together. Thus, the practice of recycling as an individual habit cannot be dismissed without simultaneously considering the influence of collective programming that provide the resources, systems, and processes to collectively engage in waste mitigation in impactful ways.

Collective Moral Consciousness

Perhaps not unrelated, the rhetorics we examined revealed a *collective moral consciousness* about recycling depicted as a shared commitment rather than an ideologically aligned or controversial practice. Despite portrayals of recycling as divisive in various policies and formal political statements, recycling appeared at this event to be overwhelmingly supported. Posted expressions revealed that rather than justifying why it was ok to skip recycling, posters instead overwhelmingly expressed regret for failing to recycle: "I wanted to recycle but didn't see any recycle bins!" Other comments went further to shame concert-goers who left waste items behind after the event, pointing out that volunteers should not be left to pick up after them since we are all responsible for making our environment better: "Too bad not enough people respect their country enough to HELP keep it clean." This last comment highlights the tension between understanding recycling as a "respectful" way of living together and recycling as an expected part of living in the world together. In this way, the incongruity between living in an ideal way and living in an expected way provides insight into the complexity of the relational aspects of norms. In this case, despite the overwhelming support expressed in online forums for the volunteers and their recycling efforts, explicit support for recycling as an expected practice of sustainable living was not nearly as apparent. Policies for recycling at the university, city, state, or federal levels all revealed shifting accountability rather than an attempt to address the discontinuity between lack of policy mandates and widespread participation in recycling programs as demonstrated both in performative and mediated forms.

While our city government has explicitly adopted opportunities for recycling, especially curbside recycling for individual households, they have not done a good job ensuring or motivating the production of clean streams of recycling. This failure significantly inhibits the success of any recycling program to mitigate waste because once a stream of recyclable material is compromised or contaminated the entire unit of material must be moved to the landfill instead. Thus, the lack of oversight in program implementation to ensure clean streams of recyclable material reveals an even larger incongruity between how recycling is practiced and how it actively (fails to) contributes to sustainable living.

Common Vision for the Future

Analyzing the rhetorics of recycling at the event itself revealed a *common vision for the future* in ways that performed recycling practices as collectively constituting the ideals embedded in a larger and more ideal discourse of sustainability. These rhetorics of recycling, in many ways, served as "good PR" for the university, displaying its commitment to recycling, which further allowed others to also identify with the university as "good" because it implemented this pilot recycling program. But "good PR" is not the same incentive for recycling as "good morals." Thus, one notable tension arose when stadium officials rejected the sustainability team's request to move a clearly-labeled "recycling" dumpster to the back of the event building. Rather than ensure easy access for the sustainability team to ensure the contents of that dumpster would not be contaminated by passers-by, the facilities staff were much more immediately concerned with "looking good" over "doing good." In this way, the incongruity between perceptions of recycling and practices of recycling left a much larger burden on the volunteers than the facilities staff.

The invisible barriers to a successful recycling program that were presented to the sustainability team remain invisible without analyses like this one that seek to embrace *both* the multi-vocal contributions of individual rhetorics of recycling and the univocal expressions of shared valued embedded in a larger discourse of sustainability. A relational approach asks that we consider these together, in the messy ways in which they align, diverge, and align again. By celebrating the ways that individuals engage in rhetorics that both align and diverge from one another while remaining in relation to a larger discourse that constitutes rhetoric's values, ideals, and norms is important. If we are to (re)consider the world's biggest challenges, it is important that we do both.

While a univocal narrative of success, like that touting the pilot recycling program, can be interpreted as evidence of a collective moral consciousness associated with a larger commitment to sustainable living, it is not always representative of the complexities that led to that success. If diverse voices work together toward a shared vision for the future, identifying the points of discontinuity inevitably embedded in a seemingly univocal narrative can prevent foundational cracks from disrupting the possibility for complex efforts such as the pilot program discussed here to succeed in the future. There is plenty to celebrate about both the success of this pilot recycling program *and* the reception of the rhetoric of recycling as an integral part of a shared vision of the future for our city (and our university), but we should be cautious about accepting the premise that this success should hide the tensions discussed here.

As Hauser (1999) reminds us, what is most significant for a study of rhetoric is how the participants in vernacular rhetorics "found it intersecting meaningfully with their experiences" and "how they appropriated it through their own critical responses" (p. 276). In other words, the diverse and often contentious ways that multiple voices engage in vernacular rhetorics should be examined in relation to one another. But they should *also* be examined in relation to a larger discourse that constitutes its ideals and norms. A healthy body is not defined as one that is *never* ill nor is it defined without an understanding of an abstract notion of what a healthy body is perceived to be by generalized others in a culture or community. In this way, points of discontinuity play an ever-important role in helping us to (re)consider perspectives by incongruity because when such tensions are recognized and addressed, the likelihood that innovative knowledge can be successfully engaged in helping us to collaboratively and meaningful invent our future together is dramatically increased.

Note

1 E.g., *Field Rhetoric* (2018) Candice Rai & Caroline Gottschalk-Druschke (Eds.) Univ. of Alabama Press (forthcoming) or Michael K. Middleton, Samantha Senda-Cook, & Danielle Endres (2011). Articulating rhetorical field methods: Challenges and tensions, *Western Journal of Communication* 75(4), 386–406.

References

Burke, K. (1969). *A grammar of motives*. Berkeley, CA: University of California Press.

Foucault, M. (1969). *Archaeology of knowledge*. Trans. A. M. Sheridan Smith. London and New York: Routledge, 2002.

Goodyear, S. (2018). "A Brief History of Household Recycling" City Lab. Available at: https://www.citylab.com/city-makers-connections/recycling/#slide-1980

Hauser, G. A. (1999). *Vernacular voices: The rhetoric of publics and public spheres*. Columbia: University of South Carolina Press.

Kirby, P. W. and Lora-Wainwright, A. (2015). Exporting harm, scavenging value: Transnational circuits of e-waste between Japan, China and beyond. *Area, 47*(1), 40–47.

Parker, L. and Elliot, K. (2018, June 20). Plastic Recycling is Broken. Here's How to Fix It. National Geographic. News. Available at: https://www.nationalgeographic.com/news/2018/06/china-plastic-recycling-ban-solutions-science-environment/

Ross, D. G. (2013). Common topics and commonplaces of environmental rhetoric. *Written Communication, 30*(1), 91–131.

7 Tensional Dynamics in Discussions of Social Responsibility

Voice Mobilization, Concern Negotiation, and Organizational Boundaries Co-creation

Alessandro Poroli

The relationship between (corporate) social responsibility ((C)SR) and communication has lately attracted increasing interest in academic research (Bruhn & Zimmermann, 2017).[1] Encouraged by the institutionalization of ethics-driven practices in business operations (Carroll, 2015), scholars have become more committed to understanding how communication functions when (C)SR is being performed (Morsing & Schultz, 2006). Primarily they have investigated *if, when*, and *how* (C)SR and related information disclosure may influence organizational legitimacy (Bachmann & Ingenhoff, 2016); affect corporate reputation (Eisenegger & Schranz, 2011); and condition organization-stakeholder relationships (Schmeltz, 2012). In this research, communication has been largely seen as a means to respond to stakeholder requirements (Groza, Pronschinske, & Walker, 2011); nurture trust in publics (Kim & Lee, 2018); and achieve financial ends (Du, Bhattacharya, & Sen, 2010).

Although this *transmission view of communication* has merit in directing the spotlight onto communication in (C)SR, it has also been questioned by scholars (e.g., Christensen, Morsing, & Thyssen, 2013), who expressed reservations about its overly mechanistic, purpose-driven, and information-disseminating understanding of communication (Schoeneborn & Trittin, 2013). This linear, representational approach has been said to account only for the message-focused and medium-based traits of communication related to (C)SR (Cooren, 2020). Considering communication as a *conduit* by which (C)SR is instrumentally conveyed to publics in functionalist terms (Christensen & Cheney, 2011), the transmission view fails to recognize the primacy of communication in creating, shaping, and perpetuating organizations and social phenomena (Schoeneborn & Trittin, 2013).

This underestimation of the formative character of communication calls for a deeper interpretation of the role and nature of communication, proposing it as the foundation of responsible acting and approaching (C)SR as *literally called into being in* and *through* instantiations, negotiations, and interconnections of interacting parties (Cooren, 2020). In the past

DOI: 10.4324/9780429297830-7

decade, this centrality of communication in (C)SR has been foregrounded by those who, adopting a *communicative constitutive view of reality* (Ashcraft, Kuhn, & Cooren, 2009), have embraced the claim that discourse has a performative strength (Fauré, Brummans, Giroux, & Taylor, 2010). Building on the language-grounded ontological turn in research that foregrounds communication to explore and explain organizational practices (Alvesson & Kärreman, 2000; Brummans, Cooren, Robichaud, & Taylor, 2014; Fairhurst & Putnam, 2004), these scholars have conceptualized (C)SR communication as being both *polyphonic* and *dialogic* (Castelló, Morsing, & Schultz, 2013; Schultz & Wehmeier, 2010). The conception of (C)SR as a negotiated process suggests that organizational social commitment is a *symbolic resource*, grounded and mediated in relations (Schultz, Castelló, & Morsing, 2013) and constantly "produced and reproduced in communication" (Schoeneborn, Morsing, & Crane, 2020, p. 18).

Thought-provoking in noting that communication is the key to understanding societal involvement for organizations, communicative constitutive arguments have suggested that (C)SR is grounded in the negotiations of various and, at times, contrasting voices (Castelló et al., 2013) and have maintained that (C)SR, like any other organizing practice, contributes to the creation of organizations (Schoeneborn & Trittin, 2013). These arguments open up intriguing paths for research, especially of unconventional and less accessible (C)SR practices. But how the multiple voices of (C)SR participate in these negotiated processes and are dealt with in everyday interaction requires more data-grounded elaboration (Koep, 2017; Schultz & Wehmeier, 2010). In addition, work pertaining to the communicative constitutive approach has begun to emphasize that the doing of (C)SR affects an organization's identity as well as the creation, maintenance, and renewal of organizational boundaries (Castelló et al., 2013; Schoeneborn & Trittin, 2013). Yet how these processes occur in practice is not yet clear, given that empirically built studies on the relationship between (C)SR discussion and organizational boundary delineation have struggled to find space in the literature.

In line with the objectives of this book, this chapter analyzes two conversational excerpts, accounting for the emergence, intervention, and effect of a plurality of voices in (C)SR and the intersection between polyphonies of interests and the organizational necessity to speak with a coherent (C)SR voice. These excerpts represent organizational discussions on (1) the management of relationships around a social responsibility project and (2) an organizational (re)positioning toward a sustainability-centred theme. The analysis embraces assumptions from what is known as *ventriloquism*, a theoretical framework proposed by Cooren (2010) to illustrate how multiple voices are made to speak and participate in interaction as people enact organizing processes. My arguments deepen the debate on the nature of voices partaking in (C)SR sense-making, a process featuring a mobilization of concerns, necessities, and constraints, which may materialize in conversation and shape (C)SR. The analysis also suggests that when making sense of (C)SR, practitioners appear to navigate between the need to respond to various interests and responsibilities and the constraining necessity to develop a consistent and clear-cut image of their (C)SR. The planning of (C)SR is, thus, marked by the intervention of many voices that may at times generate theme-focused confrontations and tensional situations. These tensions contribute to the co-construction of organizational boundaries, as illustrated in this chapter, through the emergence of dichotomous vocal oppositions in interaction.

In the next section, I introduce studies that assert the polyphonic character of (C)SR and support their argument while calling for more data-grounded research on the unfolding of voices in (C)SR-making. I then present the notion of ventriloquism (Cooren, 2010) and explain how it provides the basis for my analysis. After introducing the research context, the chapter continues with a ventriloquial examination of the two interactional extracts. In conclusion, I reflect on how this analysis may contribute to the communicative constitutive argument about (C)SR and related sense-making in organizations.

The Multivocal Nature of Organizational Social Responsibility

Extant communicative constitutive studies have contended that (C)SR should not be seen as a mere "fixed script or tool" to reach firm, settled, desirable ends (Schultz & Wehmeier, 2010, p. 13). Building on the environment-shaping understanding of communication (Putnam & Nicotera, 2009; Taylor & Robichaud, 2004) and the *equivalence approach*, which states that talk is action (Cooren, 2010; Searle, 1979), these works have started to emphasize the indissoluble relationship between (C)SR and communication (Christensen & Cheney, 2011). (C)SR has, thus, been conceptualized as *dynamic, developmental,* and *open-ended* (Christensen et al., 2013; Schultz & Wehmeier, 2010). (C)SR should be viewed as a polyphonic phenomenon, that is, according to Bakhtin (1981), a dialogical and interactional *process* in which multiple actors representing diverse sectorial and societal groups intervene to mould what being a socially responsible organization means (Castelló et al., 2013).

Therefore, (C)SR unfolds as a communication-grounded construct, a multi-party narration in which the voices of manifold stakeholders (both human and non-human; see Cooren, 2004) participate in defining practices of (C)SR (Wehmeier & Schultz, 2011). (C)SR is a process that features the staging, interaction, and confrontation of many voices that, through invocation and mobilization in interaction, express what a situation dictates and thus how it should be approached (Cooren, 2020). Given that these voices may engage in competition due to their varied nature, (C)SR should also be seen as a negotiated and "dynamic continuum of competing meanings" (Schultz & Wehmeier, 2010, p. 13).

Looking at (C)SR as fluid and processual thus amounts to recognizing that differing viewpoints, interests, and aspirations may clash with each other, generating dissonance and yet potentially ingenious outcomes for organizations, their (C)SR, and the whole society (Christensen, Morsing, & Thyssen, 2015; Cooren, Matte, Benoit-Barné, & Brummans, 2013). This interplay of contrasting voices may also be fostered by the various media that today serve as platforms for (C)SR debate, idea cultivation, and opinion-sharing (Schoeneborn & Trittin, 2013). These media are dynamic and shifting, which only bolsters the view of (C)SR as a complex process riddled with conflict. Hence, (C)SR can benefit from being considered "a forum for sensemaking, diversity of opinion, and debate" (Guthey & Morsing, 2014, p. 556). It is indeed in the processes of meaning-making, meaning attribution, and voice mobilization that (C)SR occurs. In other words, it is in the socio-material practices that organizations and their stakeholders create (C)SR actions and that organizations come to be viewed as legitimized actors committed to (C)SR (Castelló et al., 2013).

Approaching (C)SR as constituted in the communicative interventions of multiple actors means looking at it as a form of organizing (Kuhn & Deetz, 2008). Therefore, (C)SR talk, as a type of communication conducted in and by organizations, also intervenes to create, maintain, and extend the boundaries of organizations (Schoeneborn & Trittin, 2013). In line with the constitutive view that suggests organizations as precarious communicative accomplishments (Cooren, Kuhn, Cornelissen, & Clark, 2011), a "boundary" is not only set or fixed by parameters such as legal arrangements (e.g., statutes), geo-locational constraints (e.g., office buildings), and membership criteria (e.g., membership cards), which establish what organizations include or do not include (Schoeneborn & Trittin, 2013; Taylor & Van Every, 2000). An organizational boundary also needs to be unceasingly (re)created, (re) established, and (re)negotiated in or through communication (Cooren & Fairhurst, 2009). The constitutive argument invites analysts to approach boundaries as also negotiated in communicative practices and intertwined with processes of identity-making, which are defined by the participation of numerous actors in the society (e.g., stakeholders, media) (Dobusch & Schoeneborn, 2015; Kjærgaard, Morsing, & Ravasi, 2011). Boundaries are then permeable to multi-party interventions and interpretations, and open to change and contestation (Ashcraft et al., 2009).

This view represents a shared understanding in the communicative constitutive literature, one which considers organizational boundaries as emergent in communication and developing along with the construction and perpetuation of organizational identities (Dobusch & Schoeneborn, 2015). When organizations and their members do and speak about (C) SR, they thus shape their (C)SR-committed identity and communicatively enact their boundaries. Such a process builds on the interaction of stances and values nurtured by multiple actors, which include numerous third parties, such as media, international organizations, and NGOs (Schultz et al.,

2013). These actors may, thus, affect the constitution of organizational boundaries by sharing their views on (C)SR either indirectly (e.g., through the delineation of what is considered good [C]SR acting) or directly (e.g., through a critique of certain practices).

This reasoning about the polyphony of (C)SR and (C)SR talk as contributing to the construction of organizational boundaries has shown potential to enhance knowledge on organizational responsibility. Yet if on the one hand the multivocal nature of (C)SR has been well defined conceptually (Crane & Glozer, 2016), on the other hand, there have been scant analyses of how these voices unfold in (C)SR action planning, with communicative constitutive studies featuring few observations grounded in data (Koep, 2017). This lack of data calls for reflections building on practitioners' interactions, using actual data to illustrate the interplay of voices in (C)SR and the relation between (C)SR communication and the definition of organizations.

My analysis starts with the recognition that unlike other communicative constitutive studies that have pointed to organizations as being concomitantly "many and one" and "pluralistic and unitary" (e.g., Brown & Thompson, 2013; Robichaud, Giroux & Taylor, 2004), extant constitutive literature on (C)SR has had a hard time arguing that, in practice, organizations need to find a way to speak with one (C)SR voice to their publics. Primarily elaborating on the polyphony of (C)SR, communicative constitutive literature has not directly considered that organizations need to create a unified image of their (C)SR and to be externally perceived as coherent (C)SR-engaged entities (Christensen & Cornelissen, 2011). Hence, the need exists for more research on how organizations distinguish multiple voices, deal with them, and then unite them into a distinct (C)SR voice.

Aiming to analyze how voices interrelate when practitioners talk of and plan their (C)SR, and how this discussion affects the constitution of organizational boundaries, after Cooren (2010), I adopt a ventriloquial approach to communication. The ventriloquial lens has shown value in reflecting on the agentic strength of voices in communication, so appears to have theoretical and methodological potential for this argumentation. In addition, given its utility in revealing tensions in discursive practices, ventriloquism may also be helpful in identifying polyvocal forces and detecting univocal necessities of organizations in the doing of (C)SR.

Ventriloquism in Organizational Communication

In line with the assumption that social reality is constituted in communication (Craig, 1999), the idea of ventriloquism highlights a key trait of communication—i.e., the ability of interactants to make other people or beings do or say things, as they speak, write, or merely behave (Cooren, 2010, 2012). With roots in stagecraft, the art of ventriloquism consists of speaking in such a way that the sound coming from one's mouth appears to be generated from another source. Brilliantly adopted by Cooren (2010) in a theory-enriching metaphor, the ventriloquial construct depicts a ubiquitous phenomenon in human interactions: the fact that when people interact with one another, they always *act* and *speak for* or *in the name of* things to which they feel attached.

These objects of attachment—which animate interactants either consciously or unconsciously (Cooren et al., 2011)—may be principles, regulations, organizations, and, of course, other people (Latour, 1996). Saying something *on behalf of* a person or organization, thus, consists of "ventriloquizing" that person or organization. Doing so creates a relationship between the ventriloquist (the person who speaks in the name of something) and her *figure* (the name often attributed to the dummies enlivened by ventriloquists), with the latter being literally *made to speak* or *act*, i.e., participate in a certain situation and affect it (Cooren & Sandler, 2014).

Such a relationship is bidirectional, which means that a ventriloquist can also respond to her figure. She may become animated by the figure itself, which makes her say things or perform in certain ways. On that account, every interaction features a continuous oscillation between a ventriloquist and her figure (Cooren, 2012). When a ventriloquist speaks on behalf of a figure, she does not merely *make this figure present in communication*, but she is also being *ventriloquized* by it. According to Cooren (2012), when figures are made to talk and act in what humans do and say, they become actors in conversation and "*participate, as forms of agency, in these same interactions*" (p. 6; emphasis in original). This view allows us to point to the multiple forms of agency at play every time interactions take place (Cooren, 2012). Going beyond a mere attribution of agency to individuals, ventriloquism in fact underlines that non-human actors *unceasingly invite and express themselves* in human interactions (Cooren et al., 2013).

When we study meetings between CEOs and middle managers, ventriloquism may help in exploring the diverse voices that partake in and take on agency (that is, the capacity to make the difference) in the language game (Taylor & Van Every, 2011). These are those figures CEOs and middle managers feel attached to, which are *mobilized* to achieve objectives, and those that, speaking through their voices, *materialize* in dialogue and in turn ventriloquize CEOs and middle managers, thereby affecting the course of action (Cooren, 2012). In dialogue, as Cooren (2015) points out, "people act as much as they are acted upon" (p. 476).

In addition, ventriloquism accounts for what Cooren (2015) calls *effects of authority*. Invoking an agreement or mobilizing a policy, for instance, may increase one's authority through a process where these non-human figures act as co-authors of an utterance. An organization's representative may feel authorized to say something because, according to her, documents mobilized in dialogue allow her to do so (Cooren, 2015). The invocation of a figure in discussion, Cooren (2020) illustrates, leads the analyst to investigate what this figure dictates about a situation at stake. This approach maintains that these mobilized elements may become sources of authority, that is, they can author (i.e., strengthen) the validity of a position. In this view, increasing one's authority corresponds to augmenting the number of actors partaking in the definition of a situation. Yet Cooren (2015) also reminds us that other participants may take these invocations differently, questioning one's ventriloquation and counterbalancing one's authority. The mobilization of figures may, thus, generate situations in which different voices (each constituting a source of authority for interacting participants) can clash with one another, leading to tensions (Cooren et al., 2013).

Embracing ventriloquism in (C)SR suggests that (C)SR is constructed in communication, in which human beings are both actors and channels (Cooren, 2020), mobilizing and being mobilized by values and necessities. Ventriloquism, thus, invites us to look for those elements that make a difference in interaction and listen to what (C)SR situations appear to dictate when they are invoked (Cooren, 2020). For a researcher, adopting a ventriloquial lens means identifying those elements (figures) invoked by interactants when communicating (about) (C)SR (Cooren, 2016). When they are called into being in discussions, these figures represent issues people are required to deal with, but they are also voices of a situation that come to speak and point to possible courses of action.

As Cooren (2020) puts it, the task for the (C)SR-focused researcher, thus, becomes to understand how seemingly cacophonic contexts turn into polyphonic yet more harmonious situations. Helping to identify voices that can make a difference in organizing, ventriloquism is valuable to analyze situations where practitioners deal with, mobilize, and are shaped by multiple voices while planning (C)SR. Ventriloquism can also help us perceive constraints originating from organizations' need to express a coherent voice of (C)SR commitment. Given its potential to unveil conversational dynamics, uncover agentic voices, and conduct observations on meaning negotiation, the notion of ventriloquism is helpful in guiding my analysis.

The idea of voice embraced in this chapter, thus, builds on ventriloquial propositions. Accordingly, voice is first looked at as an *actantial force with performative effects* (Taylor & Cooren, 1997). By this I mean that voice is that discursive utterance in which something (e.g., an interest, an opinion, a concern) that is asserted by human actors and made present in a situation must be accounted for, as it can make the difference in the unfolding of that situation (Cooren, 2020; Trittin & Schoeneborn, 2017). Second, voice should also be viewed in its *reality-featuring* nature. Here, voice is a concept grounded in sense-making processes that reconciles, as ventriloquism allows us to do, constitutive and transmission inferences of communication. Interaction, as Cooren (2020) maintains, can indeed be viewed as a way in which the various elements of a situation are co-constructed but also transported and conveyed. In this vein, I argue, voice should also be seen as *an ensemble of negotiated and embedded polyphonies* that is presented as featuring a certain collective and can be communicated and perceived (or prospected to be perceived) in certain ways by multiple actors.

This approach to the notion of voice sets the stage for investigating how, in (C)SR sense-making, organizations navigate from polyphonic negotiations of multiple concerns and interests to formulations of actions and messages that are more oriented toward unity and account for potential perceptions by publics. For to be endorsed as committed to (C)SR, organizations must be externally recognized as having a delineated, unique, and coherent "voice" of (and about) (C)SR. Failing to achieve this unified voice may in fact result in stakeholder skepticism and distrust or affect organizations' reputation in the eyes of their publics (Kim, 2019; Kim & Ferguson, 2018). This navigation between univocity and plurivocity is, therefore, a necessity for organizations practising (C)SR and a crucial aspect that should be considered when reflecting, as I do here, on the interrelation of voices in (C)SR.

Research Context

The conversational excerpts analyzed in this chapter were purposefully selected from data collected during four months of fieldwork in the office of what I am calling DELTA. This fictionally named sectoral organization has representative and coordinating roles for a network of consumer co-operatives (nicknamed NOVA) operating in Country A. Dozens of co-operatives chose to delegate responsibilities to and be represented nationally by DELTA. Hence DELTA personnel (about 20 people at the time of data collection) work for the welfare of all the NOVA member co-operatives and relate with them in a service climate characterized by transparent sharing of information, constant participation in decision-making, and horizontal organizational relationships. Through the work of its social policy division (the focus of this research, consisting of four referents), DELTA coordinates the network's SR projects, which are supported by funds from the same individual co-operatives.[2] Coordination is achieved by organizing meetings with co-operative representatives, engaging in talk with state authorities, and allocating funds to valorize projects.

The network co-operatives are self-governing organizations that run their business in the retail sector and distribution of consumer goods. This means that they have their own decision-making bodies, individually owned facilities, and distinctive co-operative members. They arrange their mutualistic actions for the welfare of all members (which in consumer co-operatives represent the organizational ownership), implement their SR projects, and communicate about them using their information channels (e.g., co-operative magazines, social network webpages). All of this implies that they operate in well-delineated territorial contexts in Country A and have direct rapport with local associations. Yet they are also voluntarily bound to one another by the perceived need to act together as a network of organizations. This commitment originates from the pursuit of institutional, economic, and sustainable ends and the recognition that social aims and a better sharing of co-operative values can be more efficiently achieved via national unity and collaboration.

The network affiliation of NOVA members entails that each co-operative recognizes DELTA as a national coordinating body; accepts the role assigned to ALFA (a national organization responsible for communal marketing, product quality monitoring, and standard compliance); and embraces NOVA brand products (sold in all co-operative stores) as representing the foundational values of the network. Given the type of organizations in the NOVA network—co-ops characterized by consumer-owned structure and distributive practices to co-operative members—and their execution of communal SR initiatives, this network provides an interesting context in which to study the unfolding of voices in (C)SR sense-making and how (C)SR talk affects the shaping of organizational boundaries.

A Ventriloquial Analysis of Conversational Excerpts

This section analyzes two conversational excerpts taken from the same meeting, representing discussions about network projects and positioning toward SR themes. Here, DELTA spokespersons (pseudonymously, Robert, George, Lisa, and Pavel) discuss matters with several co-operative representatives (Jack, Harry, Jennifer, Kevin, and Chris).

In the first excerpt, the object of conversation is a project (named "Together for better horizons") where all co-operatives, coordinated by DELTA, commit to sensitize their members and wider fringes of Country A's population toward adopting responsible behaviours to fight the phenomenon of at-home food waste. This objective is the latest stage of a broader set of initiatives that, for years, have seen the network engaged with reducing food waste in its supply chain and stores. Co-operatives have implemented this through food donations, collaborating with territorial associations that help the needy (e.g., charities, parochial groups). Using the efficient functioning of a recently launched project website as a rationale for a sharing of information, DELTA invites co-operatives to exchange data about local collaborations with organizations. Clearly encountering the discontent of some co-operative representatives, this request results in an intense exchange that touches upon practices of information management and responsibilities of network organizations. Extract 1 illustrates the nature of voices at play when practitioners discuss arrangements of SR actions. It also spotlights how practitioners navigate between multiple voice mobilizations and self-restrictions dictated by the perceived need to speak with one organizational voice, throwing into sharp relief the tensional dynamics of this process.

Excerpt 1: Information Management and Concern
Mobilization in SR Arrangement

1	Robert:	Let's continue with the information collection on the relations
2		with associations. As said, that's valuable not only to have
3		contacts and conduct work for the *Together for better horizons*
4		website, but also to have data on the territorial relations [...]
5		That's to manage, as much as one can do, the relationships we
6		have nationally, and, conversely, to be locally aware of what
7		happens in both local and national settings. Some of you sent
8		these data. Could those who didn't update us?
9		[...]
10	George:	We had problems with Co-operative 5.[3]
11	Jack:	Yes.
12	George:	Because, as Jack can say, it has recently modified its food
13		donation policy, and it's preoccupied that engaging associations
14		in the web community could cause a backlash. You know, that's
15		for us to write an email (1.0) and you may also send it, to invite
16		subscribing to *Together for better horizons*, bringing a
17		contribution of ideas but also of territorial arrangements [...]
18		that's the goal.
19	Robert:	Actually, that's one of the goals, George.
20	George:	Yes.
21	Robert:	Let's not forget, though, that this collection of data can be
22		important for other goals.
23	George:	Sure.
24	Robert:	Indeed, when we meet associations that locally relate to Yellow
25		Association, Purple Association, and to organizations with
26		whom, more or less easily, we have a dialogue nationally, it's
27		useful to have information to understand what happens in the
28		territories. That's to know if there's a relationship or if there
29		isn't, if there's an exchange or not [...] The doubts of
30		Co-operative 5 can be handled in a sense that, for the subjects
31		they share, we don't send this email [...] Yet, aiming to picture
32		local relationships, the data would still be valuable. That's to
33		report them in the network SR report and better grasp how to
34		relate with national organizations [...] Who hasn't shared, can—
35		[...]
36	Robert:	[The shared information] may become a data circulation tool
37		on the relation between the co-operatives and their territories.
38		In some territories, indeed, there could be difficulties of
39		interaction with subjects belonging to certain organizations,
40		while in others, things may work much better. So, knowing
41		these things can help facing and overcoming difficulties locally.

42		(2.0)
43	Harry:	Robert, may I? (1.5) When signing agreements with
44		associations, we have a paragraph about the privacy norms. So,
45		if George wants this database, I need to ask if they're willing.
46		And if they aren't, I can't give the data. Besides, we have a very
47		close relationship with associations locally, so I don't get the
48		value of having a national database. It's difficult to see its
49		benefit. I want to have that clear, because to have another
50		database for its own sake without a precise goal— I don't get
51		it. Another thing. If we put them in contact, they'll start
52		making comparisons. The inclination of those doing this is to
53		reach the best. So, if I do less or more things than others—
54		I mean, I wouldn't want some co-operatives to face difficulties.
55		Associations may indeed tell them "in City B they do this and
56		in City D they don't, in City E they do this, while in City C
57		they don't." Let's be careful. We always want to have all these
58		data in hand. Yet, we also need to manage them. It's necessary
59		to be aware of what they're for. That's 'cause if they're valuable
60		only to have numbers, you've already got them. If I tell you I
61		work with 160 associations, you take and add it to the others
62		and get the national number. The rapport, and I say this
63		because I truly believe it, the rapport with the associations of
64		my territory, I want to be the one to maintain it.
65	Robert:	⌊Let me—
66	Harry:	I don't want to delegate others, speaking on behalf of a
67		national elusive NOVA that doesn't exist, this dialogue with
68		the territorial associations. That's always been our policy.
69	George:	⌊Well, yeah.
70	Harry:	So, to me that's normal to say.
71	Jennifer:	[...] Grey Association of City D isn't related at all with Grey
72		Association in City K. They have features and ways of
73		relating to the territory that may totally differ. Besides, for
74		us, but I think it happens to others too, there's often only
75		one association that is formed by many organizations and
76		handles the distribution of what's collected in the food
77		drives [...] The partner we sign agreements with can be a
78		religious association, but later it may not have the means or
79		volunteers to conduct a food distribution. They then use
80		this group of associations working with the municipality.
81		So, for us it's easy from a numerical perspective. I can tell
82		you even now how many associations we work with, but it
83		won't be illustrative of how that relation occurs locally.

This excerpt begins with Robert and George (of DELTA) inviting co-operative representatives to share information about territorial associations with whom co-operatives collaborate to fulfill their societal commitment. This collection of information emerges immediately in Robert's words as crucial to navigate two objectives, which are presented as what leads them to ask for this information. First, to provide DELTA with the necessary knowledge to strengthen a project communal to all co-operatives (lines 2–4). Second, to allow DELTA to better track the progress of this project and share this with all co-operatives, so they may learn what happens in other NOVA co-operatives (lines 6–7).

Robert maintains that the data requested would also fulfill DELTA's need for information about the territorial arrangements of individual co-operatives, to boost the relationship management that DELTA nurtures nationally on behalf of all co-operatives (lines 4–6). Robert seeks the delineation of a uniform network image around this project from an assembly of different local situations and diverging relational practices territorially. His pursuit becomes even more evident when he mobilizes the network SR report (lines 32–33), the means by which the network speaks to its publics and which therefore acts as a source of authority for the importance of this data collection. The necessities of coordination, representation, and service evidently surface in this interaction and are thus presented as dictating the gathering of this information.

Yet sharing the required information with other network organizations does not appear a trouble-free pathway for all participants. When confronted with the prospect of having partner associations engaged in the project website (lines 13–14), Co-operative 5 is said to have reservations. Co-operative 5's preoccupation materializes through the invocation of a renewed policy for food donation, which, when voiced in dialogue (lines 12–13), intervenes as a decision-shaping actor, seemingly justifying Co-operative 5's actions (or lack thereof). In invoking a policy that dictates how to proceed, Co-operative 5's concerns come to clash with DELTA's objectives.

As if to reassure co-operatives about the goodwill behind this request, George specifies that collected information would allow DELTA to send informative emails on behalf of the network (lines 14–15), which would enable DELTA to perform its coordinating role. The successful progress of the project is thus emphasized to confirm the indispensability of the data. And yet, anticipating a voice of dissent emerging among co-operative representatives, George responds to his preoccupation by suggesting that these emails could directly be shared by the co-operatives with their local contacts (line 15): an outward sign to soften his request. George's intervention seems to arise from reflection on how the paternity of the project actions would be interpreted by associations. Anticipating that local associations might be confused to receive project-related emails from DELTA, George appears to recognize that network co-operatives

might be frightened away by this prospect. Discussing SR project arrangements, therefore, features the emergence of a clash of voices. A conflict,
in fact, surfaces between the voice of DELTA (which, animated by the
search for coordination, solicits this data collection), the voice of an SR
project (the efficiency of which dictates the uniformity of information),
and the voices of concerns of individual co-operatives (which discour-
age information sharing in the name of visibility issues and anticipation
of negative returns). This clash strongly intertwines with organizational
identity questions and with the negotiation about what organizations are
or are not allowed to do (concomitantly extending or contracting their
responsibilities and, thus, negotiating their boundaries within the network). George's openness toward a circulation of project material by
the same co-operatives may, therefore, be read as a step to mitigate the
emergent tension between vocal concerns.

Yet, as Robert intervenes to again remind George and other participants
that this information would favour the representative work of DELTA
(lines 24–29), a principle of work efficiency emerges and is presented as
speaking in favour of DELTA's request; voice that appears to reinvigorate
the tension between different organizational needs. In fact, since many
of these associations are local manifestations of large national charities
and NGOs, having a clearer understanding of the territorial relationships would enable DELTA to better operate in its relation-building task
nationally (lines 33–34).

As the tension unfolds, animated both by task-effectiveness and
DELTA's mission, Robert proposes a compromise that would allow
Co-operative 5 to overcome alleged concerns, while providing DELTA
with the necessary information to execute its function (lines 29–32).
SR discussion manifests then as a negotiation of concerns and objectives. Here, task-effectiveness, missions, SR projects, and policies are
the main actors that come to speak through the words of DELTA and
co-operatives' representatives and have a voice in conversation. SR progress is then often constrained by the need to incorporate, answer to, and
balance all these voices.

Accordingly, Robert's next intervention may be viewed as another
attempt to rebalance the conflict between the voice of efficiency (surfacing in DELTA's necessities of coordination and task fulfillment) and
the voice of relatedness (manifested in the co-operatives' concerns for
visibility and the search for protection of their members as inherent to
their identity). By implicitly voicing the principles of service intrinsic
to the nature of DELTA, Robert (re)underlines that the acquired information may then be shared with all co-operatives, thus becoming an
informative instrument each co-operative may use to learn situations in
other territories. Real or potential scenarios in which co-operatives face
difficulties in relating with associations locally (lines 36–41) are, thus,
ventriloquized as authorizing his and DELTA's position regarding the

validity of the information request. Through knowing that relationships work better in other contexts, Robert upholds, co-operatives may act to solve their local issues.

Despite Robert's efforts to attenuate this conflict that materializes through the staging of multiple voices he recognizes and tries to appease, the dissonance between DELTA's objective and the needs of some co-operatives worsens in the following turn of talk. Taking the floor to voice several concerns, Harry promptly ventriloquizes a privacy norm in Country A (lines 43–44), which, according to him, dictates precise actions for his organization. Entering this interaction through Harry's words, the regulation and its intersection with the agreements signed by Harry's co-operative with collaborating associations act to prevent alignment with Robert's request.

If the privacy norm is ventriloquized by Harry as speaking against his participation in the arrangements proposed by DELTA, the prospect that associations may not welcome the decision to share their data with third parties (lines 45–46) does the rest, prescribing that Harry's co-operative stand aside. In addition, the acknowledgement of strong relationships between his co-operative and local associations (lines 46–47) suggests opposition to a proposal that, in Harry's words, does not seem beneficial and goes beyond DELTA's responsibilities (lines 47–49). Further, showing concern for information circulation, which may possibly reach associations and give them a motive of comparison, Harry ventriloquizes the complaint of associations disgruntled by the potentially uneven actions conducted by co-operatives territorially (lines 55–57). By becoming actors in the discussion, the voices of these associations strengthen Harry's position to refrain from sharing the requested data and advise caution, given that an improper management of data may harm the co-operatives rather than help them (lines 54 and 57–58). Here past DELTA actions appear to surface in Harry's words, for he uses the adverb "always" to question what appears to be a frequent behaviour of the network and DELTA in particular, which is to collect data prospected as valuable but then used merely for network statistics (lines 58–62).

A fierce tension manifests in the interaction, as various concerns now converge toward a more defined discursive opposition. Robert's ventriloquation of the necessity to build a more uniform, coordinated image of the network around a project appears to clash with the co-operatives' needs to preserve more independent, distinct, and tailored relationships with their territories. This dichotomy of needs reaches its peak when Harry talks of the rapport with local associations. Claiming that the relation with associations should be a prerogative of his co-operative, he shows evident aversion to delegate this rapport to other network organizations (lines 62–64). Heatedly questioning the existence of NOVA as a network that could take charge of relating with the partner associations of his co-operative (lines 66–68), he reminds others that the raison d'être of DELTA should be found in the co-operatives' decision to create a network so they could be more efficiently supported and not hampered. The many preoccupations of participating actors unfold then in a theme-related opposition, a "we" (co-operative) against "you" (DELTA) dichotomy that (re)defines the responsibilities of the network organizations and moulds their identities, contributing to the (re)negotiation of the organizations' boundaries.

In addition, Harry himself appears torn by divided loyalties. As a representative of a co-operative participating in a network project, he is constrained by the need to balance the necessity to be part of the project—which means acting as a unitary organization—and the vocal needs of his co-operative—that is, to respond to matters of visibility in SR. This interplay of concerns both at the individual and organizational level becomes even more intricate with Jennifer's intervention. Given the nature of local associations, she claims, collecting data may be useful only from a numerical perspective, as national associations may differ greatly in how they operate locally (lines 71–73). Displaying doubt for DELTA's request for information by mobilizing examples from her territory (lines 73–80), she seems to stress that co-operatives are those that can fully make sense of the territorial complexity (lines 81–83). What, therefore, seemed like an opposition between a single co-operative and DELTA extends to other co-operatives, making this a disharmonious, tension-generating situation for more participants.

In the second excerpt, thinking of planning a network-sponsored seminar about the use of genetically modified organisms (GMOs), NOVA representatives display an apparent need for a turnaround in the network stance toward GMOs in the food industry. For decades, the network has prohibited their use as a responsible choice, dictated by the objective to protect the health of co-operative members and safeguard biodiversity of goods while supporting local small producers. A repositioning of this stance seems challenged by vocal elements that, grounded in the network identity and connected with a rather conservative organizational culture, act as limiting actors for the plan and generate tensions in the network. Beyond adding to the argumentation on the polyphony of (C)SR, a ventriloquial analysis of this extract helps us reflect more deeply on how (C)SR sense-making partakes in the co-construction of organizational boundaries. This co-construction occurs in the creation of dichotomous oppositions in discussion, at times showing, as I will illustrate, embryonic forms of theme-centred "othering" (see, e.g., Chen & Eriksson, 2019; Marzorati, 2013). I conceptualize this "othering" as a narrative-grounded, identity-forging construction of clashing antagonisms between groups carrying significantly different positions and/or value systems.

Excerpt 2: Topic (Re)positioning and
Organizational Co-construction

200	Robert:	This event [seminar] may also be an occasion to promote a
201		comprehensive exchange of ideas on the GMOs, 20 years after
202		the first caution-led decisions taken by ALFA. Even here,
203		probably, the younger generations expect something more
204		than a constant repetition, 20 years after those claims, which
205		states that we're against GMOs.
206	Kevin:	Well, but doctors and researchers say—
207	Robert:	⌊Well, no. Those are, truth be told, the
208		people making fun of us, to use a mild euphemism, when we meet
209		them. But anyhow, it's a topic requiring attention and further
210		exploration. As we talked of that last time and shared the latest
211		document by ALFA, are there considerations from somebody?
212	Jack:	Yes. Besides, the document by Research Institute A of City J
213		was released last week.
214	Harry:	Yes, I saw it.
215	Robert:	What document?
216	Jack:	Research Institute A of City J has conducted studies on GM
217		food for the last 20 years and certifies that—
218	George:	⌊The NOVA network
219		isn't connected with it, though.
220	Lisa:	Well, but she's left. Isabel left. She had to go.[4]
221	Jack:	Well, as I was saying, it [the document by Research Institute
222		A] certifies no harm for people's health based on 20 years of
223		study on GMOs conducted worldwide.
224	Harry:	Well, (1.0) quite the opposite—
225	Jack:	Indeed, quite the opposite to no harm [...] This reinforces even
226		more the need for a NOVA reasoning about this, given that the
227		last evaluations are 10 years old. They were correct based on the
228		caution principle. Yet, after many years and developments, I think
229		it's appropriate to reflect again on the position that the NOVA
230		universe has toward GM food. I've no doubt to say that the
231		caution principle was a proper answer. Let me tell you, though,
232		that Country N, for example, accepted GM food based on studies
233		that, published back then, didn't highlight any harm for human
234		health. Of course, there's [...] a financial theme and one of
235		popular sensitivity, and these should be carefully considered. But
236		reflecting on this would lead us (1.5) a step forward in how
237		NOVA relates to popular awareness, which recently [...] has
238		shown extraordinary peaks of rationality. So, thinking that
239		NOVA perceptions are consistent with scientific findings, that we
240		don't rely on the "it's said that" but on scientific data, could help
241		us think about the future. 'Cause in this historic moment where
242		any screwy belief may gain followers due to the web [...] I think
243		that we, being an association of enterprises but also a network of
244		associations - 'cause a co-operative is above all an association of
245		consumers - should retake control of this issue more carefully,
246		especially considering the things said 10 years ago.

247		[...]
248	Robert:	We agree on that. Let's try to—
249	Chris:	[Only one observation.
250	Robert:	Chris, please.
251	Chris:	[...] Let's put this well into focus from a policy perspective
252		and use it for this event [...] Do we want to send a strong
253		message on what NOVA has done for the environment and
254		human health over these years? At this point, this may be a bit
255		self-critical on the GMO-free topic, on the "GMO-free label,"
256		and on the fact that perhaps this wasn't always necessary.
257		Obviously, we can discuss it here. Yet, if we go for it, let's go
258		through well-thought-out reflections in our organizations.
259	Robert:	[Good.
260	Chris:	And with those colleagues we've worked for years [...] We
261		also could do something in the SR report that [...] could make
262		of the NOVA SR a further unifying moment, right
263		when all co-operatives share on their own about economic
264		and social results [...]
265	Robert:	Pavel, please.
266	Pavel:	[...] I agree with this. The topic isn't unimportant. A seminar
267		can certainly help but [...] in this world, which still is a rather
268		conservative one, when you propose a change of line, the first
269		reaction is to go against it. For Fair A, we had prepared a
270		document having just a reference to a science-based GMO
271		re-evaluation. Well, it wasn't released. That's to give you an
272		idea of how things are.
273	Jack:	Indeed, we didn't see that.
274	Pavel:	The issue is there. I think we need to make up for the lost time
275		because scientific evidence on some GMOs— but in this, it's
276		not that somebody should stay on one side or on the other. Yet
277		a reflection is needed mainly with ALFA, which has often
278		staked, let's say, a claim on these issues.

This excerpt exhibits practitioners (re)discussing NOVA's position toward GMOs, which has always been the object of cast-iron aversion. Proposing a reconsideration of the positioning toward GMOs, Robert starts off by voicing pressing concerns that he presents as dictating this change of line. In a fast-changing world, he argues, mere repetition of a contrary position for years may no longer suffice, as this may not meet the expectations of the younger generations (lines 202–205). By being ventriloquized in this discussion, the demands of these "younger generations" emerge as supporting a turnaround of NOVA's approach to this SR theme, and yet pursuing this about-face may be challenging. This immediately appears clear when Kevin shows traces of support for those researchers who oppose GMOs (line 206), before being interrupted. It is then Robert who, unlike Kevin, intervenes to voice what he presents as the positioning of scientists, who are ventriloquized as mocking the network's rigid position (lines 207–209). An opposition implicitly manifests here, one having identity-shaping traits. The opposition counterposes a community of scientists apparently positively disposed toward GMOs and the network, which has supported the GMO-free argument for decades. This clash, along with what are presented as pressures originating from the flow of time and mounting expectations in the population, generates a tension in this interaction, a tension that is ventriloquized as calling for a change of view by the network. The fact that the same scientific evidence, as seemingly voiced by Kevin, is approached differently by different scientists only adds complexity to the situation.

If most participants' interventions emerge in support of Robert's stance, decisional complexity is nevertheless evident in the interaction. When Jack, for instance, ventriloquizes study results apparently confirming the non-harmful nature of certain GMOs (lines 216–217 and 221–223), we see George and Lisa (of DELTA) showing signs of caution. George reminds participants that the institute releasing the study is in no way connected with the network (lines 218–219), which can be heard as decreasing the importance of this voice in the discussion. This comment, thus, appears to be a way to pour oil on waters troubled by a potential clash of perspectives. Similarly, Lisa's apparent concern for the absence of Isabel (line 220), the representative from ALFA responsible for this SR theme, displays an inclination to the prudent side. Hence, if the co-operative members' invocation of a study authorizes the nascent discussion toward a reconsideration of the GMO theme, Lisa and George's preoccupations call for caution and, thus, act against audacious moves. The fact that Robert (on the pushing side) seems on a different page compared to his DELTA colleagues (on the prudent side), as the latter possibly intervene by implicitly voicing diverse mindsets within the network, suggests SR discussion as a complex negotiation between the voice of caution and the voice of innovation (both interacting with elements of organizational tradition and identity).

And yet, even if Jack acknowledges the pertinence of the prudence principle that he ventriloquizes as guiding actions in the past (lines 227–228), his support for a network repositioning toward GMOs, animated by science-backed developments, continues to unfold. To strengthen this, he invokes the choice of another country, which even based on older scientific evidence, embraced GMOs (lines 231–234). Jack's ventriloquation of Country N's example adds to the need for network action on the topic.

Yet even the strength of Jack's conviction appears tempered by the sudden manifestation of elements intrinsic to the GMO issue. Possible public reactions emerge as sources of preoccupation for Jack when he indirectly speculates about the risks that NOVA's repositioning might be attributed to an economics-driven motive and, thus, questioned (lines 234–235). This concern surfaces as another actor in this discussion and invites a careful assessment before decisions are made and actions taken. However, voicing the fact that NOVA's publics are becoming increasingly knowledgeable (lines 237–238) and mobilizing the observation that, even so, this rationality is constantly tested by the fake content that circulates on the internet (lines 241–242), Jack continues to lean toward the necessity to change. It is indeed a full responsibility of the network, he says, to guide its members toward an informed consciousness. Founding traits of the co-operative identity manifest here, supporting the emergent orientation toward the reassessment of an SR topic based on scientific evidence (lines 238–241), while reinstating and, thus, strengthening the purpose and mission of the network as an association of consumer organizations (lines 242–246).

What appears as an inclination, though featured by manifestations of concerns, favouring a reconsideration of the network's position toward GMOs, is nevertheless weakened by the voicing of a striking opposition in the second part of the extract. Suggesting a policy clarification and the planning of an event built on self-reflexivity (lines 251–254), with this possibly implying the voicing of self-critical reflections toward some steps adopted by NOVA about GMOs (lines 254–256), Chris expresses the need to bring this argumentation to the attention of all organizations' boards (lines 257–260). In emphasizing the need for a talk within each organization, he seems to presage difficulties on the horizon. His position highlights the complexity of this topic. If, in fact, he shows openness toward a network repositioning (strengthened by his invocation of the network SR report in lines 260–264—an actor mobilized as granting the needed unity to the network in a moment during which co-operatives have followed different paths), he also appears concerned about possible contrasting opinions within each co-operative.

Pavel (of DELTA) agrees with Chris. Ventriloquizing what he defines as the conservative essence of the co-operative universe (lines 267–269), he suggests other spokespersons' potential lack of will for a reversal of thought on the theme of GMOs. This insertion reinforces an opposition forming between those who recommend being more open to GMOs, and a rather unspecified within-network group that appears to have the authority to contrast that view. ALFA appears to be part of this latter group (lines 277–278), and is said to have always been closed-minded toward the theme of GMOs (which also better explains now Lisa's concerns in the beginning of the extract). The invocation of a recent episode in which a document was ostracized for containing a somewhat positive inclination toward GMOs (lines 269–271) brings the clash between opposing perspectives to a new level, one in which two different groups seem to surface in interaction.

Presented as carriers of unbreakably sealed value systems oriented in the past and reluctant to flexibility, the group of GMO opponents is ventriloquized as totally clashing with the group of participants in the conversation. The dichotomy between the two visions, thus, unfolds as containing traits of a within-network theme-related "othering" narration, in which the "other," in this case, are those who close the door to even a preliminary discussion about GMOs. This narrative construction strongly intersects with the definition of organizational identities, negotiates what the diverse components of the network can or cannot do, and, reconciling the views of the meeting participants while opposing their common views to those of other network members, affects the constitution of the responsibilities of DELTA and individual co-operatives, thus moulding the boundaries of their social policy divisions.

This ventriloquial analysis has shown how in practice (C)SR discussions and planning feature a continual emergence of differing voices in interaction. Invoked and mobilized by participants in dialogue, these voices constitute sources of authority to strengthen interactants' positions and dictate specific courses of action to pursue. The intervention of these voices generates in-dialogue tensions that require negotiation, debate, compromise, and a search for balance between divergent stances. In addition, this ventriloquial analysis sheds light on how (C)SR interaction is characterized by a constant process of negotiation between univocal and polyvocal needs and positions. Deeply intertwined with organizational identities and marked by frequent discursive oppositions among contrasting actors, concerns, and visions, this process renews the responsibilities of participating organizations and, as such, contributes to the creation and redefinition of organizational boundaries.

Concluding Remarks

This chapter adopted a constitutive approach to communication (Ashcraft et al., 2009) to explore how voices intervene and are dealt with by practitioners in (C)SR interactions and to look into how (C)SR discussion affects the construction of organizational boundaries. Acknowledging the need for reflections grounded in data, this work engaged in a ventriloquial analysis of two conversational excerpts to reveal how (C)SR polyphony unfolds in the making of social responsibility and planning of arrangements for action (Castelló et al., 2013). My research focused on dialogue between representatives of a co-operative network—a novel and appealing case study, since co-operatives are democratic, equality-driven, and SR-committed organizations, which, however, pursue economic ends for the welfare of their members and society. The analysis reflected on the essence of voices and their intervention(s) in interaction, adding to the communicative constitutive understanding of (C)SR (Schultz et al., 2013) with insights from a collaborative and multi-organizational context.

This ventriloquial analysis (Cooren, 2010) pointed to (C)SR discussions as processes featuring the invocation of multiple voices by interacting participants. In line with a polyphonic understanding of (C)SR organizing (Castelló et al., 2013), when mobilized in communication, these voices (including regulations, documents, organizations) become actors by directing specific courses of action (Cooren, 2020). The analysis contributes to the assertion by Schoeneborn and Trittin (2013) that non-human figures partake in (C)SR-centred negotiation, for it empirically showed that these voices are often invoked to strengthen a claimed position and, at times, to question the apparent development of an argument.

The analysis also adds to our knowledge about the variety of voices participating in (C)SR and their intersection in communication. First, it illustrates that economics-driven, visibility-informed, and preoccupation-untangling reflections are always at play when discussing (C)SR. This leads me to argue that (C)SR-making consists of a mobilization of interests, concerns, and necessities, which are steadily voiced as the interaction unfolds. Second, the analysis highlights that the materialization of these voices in conversation may generate theme-related contrasts between participants and lead to vocal clashes, engendering tensions.

As Cooren (2015) reminds us, voice mobilization in interaction may be interpreted differently by participants, producing a plurality of responses that, in turn, may feed these tensions. The negotiation of (C)SR meaning and action, thus, becomes a polyphonic, tensional process in which multiple standpoints and figures intervene as co-actors in planning actions. Accordingly, progress toward (C)SR goals is often constrained by the surfacing need to incorporate, answer to, and balance all these voices. This reflection on the participatory nature of (C)SR furthers research on (C)SR sense-making, which has mainly focused on how individuals cognitively elaborate and behaviourally respond to their perception of how organizations position themselves in relation to what is presented as the common good.

In addition, extending the argument on the unfolding of voices in (C)SR, this analysis suggested situations of conflict between univocality and polyvocality. Practitioners found themselves constrained between the necessity to account for their role as speaking on behalf of individual organizations and the need to accommodate the requests of being part of a network. Building on the insights from Christensen and Cornelissen (2011), this observation suggests that (C)SR is a process of incessant oscillation between the construction of a coherent, univocal, and clear-cut (C)SR image and the pressing requests to listen, attend, and respond to the voicing of multiple interests, concerns, and objectives. This finding may serve as a warning for the extant research—which often investigates only one side of this process—and invite studies that would account for the multivocal character of (C)SR while also recognizing the organizational necessity to build a coherent, uniform image of a (C)SR-committed organization.

In addition, this chapter adds to the proposition that (C)SR talk contributes to the (re)definition of organizational boundaries (Schoeneborn & Trittin, 2013). By unfolding through the creation of discursive oppositions established more or less purposefully by interacting participants, boundary constitution intertwines with the formation and negotiation of organizational identities. The oppositions emerge with strength when concerns mobilized by interactants surface as antagonistic clashes between delineated positions supported by specific actors. These dichotomies may vary in type, nature, and the number of subjects involved. Participants, alternately and depending on the topic under discussion or their position, may oscillate from questioning the very existence of an organization they are part of to calling for a strengthening of its unity, thereby elevating its importance. In line with a communicative constitutive view that understands boundaries as fluid and steadily defined in communication (Dobusch & Schoeneborn, 2015), (re)shaping the responsibilities of organizations and individuals through a negotiation of what can or cannot be done and should or should not be allowed unavoidably affects the constitution and maintenance of the network organizations' boundaries. In addition, the ventriloquial analysis underlines that when oppositions are constructed as dissonant dichotomies between delineated groups with markedly contrasting values, the ongoing positioning of interactants may take on the initial traits of an "othering" narration, thereby shaping identity construction and the role of interacting network organizations. So far, the concept of "othering" has been primarily used for studies about topics such as urban neighbourhoods and community relations (Marzorati, 2013), marketing strategies (Chen & Eriksson, 2019), and media framing (Ibrahim & Howarth, 2017). The observation that "othering" practices may occur when planning (C)SR actions suggests an additional applicability of the "othering" narration to research on (C) SR-making.

In conclusion, these reflections add complementary arguments to the conventional views on (C)SR, those primarily taught in business and communication schools. This analysis suggests that (C)SR-making is a negotiated and tensional process marked by the continual intervention of interests, concerns, and oppositions. The training of tomorrow's practitioners in (C)SR should feature curricula that include practice-grounded exercise of (C)SR as a fluid and emergent process, so students may develop a mindset to prepare for a demanding but fascinating work journey.

Acknowledgements

A very heartfelt thanks goes to Timothy Kuhn and Boris H. J. M. Brummans for their valuable comments on a former version of this chapter. Profound gratitude is extended to François Cooren for his valuable feedback during the data analysis phase. Sincere gratitude goes also to Chantal Benoît-Barné and Thomas Martine for their continual guidance toward the completion of this chapter.

Notes

1 This chapter uses the term (corporate) social responsibility, (C)SR, to emphasize that social responsibility relates to a vast range of organizations, from corporations, which are committed to doing *CSR*, to volunteer and nonprofit groups, which implement *SR* projects.

2 Given the type of organization, the term social responsibility (SR), rather than (C)SR, better describes the essence of the network's social commitments.

3 To assure anonymity, extracts refer to co-operatives with the use of numbers (e.g., Co-operative 5). Associations are referred to using colours (e.g., Grey Association). I use fictional names for projects and allude to cities, events, and other entities using letters of the alphabet (e.g., City B). Numbers between parentheses represent seconds of pause in turns of talk. Square brackets between lines mean that persons are talking over each other.

4 Isabel is an ALFA representative who left the meeting before the discussion on this topic.

References

Alvesson, M., & Kärreman, D. (2000). Taking the linguistic turn in organizational research: Challenges, responses, consequences. *Journal of Applied Behavioral Science, 36*(2), 136–158.

Ashcraft, K. L., Kuhn, T. R., & Cooren, F. (2009). Constitutional amendments: "Materializing" organizational communication. *Academy of Management Annals, 3*(1), 1–64.

Bachmann, P., & Ingenhoff, D. (2016). Legitimacy through CSR disclosures? The advantage outweighs the disadvantages. *Public Relations Review, 42*(3), 386–394.

Bakhtin, M. M. (1981). *The dialogic imagination: Four essays* (M. Holquist, Ed.; C. Emerson & M. Holquist, Trans.). Austin, TX: University of Texas Press.

Brown, A., & Thompson, E. (2013). A narrative approach to strategy-as-practice. *Business History, 55*(7), 1143–1167.

Bruhn, M., & Zimmermann, A. (2017). Integrated CSR communications. In S. Diehl, M. Karmasin, B. Mueller, R. Terlutter, & F. Weder (Eds.), *Handbook of integrated CSR communication* (pp. 3–21). Basel, Switzerland: Springer.

Brummans, B. H. J. M., Cooren, F., Robichaud, D., & Taylor, J. R. (2014). Approaches in research on the communicative constitution of organizations. In L. Putnam & D. K. Mumby (Eds.), *The Sage handbook of organizational communication: Advances in theory, research, and methods* (3rd ed., pp. 173–194). Los Angeles, CA: Sage.

Carroll, A. (2015). Corporate social responsibility: The centerpiece of competing and complementary frameworks. *Organizational Dynamics, 44*(2), 87–96.

Castelló, I., Morsing, M., & Schultz, F. (2013). Communicative dynamics and the polyphony of corporate social responsibility in the network society. *Journal of Business Ethics, 118*, 683–694.

Chen, A., & Eriksson, G. (2019). The making of healthy and moral snacks: A multimodal critical discourse analysis of corporate storytelling. *Discourse, Context & Media, 32*, 1–10.

Christensen, L. T., & Cheney, G. (2011). Interrogating the communicative dimensions of corporate social responsibility. In Ø. Ihlen, J. Bartlett, & S. May (Eds.), *The handbook of communication and corporate social responsibility* (pp. 491–504). Chichester, UK: Wiley-Blackwell.

Christensen, L. T., & Cornelissen, J. (2011). Bridging corporate and organizational communication: Review, development and a look to the future. *Management Communication Quarterly, 25*(3), 383–414.

Christensen, L. T., Morsing, M., & Thyssen, O. (2013). CSR as aspirational talk. *Organization, 20*(3), 372–393.

Christensen, L. T., Morsing, M., & Thyssen, O. (2015). Discursive closure and discursive openings in sustainability. *Management Communication Quarterly, 29*(1), 135–144.

Cooren, F. (2004). Textual agency: How texts do things in organizational settings. *Organization, 11*, 373–394.

Cooren, F. (2010). *Action and agency in dialogue: Passion, incarnation, and ventriloquism*. Philadelphia, PA: John Benjamins.

Cooren, F. (2012). Communication theory at the center: Ventriloquism and the communicative constitution of reality. *Journal of Communication, 62*(1), 1–20.

Cooren, F. (2015). Studying agency from a ventriloqual perspective. *Management Communication Quarterly, 29*(3), 475–480.

Cooren, F. (2016). Ethics for dummies: Ventriloquism and responsibility. *Atlantic Journal of Communication, 24*(1), 17–30.

Cooren, F. (2020). A communicative constitutive perspective on corporate social responsibility: Ventriloquism, undecidability, and surprisability. *Business & Society, 59*(1), 175–197.

Cooren, F., & Fairhurst, G. T. (2009). Dislocation and stabilization: How to scale up from interactions to organization. In L. L. Putnam & A. M. Nicotera (Eds.), *Building theories of organization: The constitutive role of communication* (pp. 117–152). Oxford, UK: Routledge.

Cooren, F., Kuhn, T., Cornelissen, J. P., & Clark, T. (2011). Communication, organizing and organization: An overview and introduction to the special issue. *Organization Studies, 32*(9), 1149–1170.

Cooren, F., Matte, F., Benoit-Barné, C., & Brummans, B. H. J. M. (2013). Communication as ventriloquism: A grounded-in-action approach to the study of organizational tensions. *Communication Monographs, 80*(3), 255–277.

Cooren, F., & Sandler, S. (2014). Polyphony, ventriloquism, and constitution: In dialogue with Bakhtin. *Communication Theory, 24*, 225–244.

Craig, R. T. (1999). Communication theory as a field. *Communication Theory, 9*(2), 119–161.

Crane, A., & Glozer, S. (2016). Researching corporate social responsibility communication: Themes, opportunities and challenges. *Journal of Management Studies, 53*(7), 1223–1252.

Dobusch, L., & Schoeneborn, D. (2015). Fluidity, identity, and organizationality: The communicative constitution of anonymous. *Journal of Management Studies, 52*(8), 1005–1035.

Du, S., Bhattacharya, C. B., & Sen, S. (2010). Maximizing business returns to corporate social responsibility (CSR): The role of CSR communication. *International Journal of Management Reviews, 12*(1), 8–19.

Eisenegger, M., & Schranz, M. (2011). Reputation management and corporate social responsibility. In Ø. Ihlen, J. Bartlett, & S. May (Eds.), *The handbook of communication and corporate social responsibility* (pp. 128–146). Chichester, UK: Wiley-Blackwell.

Fairhurst, G. T., & Putnam, L. (2004). Organizations as discursive constructions. *Communication Theory, 14*, 5–26.

Fauré, B., Brummans, B. H. J. M., Giroux, N., & Taylor, J. R. (2010). The business of calculation or the calculation of business? Accounting as organizing through everyday communication. *Human Relations*, *63*(8), 1249–1273.

Groza, M. D., Pronschinske, M. R., & Walker, M. (2011). Perceived organizational motives and consumer responses to proactive and reactive CSR. *Journal of Business Ethics*, *102*(4), 639–652.

Guthey, E., & Morsing, M. (2014). CSR and the mediated emergence of strategic ambiguity. *Journal of Business Ethics*, *120*, 555–569.

Ibrahim, Y., & Howarth, A. (2017). Contamination, deception and 'othering': The media framing of the horsemeat scandal. *Social Identities*, *23*(2), 212–231.

Kim, H., & Lee, T. (2018). Strategic CSR communication: A moderating role of transparency in trust building. *International Journal of Strategic Communication*, *12*(2), 107–124.

Kim, S. (2019). The process model of corporate social responsibility (CSR) communication: CSR communication and its relationship with consumers' CSR knowledge, trust, and corporate reputation perception. *Journal of Business Ethics*, *154*, 1143–1159.

Kim, S., & Ferguson, M. A. T. (2018). Dimensions of effective CSR communication based on public expectations. *Journal of Marketing Communications*, *24*(6), 549–567.

Kjærgaard, A., Morsing, M., & Ravasi, D. (2011). Mediating identity: A study of media influence on organizational identity construction in a celebrity firm. *Journal of Management Studies*, *48*(3), 514–543.

Koep, L. (2017). Investigating industry expert discourses on aspirational CSR communication. *Corporate Communications: An International Journal*, *22*(2), 220–238.

Kuhn, T., & Deetz, S. (2008). Critical theory and corporate social responsibility: Can/should we get beyond cynical reasoning? In A. Crane, D. Matten, A. McWilliams, J. Moon, & D. S. Siegel (Eds.), *The Oxford handbook of corporate social responsibility* (pp. 173–196). Oxford: Oxford University Press.

Latour, B. (1996). On interobjectivity. *Mind, Culture, and Activity*, *3*(4), 228–245.

Marzorati, R. (2013). Imagined communities and othering processes: The discursive strategies of established Italian residents in a Milan city neighbourhood. *Journal of Language and Politics*, *12*(2), 251–271.

Morsing, M., & Schultz, M. (2006). Corporate social responsibility communication: Stakeholder information, response and involvement strategies. *Business Ethics: A European Review*, *15*, 323–338.

Putnam, L. L., & Nicotera, A. M. (Eds.) (2009). *Building theories of organization: The constitutive role of communication*. Oxford, UK: Routledge.

Robichaud, D., Giroux, H., & Taylor, J. R. (2004). The metaconversation: The recursive property of language as a key to organizing. *Academy of Management Review*, *29*(4), 617–634.

Schmeltz, L. (2012). Consumer-oriented CSR communication: Focusing on ability or morality? *Corporate Communications: An International Journal*, *17*(1), 29–49.

Schoeneborn, D., Morsing, M., & Crane, A. (2020). Formative perspectives on the relation between CSR communication and CSR practices: Pathways for walking, talking, and t(w)alking. *Business & Society*, *59*(1), 5–33.

Schoeneborn, D., & Trittin, H. (2013). Transcending transmission: Towards a constitutive perspective on CSR communication. *Corporate Communications: An International Journal, 18*(2), 193–211.

Schultz, F., Castelló, I., & Morsing, M. (2013). The construction of corporate social responsibility in network societies: A communication view. *Journal of Business Ethics, 115,* 681–692.

Schultz, F., & Wehmeier, S. (2010). Institutionalization of corporate social responsibility within corporate communications: Combining institutional, sensemaking and communication perspectives. *Corporate Communications: An International Journal, 15*(1), 9–29.

Searle, J. R. (1979). *Expression and meaning: Studies in the theory of speech acts.* Cambridge, UK: Cambridge University Press.

Taylor, J., & Cooren, F. (1997). What makes communication "organizational"? How the many voices of a collectivity become the one voice of an organization. *Journal of Pragmatics, 27*(4), 409–438.

Taylor, J. R., & Robichaud, D. (2004). Finding the organization in the communication: Discourse as action and sensemaking. *Organization, 11*(3), 395–413.

Taylor, J. R., & Van Every, E. J. (2000). *The emergent organization: Communication as site and surface.* Hillsdale, NJ: Lawrence Erlbaum Associates.

Taylor, J. R., & Van Every, E. J. (2011). *The situated organization: Case studies in the pragmatics of communication research.* New York, NY: Routledge.

Trittin, H., & Schoeneborn, D. (2017). Diversity as polyphony: Reconceptualizing diversity management from a communication-centered perspective. *Journal of Business Ethics, 144,* 305–322.

Wehmeier, S., & Schultz, F. (2011). Corporate communication and corporate social responsibility: A storytelling perspective. In Ø. Ihlen, J. Bartlett, & S. May (Eds.), *The handbook of communication and corporate social responsibility* (pp. 467–488). Chichester, UK: Wiley-Blackwell.

8 "Centering [Voices From] the Margins"

Negotiating Intersectionality as a Consultative Framework

Khaoula Zoghlami

Introduction: Voicing Systemic Racism in Quebec

It is hard to talk about racism. The word *racism* is "very sticky" and just uttering it "introduce[s] a bad feeling" and "does things," notices Sara Ahmed (2009, p. 47). It is usually replaced by feel-good and "cuddly" words like "diversity" or "inclusion," words that project a "happy image of people who 'look different' just getting along" (p. 48). This situation holds in Quebec as elsewhere. Discussions about racial discrimination and systemic racism in the Canadian province are continually met with defensiveness by politicians and op-ed pundits who consider these conversations "[an] effortless ammunition to those who seek to disparage Quebecers" (Drimonis, 2017, para. 8). This was the case in summer 2017, when, after months of pressure from anti-racism activists, the provincial Liberal government announced a public consultation on systemic racism. According to the president of the Quebec Human Rights Commission, appointed by the government to lead the initiative, "the goal [of the consultation] is for people to be listened to and to hear their voice[s]" (quoted in CTV Montreal, 2017, para. 18). This opinion was shared by community organizations, for whom a consultation on systemic racism was an opportunity to "allow participants to have their specific stories heard, instead of perpetuating generalized ideas of what it's like to experience racism" (CBC News, 2017, para. 13). However, the announcement of a government-led consultation on racism also sparked fierce criticism from the opposition parties, who claimed this consultation amounted to "putting Quebec society on trial" (Montgomery, 2017, para. 4) and "demonize[d] the province as inherently racist" (Valiante, 2017, para. 2).

Realizing it was navigating a political minefield that had started to cause electoral losses,[1] the government finally backtracked on its promise and changed not only the name but also the focus and the leadership mandate of the consultation. Systemic racism was reframed as a "diversity problem" restricted to new immigrants experiencing difficulties accessing the job market. In the end, a public consultation on systemic racism was turned into one-day "Forum on valuing diversity and fighting against

DOI: 10.4324/9780429297830-8

discrimination." As a *Montreal Gazette* journalist pointed out, "Lost in the makeover were the voices that have long clamoured for a microphone to talk about their experiences with systemic discrimination and how to fix the system" (Solyom, 2017, para. 6).

It is to offer a platform to those neglected voices that the project of an independent popular consultation on systemic racism (IPCSR) was born.[2] Feeling betrayed by the sudden *volte-face* of the government, a coalition of more than 40 groups (unions, student organizations, community-based organizations, cultural and religious minority associations, feminist groups, etc.) decided to go through with the initial consultation independently. Unlike the government, the IPCSR did not question the existence of systemic racism in Quebec. It recognized not only its existence but also its structuring of all areas of life in Quebec society as well as its impact on Indigenous and racialized people's lives.[3] Amid a political and social environment where the voices of people who experience racism are met with defensiveness, hostility, and denial, the IPCSR was conceived to be a counter space where those voices would be welcomed, listened to, and validated. Unfortunately, due to lack of funding and mobilization, the IPCSR did not get past the design process. I believe this "failure" does not diminish the importance of the process and the efforts poured into the initiative by members of the coalition. Failure is often associated with "futility, sterility, emptiness, loss, negative affect in general and modes of unbecoming" (Halberstam, 2011, p. 23). However, following Halberstam, I rather conceive of failing as a counterintuitive and alternative mode of knowing. Therefore, to me the most important part of this citizen project was the organizing process and the collective and individual lessons everyone, including myself, experienced while being involved in it. The consultation was the subject of many discussions and debates spread over two years and involving dozens of activists. I joined the initiative as an activist-researcher member of the IPCSR's Coordination Committee a few months after it was publicly announced and stayed on until the project of holding a consultation on systemic racism was abandoned. This involvement was part of a critical-militant ethnography I conducted for my doctoral research about the anti-racism movement in Quebec. This chapter aims to reflect on the challenges surrounding the implementation of an intersectional consultative framework by investigating the discussions and debates we had inside the coalition and the IPCSR's Coordination Committee about the best strategies to design a popular consultation that values voice.[4]

I begin by defining the key concepts I rely on in this chapter—*intersectionality* and *voice*—and provide the research questions I developed. Then I focus on one significant event I experienced in my critical-militant ethnography with the IPCSR and how this event destabilized the dominant framework through which we used to think of consultations and intersectional work. Next, I elaborate on the two different understandings of intersectionality that were manifest during the event, highlighting the limits of the first and the potentialities of the second. Finally, I conclude by summarizing the key findings of this chapter while emphasizing the inherent difficulty of intersectional anti-racism organizing in general, and consulting in particular.

What Is a Consultation and How Do We Consult?

During my interview for the position of co-coordinator of the IPCSR, I was asked about my vision for an independent popular consultation on systemic racism. Back then, the idea of a consultation was simultaneously very clear and very elusive to me. When I thought about "a consultation," I mostly pictured an event with two or more high-profile commissioners (usually White men who would give their names to the process, just like the Bouchard-Taylor Consultative Commission)[5] sharing the front stage of a wide room full of "witnesses."[6] One at a time, the witnesses would come forward to share their testimonies and the commissioners would listen attentively while taking notes. At the end of the consultation process, the commissioners would produce a report that summarized their observations and conclusions along with a set of recommendations. At that time, I naively believed the main difference between a consultative commission like Bouchard-Taylor and the IPCSR lay in the identities of the commissioners, who in the case of IPCSR should be from racialized communities. Sitting in front of the two activists in charge of the interview, I remember feeling very embarrassed by my superficial answer to their question. Surprisingly, the interviewers did not seem shocked by my lack of vision. They did not even comment on it and, a few days later, they told me I was hired. I later found out that I was not the only one to entertain this vision of the consultation, and that it was the dominant framework through which we usually think about consulting processes. I also noticed a widely shared belief among the coalition's members that the IPCSR had the responsibility to be *"un porte-voix"* (which literally translates as "voice carrier") for racialized people in Quebec, especially those who do not have alternative spaces where they may narrate their experiences of racism. The IPCSR—through the commissioners at its head—would give shape to people's voices by translating them into recommendations in order to pressure the governmental institutions to dismantle systemic racism. Thus, after hearing and analyzing the narratives of hundreds of racialized people across the province, the commissioners would act as the faces and voices of the consultation and the representatives of those who trusted them with their experiences.

However, as has been pointed out by many critical theorists and activists, being *porte-voix* for those who cannot speak is a double-edged sword (Alcoff, 1991; Spivak, 1988). While it can be crucial to convey the voices, and defend the interests, of those without access to institutional representation, "the practice of privileged persons speaking for or on behalf of less privileged persons has actually resulted (in many cases) in increasing or re-enforcing the oppression of the group spoken for" (Alcoff, 1991, p. 7). Consequently, to make sure the sensitive and power-laden consultative process was not oppressive for the people who would give it their voices and did not reproduce and consolidate relationships of privilege or marginalization, it was widely agreed by those involved in the design process that intersectionality should be adopted as one of the guiding principles of the IPCSR. Before going further, I will define the two key concepts of this chapter: *intersectionality* and *voice*.

Intersectionality

Intersectionality is a militant knowledge rooted in the struggles for liberation of Black women who, as far back as the 19th century, wrote and spoke about the racial construction of gender and its violent effects on their lives and their bodies. It is from the writings and speeches of these women and other women-of-colour feminists, working-class feminists, and lesbians that Black feminist legal scholar Kimberlé Crenshaw (1989, 1991) elaborated a theory of intersectionality. Intersectionality exposes how the experiences of people at the intersection of multiple "formations of difference"[7] (i.e., race, class, sexuality, gender, dis/ability, nationality, immigration status, religion) may be erased and rendered invisible in legal practices, political decisions, and even in social movement strategies. These formations of difference intersect and co-produce one another to result in unequal material realities and distinctive social experiences that marginalize or privilege certain bodies and subjectivities (Collins, 2015). Therefore, implementing an intersectional strategy in organizations and social movements can help grant special attention to people at the crossroads of multiple oppressions and prevent their voices from "falling through the cracks" (Crenshaw, 1991, p. 1275).

McDonald (2019) reminds us of the imperative, while conducting intersectional scholarship, to conceive of these categories or formations of difference "as fluid, changing and interwoven with each other" (p. 274). "Conceiving of categories in this way helps underscore that even as we may foreground particular intersections of difference, these categories should not be taken to be stable and fixed features of social life" (p. 274).

Intersectionality was introduced in activist circles in Quebec in the early 2000s, mostly through feminist organizations (Lopez, 2017). It is also through the entanglement between feminist and anti-racist activist networks and the involvement of many intersectional feminists in the coalition that intersectionality was suggested as an important tool to implement an anti-oppressive consultative process. However, the operationalization of intersectionality often brings challenges, and many "movement actors attempting intersectional tactics still struggle to translate their insights into practice" (Luft & Ward, 2009, p. 29).[8] As I discuss later, even if there was an agreement among coalition members about the theoretical definition of intersectionality, different activists and groups shared paradoxical visions of how to build an intersectional consultative framework.

Voice

My conceptualization of "voice" follows the feminist and critically oriented organizational communication works that share "an understanding of voice as tied to meaning making and sees its suppression, amplification, omission, or protection as a fundamentally political process" (Dempsey, 2017, p. 4). Hence, I will use the notion of voice to refer to "the process of giving narratives about one's life and its conditions" and being heard and acknowledged as doing such (Couldry, 2010, p. 7). I approach voice as more than just speaking and the growing incitements to speak, since people also need practical resources, like language, and other social resources, like showing people that their voices matter (Couldry, 2010, p. 8).[9] Therefore, we have to pay attention to the conditions that value voice, that is, "the conditions under which people's practices of voice are *sustained* and the outcomes of those practices validated" (Couldry, 2010, p. 113, italics original). Indeed, according to Couldry, "[V]oice does not simply emerge from us without support" (p. 9); "without material resources, voice is impossible" (p. 8).

In this chapter, I follow the line of research in critical organizational communication that aims to highlight the role of power in shaping or limiting voice (Deetz, 1995; Dempsey, 2007, 2017; Parker, 2014). I agree with Dempsey's statement that it is not enough to detail "how voice may be constrained or systematically narrowed" and that researchers need to "understand the mechanisms for ensuring egalitarian, transformative, and robust voice in the workplace and beyond" (2017, p. 5). The study of participative, feminist, anti-racist, and democratic forms of organizing, like the IPCSR, is the perfect opportunity to investigate these mechanisms.

Research Questions

My approach to intersectionality and voice is anchored at the crossroads of critical feminist/race theories and critical organizational communication and leads me to ask the two following questions. First, how did members of the IPCSR negotiate meaning about intersectionality and how did they/we operationalize it through an anti-racist consultative framework? Second, what are the material arrangements—or material supports, in Couldry's phrasing—to value voice that ensued from those understandings—and how do those arrangements "organize in" or "organize out" some formations of difference? As a whole, I argue that two conceptions of intersectionality emerged: intersectionality as inclusion and intersectionality as centering the margins. These conceptions did not surface necessarily during discussions about intersectionality, but more generally, during conversations about (1) how to negotiate difference and guarantee a representative and inclusive process, and (2) what kind of material arrangements or supports we should implement and what consulting practices we should adopt (e.g., recruitment strategies, accessibility measures, committee creations, spokespersons election, timelines, etc.). Hence, to paraphrase Cho, Crenshaw, and McCall (2013), my focus in this chapter goes beyond the debate about what intersectionality is to reflect on what intersectionality does (or could do) when put into practice, specifically as a consultative framework for a popular and independent consultation on systemic racism. I argue that a consultation on systemic racism designed and conceived through an intersectional lens that aims at centering the margins is an organizing process that would have the potential to effectively value voice. As I elaborate in the next section, intersectionality as "centering the margins" was introduced during one event, a public assembly we organized in summer 2018, four months after the beginning of my involvement as co-coordinator. This assembly caused a radical shift not only in the Coordination Committee's understanding of intersectionality as a practice, but most importantly, in how we understood what it means to consult.

A Key Moment in the Organizing Process

During my critical-militant ethnography, I participated in every event regarding the IPCSR (general assemblies, panels, workshops, and meetings) where the consultation's design was discussed and debated.[10] Moreover, since I had forged deep friendships with other activists from the coalition, we discussed the IPCSR on several informal occasions. However, one event was particularly important: the public assembly that took place in summer 2018. Indeed, it was my first public event since I was hired and a tipping point in the way I/we envisioned consultative work. During this public assembly, after months of organizing, I came to realize the scale and the complexity of the endeavour I was engaged in with the consultation.

According to Pavoni and Citroni (2016), events "do not occur in a vacuum"; they rather emerge "out of a dense spatiality of bodies, forces and intensive becoming" (p. 233). They are the coming together of a "constellation of processes," previously unrelated (Massey, 2005, pp. 140–141). The public assembly included about 30 participants representing 20 different organizations. It was divided into two sessions: first, a roundtable composed of seven activists with experience in designing popular consultations on social justice issues, who were invited to give us their inputs on the best consultative practices; second, a workshop to exchange ideas about the first draft of the consultation's design submitted by the Coordination Committee, in light of the best practices presented in the first session. Hence, the assembly was the meeting point of various experiences, perspectives, and visions about what a consultation is and how to do intersectional, anti-racist, and non-oppressive consultative work.

In my case, the assembly was a "destabilizing" event, a "moment of discontinuity" and "rupture" that made visible what was not formerly seen, and that made audible the voices not previously heard (Pavoni & Citroni, 2016, p. 234). This experience resonates with Pavoni and Citroni's observation about the "conflictual" and "radically political quality" of events: "Essentially, events *are* conflict. Here lies their radically 'political' quality, the affective resonance they generate, re-articulating the atmosphere and rhythm of being-together, 'mak[ing] visible what had no business being seen, and mak[ing] heard a discourse where once there was only place for noise' (Rancière, 1995, p. 30)" (2016, p. 234). According to the authors, the conflictuality of events is where "their dialectics and politics (management, participation, outcome, etc.) are played out" (p. 234). Consequently, studying events is best accomplished through an immersive ethnographic position where the activist-researcher develops "an insider knowledge of the event in its unfolding" in order to "grasp how it takes shape and resonates through space and time" (Pavoni & Citroni, 2016, p. 237). Therefore, undertaking an immersive critical and militant ethnography allowed me to be attuned to the dynamics of the movement I was studying and perceive the importance of the public assembly and how it was a key moment in the organizing process.[11]

Pavoni and Citroni (2016) point out that during an immersive ethnography, the activist-researcher becomes "a sort of 'radio receiver', constantly attuning the frequencies of this being-together and that s/he is tuned by them, or indeed a *seismographer* [italics added], capable of detecting the telluric waves generated by the encounter between the event and the space in which it takes place" (p. 247). The analogy with a radio receiver and a seismographer is particularly compelling to me since I was fully involved in the ethnography, "build[ing] long-term relationships of mutual commitment and trust," being "entangled with complex relations of power," and living the emotions associated with feminist and anti-racism work (Juris, 2007, p. 165). The frequencies I detected and recorded are the product of the interaction of my "body among other bodies (tangible and intangible, human and non-human)" during events that "occur in and through a dense spatiality made of practices, assumptions, affects, bodies, and a complexity shaped into shared rhythms [...]" (p. 247). Thus, the analysis shared in this chapter is based on the transcript of the assembly's video recording and on my field diary (audio and written), where I systematically noted my "seismographic" observations and impressions before, during, and after the public assembly. As discussed in the next sections, it is through this assembly that not only did I realize the possible transformative and emancipatory impact the consultative process could have on racialized persons and communities, but I also became aware of the violence and oppression we would perpetuate and reinforce if we—i.e., members of the Coordination Committee and other members of the coalition—were not careful and attentive enough during each step of our work.

The Limits of Intersectionality-as-Inclusion

Up until the assembly, the coalition's key answer to a more representative and inclusive process was to "value the inclusion of the greatest possible number of citizens and groups in the consultation process" and "not leave anyone behind" (field diary). Since we could not possibly bring in every single racialized person in Quebec, we wanted to represent as many intersectional experiences as possible by including people situated on various intersections of race, gender, sexuality, class, status, religion, and dis/ability. Moreover, to ensure the legitimacy of the coalition and the IPCSR to speak for racialized people and represent their interests, we took steps to reflect the diversity of racialized communities through the coalition's composition. Hence, the coalition members elected an Executive Committee comprising representatives from different organizations and various racialized groups situated at the intersection of multiple formations of difference. The same procedure was then followed for the IPCSR's Coordination Committee, where all three co-coordinators were women of colour (including myself). This "descriptive representation"—when the representatives share similar traits to those they represent—aimed to project an image of the IPCSR as a legitimate consulting process where people of colour organize for and speak for other people of colour.

However, researchers have shown that translating intersectionality into the representation of demographic categories is problematic. According to many intersectionality scholars, this is a result of the "institutionalization" (Nash, 2014, p. 45), "whitening" and "depoliticization" (Bilge, 2013, p. 405) of intersectionality, where it is reduced to a mere "labelling process" (Carastathis, 2016, p. 211). Moreover, this understanding of intersectionality shares many similarities with the "politics of diversity management," which, in the words of Sara Ahmed, "reifies difference as something that already exists 'in' the bodies of others (we are diverse because you are here)" (2009, p. 43). Indeed, addressing minorities "as demographic representations of a superficial diversity" almost always lapses into tokenism, where people are only symbolically included, giving the appearance of inclusivity and diversity (Roshanravan, 2014, p. 57).

During the assembly, several critiques of this version of intersectionality were expressed by activists from various backgrounds. One comment came from "Salma", who, after a long experience in the feminist movement, said she now refuses to participate in "structures that claim to be for us but are thought without us" (June 20, 2018). She denounced a feminist consultation that she helped organize and where the "participation of women of colour was welcome but not considered essential." She added, "When you accept to just be included, you recognize the legitimacy of the norm, of the majority." This was also the opinion of "Gregory", an activist for people without status, who reminded the assembly to be wary of calls for inclusion from self-proclaimed White allies because they can serve to absorb dissent:

"[they] include us, they swallow us and then they dissolve us" (June 20, 2018). Mostly addressed to initiatives led by White organizations, these critiques were supported by many other activists. However, not until the intervention of "Melissa", a Mohawk activist, invited by the Coordination Committee to share her insights on the best consultative practices from an Indigenous perspective, was the problem of inclusion within communities of colour raised. Indeed, the limits to inclusion are usually mentioned by critiquing the unequal power relationships between racialized people and the White majority and overlook how relationships of privilege or disadvantage exist and shape organizing work within communities of colour. When asked about how to include Indigenous organizations in the coalition, Melissa explained why many Indigenous people are usually reluctant to join the anti-racism movement, including participating in consultations about racism:

> This is a question I hear quite often in circles that are oriented to combat racism. I think it has to do with homogenization. And it is not the homogenization of Indigenous Peoples, but it is the grouping of Indigenous Peoples in or with all the other peoples that are all trying to bring down systemic racism. But there is a fundamental difference when it comes to Indigenous Peoples in Canada. Indigenous Peoples in Canada have a direct political relation that has never been resolved with the settler colonial government. So often you will see that Indigenous Peoples will shy away from broader circles like these because of that simple fact. And to be honest, there is so much energy that is being poured into trying to change that power imbalance and to really be talking, you know … You've got politicians out there throwing around words that they don't know what they mean. You've got Trudeau out there talking about nation to nation. If he was really talking nation to nation, we would be talking about land … and so the degree of the systemic racism that is built into that power imbalance with Indigenous Peoples, specifically, the legal framework and the legal relationship that is there, is really quite distinct to that particular group of people (June 20, 2018).

As expressed by Melissa in the above quotation, a consultation about racism that regroups Indigenous peoples with other racialized people cannot adequately address the specificity of Indigenous experiences. Even if the coalition officially recognized settler colonialism in Canada and had elected an Indigenous activist on the Executive Committee, our inclusive approach only ran "a colonialism road through the intersection" and did not take into account the intertwining of colonialism and racism (Carastathis, 2016, p. 203). Other Indigenous activists and scholars have already shown that Indigenous political resistance and the struggles of other racialized minorities can be incommensurable if the latter do not centre the fight against colonialism within their political strategy (Arvin, Tuck, & Morril, 2013). Racialized minorities in Quebec cannot assume they share the same oppression—racism and White supremacy—without recognizing that, as settlers, they are complicit in it as well (Smith, 2016). Following from this idea, what we needed to do when planning and designing the IPCSR was not merely include more Indigenous activists and organizations in the consultation's design to cover some blind spots, but instead, as later suggested by Melissa, to work on a design that targeted specifically Indigenous Peoples and was adapted to hear their perspectives: "I think if you really want to have that conversation, you have to target particular groups that you want to bridge that kind of relation with, and you are going to hear what they want to bring to the table, 'cause I am not sure it is the same as what people envision when they think about breaking down systemic racism" (June 20, 2018).

Melissa's critique of inclusion resonates with the argument that Crenshaw has been advancing since her first paper about intersectionality in 1989, where she explicitly states that "problems of exclusion cannot be solved simply by including Black women within an already established analytical structure" (1989, p. 140). According to her, an intersectional critique urges us to "rethink the entire framework that has been used as a basis for translating 'women's experience' or 'the Black experience' into concrete policy demands" (p. 140). Therefore, to develop a more equitable consulting process that does not create further marginalization, we ought to "target" specific marginalized groups and rethink both the "analytical structure" that enables them to speak and the framework through which their voices are translated. But Melissa's critique goes even further than Crenshaw's quote above; she not only calls for rethinking the consultative framework but also, more radically, for rethinking the possibility of a common framework altogether. Indeed, grouping Indigenous Peoples' experiences with other communities would only dilute their experiences, their unique take on what systemic racism is and how it is lived—as pointed out by Melissa—and, thus, render them, again, invisible. By criticizing the homogenization of Indigenous Peoples, she indirectly pushed toward many frameworks rather than a unifying one.

My analysis of the discussions that took place on that day shows that other activists shared this critical understanding of intersectionality, and they referred to it as "centering the margins."[12] In the next section, I further develop their approach to intersectionality and explain how it could help rethink and redesign a popular and independent consultation on systemic racism.

Centering the Margins

> To be in the margin is to be part of the whole but outside the main body.
>
> (bell hooks, 2015, p. xvii)

Centering the margins means emphasizing and treating as salient what is usually excluded by bringing it to the forefront, to the centre stage (Putnam, Jahn, & Baker, 2011). McKittrick (2006) points out that the margin to which activists and writers refer is not only metaphoric; it is a space occupied by those who are excluded from the main body—to paraphrase bell hooks's above quotation—and experience processes of marginalization within various arenas of social justice. Collins (1998) reminds us that Black feminist scholars used this metaphor to draw attention to "Black women's experiences within hierarchical power relations in the United States" that constructed "whiteness, maleness and wealth as centers of power" and, in turn, "relegated African-American women to positions of marginalized others" (p. 128). However, writers such as bell hooks claim the margin as a space "of radical openness," creativity and resistance and call for transforming marginality from "a site of deprivation" into "a site of radical possibilities, a space of resistance" (hooks, 1990, pp. 149–150). She adds, "[L]ocating oneself there is difficult yet necessary. It is not a 'safe' place. One is always at risk" (p. 90). Through her work on Black women geographies, McKittrick (2006) asserts that the margin is "a descriptive and analytic tool" that "allow[s] black feminists and other subaltern communities to locate the complexities of their unique relationship to patriarchy, whiteness and white femininity, struggles for liberation, and feminism" (p. 56). The margin is therefore redefined as a potential source of strength for African-American women "fostering a powerful oppositional knowledge" (Collins, 1998, p. 128).

During the assembly, the metaphor of the centre/margin was repeatedly used by some panellists and echoed later by many activists. Building on the conceptualization of the margin given by Black women scholars and on the ideas shared by some activists during the assembly, the last section of this chapter is dedicated to highlighting the material arrangements and practices put forward by those who called for centering the margins. This allows me to outline the meanings of this metaphor and show how it may be operationalized in a popular and independent consultation on systemic racism that aims to value voice. However, before delving into the specificities of what it means to center the margins, I make a conceptual detour to reflect on and redefine difference and coalitions. To adopt a "centering the margins" mindset, we should first shift our understanding of alliances built on difference.

Coalitional Difference and Plural Voices

In contrast to identity-based groups that are often conceived as "spaces of similarity, seclusion, and safety," a coalition formed by many groups is usually seen as a "space of difference, confrontation, and risk" (Carastathis, 2016, p. 184). Hence, managing and organizing through difference has long been a preoccupation for many coalitions, who usually see difference as threatening. Indeed, the impulse to "manage" and "negotiate" difference when working with multiple groups reflects an understanding of difference as an obstacle, an impediment, and a challenge to harmonious and united coalitions. However, approaching difference from the nexus of critical organizational communication and intersectionality, I instead conceptualize it as a communicative and constitutive feature of organizing (Mumby, 2011, p. ix; Parker, 2014, p. 620) and "the condition of possibility [...] of any collective political act" (Carastathis, 2016, p. 206).

This shifts the understanding of difference "from being an essentializing property of individuals, groups and organizations" (Parker, 2014, p. 620) to being "an organizing principle of the meaning, structure, practice, experience and economy of work" (Ashcraft, 2011, p. 8).[13] According to Mumby (2011), "difference is both the mechanism through which meanings and identities are organized and the product—intended or unintended— of everyday organizing and collective sense-making" (p. ix). Therefore, instead of being an obstacle and an impediment to coalitions, difference is apprehended as "a productive or generative force within cross-sector partnerships and other organizational forms characterized by diverse members" (Dempsey, 2011, p. 6). This conceptualization echoes Barvosa-Carter's statement that "[d]ifferences within us can enable radical alliances among us" (1999, cited in Carastathis, 2016, p. 187). Simply put, difference is what makes coalitions possible.

In addition to de-essentializing our understanding of difference, "[i]ntersectionality usefully deconstructs the false dichotomy between identity and coalition" (Carastathis, 2016, p. 192). For example, the category (or formation) of race should be conceptualized, according to Crenshaw (1991), as a coalition among racialized people. Therefore, all racialized identities could be apprehended as coalitions, "internally heterogenous [and] complex unities constituted by their internal differences and dissonances and by internal as well as external relations of power" (Carastathis, 2016, p. 7). This intersectional conceptualization of identities-as-coalitions highlights how experiences of racism are never lived in a singular and internally consistent way but are always intertwined with other formations of difference. Following the same vein of thought, I want to suggest— with Couldry (2010)—that voicing racism (and any other form of injustice), both at the individual and collective levels, is also "irreducibly [and inevitably] plural":

> It would be absurd to imagine that a life comprised just one story, or just one continuous sequence of action. The inherent internal plurality of each voice encompasses the processes whereby we reflect from one narrative stream on to another, and think about what one strand of our lives mean[s] for other strands. [...] To block someone's capacity to bring one part of their lives to bear on another part—for example, by discounting the relevance of their work experience to their trajectory as a citizen—is, again, to deny a dimension of voice itself.
>
> (Couldry, 2010, p. 9)

In this passage, Couldry does not mention intersectionality per se but he deftly points to the co-construction and entanglements of multiple inter-sectional voices—and stories—that constitute each person. Therefore, the voices of racialized persons and groups were already plural, coalitional, and constituted by difference before they joined the coalition. Nevertheless, if difference is usually seen as threatening a coalition's unity it is because, Black feminist author Audre Lorde (1984) points out, "the need for unity is often misnamed as a need for homogeneity" (p. 226). Yet an intersectional lens seeks "unity without uniformity" and mobilizes identities "without demanding that people be identical" (Chun, Lipsitz, & Shin, 2013, p. 923). Thus, according to this perspective, instead of being an obstacle to unity, the plurality of voices is precisely what sustains it. Indeed, Sharon Parker rightly observes that "unity is not achieved through homogeneity, but by bringing heterogeneous elements into a whole" without losing their par-ticularities (1991, cited in Carastathis, 2016, p. 215).

If difference renders coalitions possible, then why are organizing through difference and keeping coalitions united such hard and tiring work? According to Carastathis (2016), "the true threat to alliances across lines of power is not difference but rather the reproduction of relations of dom-ination within a coalition" (p. 195). As mentioned earlier, hierarchical relationships should not be considered as external to racialized groups or limited to White majority/racialized minority relationships. Instead, "rela-tions of domination express themselves horizontally, quickly reconfiguring internal hierarchies and producing internalized oppression" among racial-ized minorities (Carastathis, 2016, p. 195). This is particularly salient for the IPCSR as it was intended to be a space for voices, which made it also inherently a space of power (Couldry, 2010). "Marya", co-coordinator of the IPCSR, raised this point during the panel discussion:

> Now that we are doing it [i.e., the consultation] on our own, we are independent, in the sense that we can do things in the way we want: how do we work with power dynamics and questions of privilege within communities of colour? And how do we take into consideration this difference of privilege and power dynamics? [...] How do we make sure that these issues ... that we can go above them? (June 20, 2018)

The main answer to Marya's question, mostly given by feminist panellists, evolved around the idea of "centering the margins." The metaphor had been brought forward all day long as an intersectional strategy, sometimes even used as a synonym for intersectionality. In the next subsections, I explain and comment on the two strategies suggested by the activists who called for centering the margins by drawing parallels with intersectional feminist lit-erature. While the first strategy requires us to "de-center" ourselves, bring our critical gaze inward in a reflexive way to analyze our own positionali-ties in systems of power, the spaces we occupy, and how to be accountable for our privileges, the second strategy compels us to take a step backward and answer the difficult question: Why are we doing this consultative work and for whom?

De-centering

According to "Lily", an anti-oppression organizer, the feminist intersectional lens prompts us to ask two questions: First, who are we not listening to and whose experience is overlooked in our conversations about racism? Second, who is taking up all the space and dominating the conversation?[14] She argued that these two questions are interrelated and need to be asked simultaneously; it is because of the space some of us occupy in the centre that others remain relegated to the margins. Hence, "centering the margins" requires a complementary and necessary movement of de-centering, "namely unseating those who occupy centers of power" (Collins, 1998, p. 127). To unseat the centres of power and center the margins, some activists suggested that we need to be self-aware of our privileged positionalities and transparent about them, and work on an accountable consultative process that gives back control to those who entrust it with their voices.

Self-awareness of Our Privileged Positionalities and Transparency

A consulting process is a space for voice and power built by those who have the resources to create it (even if the resources in question are minimal and not equally distributed among the organizers) for those who do not have the same opportunities and resources. That is why Lily stressed the importance of "having that hard conversation of being cognizant about the space we are taking" when we organize for the IPCSR (June 20, 2018). Her comments have two important implications that need to be unpacked. First, they mean we need to recognize that the space we come to occupy when we organize is intimately related to our positionalities, which, in turn, are contextual and relational (Collins & Chepp, 2013). Indeed, our social positions and experiences may sometimes be contradictory, in such a way that we are marginalized in certain situations (in White spaces, for instance) and privileged in others (for example, when working with other racialized persons). Second, Lily's comments imply recognizing, in the words of Dempsey (2017), that "the social location of a speaker always bears on what is said, how it is heard, and whether that voice is likely to be heard and have the ability to make a difference" (p. 1). Therefore, when we use our privileged space to carry the voice of other marginalized persons, we may only reinforce their invisibilisation. Furthermore, Couldry (2010) rightly states, "[I]f through an unequal distribution of narrative resources, the materials from which some people must build their account of themselves are not theirs to adapt or to control [which happens when others speak for you or do not leave a space for you to speak], then this represents a deep denial of voice, a deep form of oppression" (p. 9). He draws a parallel with W.E.B Dubois's "double consciousness," which refers to the "sense of always looking at oneself through the eyes of others" (Couldry, 2010, p. 9).

This self-awareness about our own positionalities and how they can foster power and voice inequalities should be followed, according to Melissa, by being "upfront" about it. She considers this act of transparent recognition unavoidable if we aim to create "a safe space and a place for trust." This point is even more salient since a consultation is also a space of representation:

> One of the obvious factors is, who is going to wear the face of consulting? Is it a male? A female? A White person? Being cognizant about who you are coming to the process [...]. You can't change the simple fact of who you are, the colour of your skin or your gender. You are who you are. The act of being able to put that out there and say, "This is who I am and I am coming to this with an open mind" is a very powerful thing when you are going to be consulting.
>
> (Melissa, June 20, 2018)

To complete Melissa's recommendation, Lily added that those who organize for the IPCSR should not only be transparent about who they are and what they can bring, but also—and most importantly—"about what they can't bring." "So, it is honouring both sides of those things and being transparent about it" (Lily, June 20, 2018).

As we can see, centering the margins goes hand in hand with fostering discussions about privilege, marginalization, and how they are constituted by power relationships within communities of colour. It also requires unseating or decentering those who occupy all the space when we speak about racism in Quebec and instead put at the forefront those who are usually not heard and not seen. Crenshaw (1991) stresses that recognizing the way racial discrimination works in differentiated ways does not mean thinking of suffering quantitatively (who is suffering more or has worse oppression), falling, therefore, into what Martínez (1993) calls "the Oppression Olympics." It is rather recognizing that experiences of racism are qualitatively different and are always shaped by other formations of difference, such as gender, sexuality, class, religion, dis/ability, and status. Thus, placing at the centre of our consultative strategy—and any resistance strategy, actually—the most marginalized among us (because they are at the crossroads of multiple disadvantages) means that we are fighting for the emancipation of those "whose freedom necessitates the destruction of all systems of oppression" (CRC, cited in Carastathis, 2016, p. 7).

Building an Accountable Process

Because consulting is a process to which people are asked to entrust a precious part of themselves and, in Lily's words, it "can hurt people," some activists stressed the importance of taking precautions so the IPCSR would not become an exploitative and extractive process. In order to prevent this, they apprehended the consultation as a research process and called for the implementation of decolonial and anti-oppressive research methodologies. Moreover, Melissa insisted that consulting, like any other research endeavour, could be particularly violent to Indigenous Peoples. Therefore, she reminded us that "First Nations across the country are continually researched to death" and are fed up with external researchers "coming into a community, conducting research, and then walking away." Thus, a consultative process should be accountable to the people who participate in it, it has to guarantee that people "feel that they have access, control, and ownership over the process that harvests their voices" (Melissa, June 20, 2018). She added, "When you are someone who is being consulted, you want to know how your information is being used. You want to know what it is going to influence. You want to know that what you've said is appropriately reflected, it is *accurately* reflected" (Melissa, June 20, 2018, italics added). In keeping with this, Lily added, "[We should] create a space where people would be able to criticize the process and ask for change or for reparations; [this would] help build trust and make people feel in charge and fully part of the process to which they give their voices" (June 20, 2018).

These statements converge with Couldry when he writes about the importance of recognizing one's individual voice in the collective voice that speaks for him or her. "For me to feel that a group of which I am a member speaks for me, I must be able to recognize my inputs in what that group says and does; if I do not, I must have satisfactory opportunities to correct that mismatch" (Couldry, 2010, p. 114).

In the last subsection, I address another fundamental and important question, asked by "Sherine"—a sexual rights and anti-racism activist—which is, according to her, fundamental if we are to engage in a genuine consultative process that centers marginalized voices: Why are we doing this work, and for whom? Are we doing it for ourselves, for racialized communities, or for the government?

Reviewing Our End Goal: Why Are We Consulting?

"The end goal of the consultation should be first and foremost about the people who participate in the process," asserted Sherine (June 20, 2018). She believes that harvesting the voices of marginalized people should not be a means toward an end. Rather, safeguarding an anti-oppressive and a caring space for those voices should, in itself, be the end goal. This opinion was shared by Lily, who added, "I think that the end goal of any consultation on racism and all the other 'isms' … should ultimately be healing [...] By allowing that natural process of connection to be settled, you can get this deep richness in terms of the testimonials that you are hearing" (June 20, 2018). Lily's comment highlights the collective process that is consulting and how it is "a shared act of interpretation" that could (and should) lead to healing (Couldry, 2010, p. 130). It aligns with Couldry's understanding of voice and how "our stories are entangled with others" (p. 98), in such a way that making sense of our lives and gaining voice is "an ongoing process of reflection, exchanging narratives back and forth between our past and present selves, and between us and others" (p. 8). In the same vein, "Samuel", a long-time activist against police brutality, considered the consultation as an opportunity "to break the isolation," to provide a safe space shared with people with similar experiences, where everyone could speak freely (June 20, 2018).

Enabling healing, breaking the isolation, nurturing trust, and creating safe spaces were the main objectives advanced by activists calling for an approach centered around the needs of the participants in the consultation. This reflects an understanding of the consultation as a space that gives material form to a collective memory, "a particular organization of time and place whereby acts of remembering [are] performed" in the presence of other bodies (Couldry, 2010, p. 130). Yet during the panel's discussion, "Azyz", an activist against Islamophobia, expressed another end goal to the consultation that provoked an interesting conversation. According to Azyz, we (those who would design and build the consultation) also had "an obligation for results," and therefore "we would be missing the point of the consultation" if we focused only on healing (June 20, 2018). From this standpoint, the main outcome of the consultation should be to publish a final report and to address the recommendations made by the commissioners to the relevant institutions. He added, "We cannot ask less of ourselves than to dismantle systemic racism," which could be partly done through the enactment of our recommendations by the government (June 20, 2018). Azyz was obviously not opposed to healing; on the contrary, he considers it a desirable and a welcome result. However, in his opinion, it should not be the end goal of the consultation.

Many other activists agreed with Azyz's statement but that was not the case for Lily and Sherine, both intersectional feminists. According to Lily, too many recommendations and reports have already been written over the years and are now sitting on many institutions' shelves. Therefore, designing and building up another consultation that would culminate in an endless list of recommendations was not only useless but also draining. "I think one thing that has continuously come to mind throughout this process is how many reports have there been written over the years? How many recommendations and suggestions have been written out after years of work? How often have these recommendations been lived?" (Lily, June 20, 2018). According to feminist activists who call for centering the margins, only valuing measurable results—like recommendations and reports—while dismissing less measurable ones—like individual and collective healing— is an effect of "white supremacy culture."[15] White supremacy thinking is insidiously promoted through "norms and standards without being proactively chosen or named by the group" (COCo, 2019, p. 7), which leads many organizations (even ones that oppose White supremacy) to direct more "time and money resources toward producing measurable outcomes" (COCo, 2019, 37). White supremacy culture is also entangled with neoliberalism in such a way that "success and progress are synonymous with 'bigger' and 'more'" (COCo, 2019, p. 33). Hence, through the lens of "White supremacy culture," an alternative consultation to the one previously planned by the government should only be bigger (including more people and more areas of inquiry) and produce more measurable results (i.e., more recommendations).

White supremacy culture also falls within what Couldry (2010) calls "voice-denying rationalities," that is, rationalities that "take no account of voice" and promote subtle practices and ways of organizing social relations "that exclude voice or undermine forms of its expression" (p. 10). Couldry argues that neoliberalism is a voice-denying rationality that does not "deny the value of voice outright," it may even celebrate it, but works in other ways to weaken it on various levels (p. 10). However, racism is also a fundamental dimension of how the material conditions of voice are shaped and undermined, and, from an intersectional perspective, neoliberalism is entangled, sustained, and co-constructed with White supremacy. Therefore, we should apprehend both neoliberalism and White supremacy as voice-denying rationalities that permeate how we organize against racial injustices and what kind of end goals we envision for our initiatives. [16] Hence, if we follow Audre Lorde's famous statement, "The master's tools will never dismantle the master's house" (1984), to accomplish effective and voice-valuing anti-racism work, we must break away from the thinking of White supremacy and neoliberalism.

It is with this goal in mind that Lily asserted that a better consultation is not necessarily a bigger one: "Sometimes less is more." The most important thing according to her was to set realistic objectives and "go for what we commit for." This means that consulting differently does not signify doing more of the same by adding more people—and more intersections—all the while trying to make the process fit in an unrealistic time frame conditioned by political agendas. An approach that centers the margins requires prioritizing those who never had the opportunity to speak and make themselves heard, and then building a consultation that places *their* needs, in terms of accessibility measures and timeline, first. Sherine summed up this point perfectly when she said:

> If we want to do things differently from the government, we have to think about and conceptualize what consulting means. For us, it means doing it in an ethical way, while keeping our values, and don't make it live on a shelf. It is not about points, listing points, but it is about how to bring it back to the community. How do we do workshops and talk to the community about how they are living their experiences and how

we could together build tools. Because I think fundamentally […] we need to be working with our community to come up with those solutions. It is not that we should not work with or talk to government, but, ultimately, the liberation comes from us (June 20, 2018).

Conclusion

At the beginning of our organizing for the IPCSR, we believed intersectionality would help us guarantee an organizing process that was both inclusive and representative of the heterogeneity of racialized people's voices. However, we discovered along the way, thanks to the inputs of Indigenous and intersectional feminist activists, that intersectionality is not necessarily a solution to dealing with difference or to work with interlocking oppressions. It is rather a tool that can help us reveal what or who is missing and what or who is invisible. In revealing these things, intersectionality is a "point of departure for a liberatory and coalitional project" (Carastathis, 2016, 225).

This chapter highlighted how "centering the margins" was put forward during the IPCSR's assembly as a consultative approach that takes our attention away from questions like "How could we include the greatest number of racialized communities?" to focus instead on questions like "How could we maximize the possibilities of voice for the most marginalized and silenced racialized communities?" Moreover, I tried to show how the focus on building numerical and political power, usually important in order to pool resources and resist marginalization, could easily subsume the perspectives, demands, and objectives of the most disadvantaged within the coalition (Luna, 2016). An intersectional consultative approach that centers the margins may require, as in the case of the IPCSR, working with fewer people and collecting fewer resources. However, as we can see based on the suggestions and recommendations made by Indigenous and intersectional activists, this approach also means closely examining the experiences of the most disadvantaged racialized groups, prioritizing their voices all along the consultative process, creating safe spaces for collective remembrance and healing, building tools with the community, fostering self-reflection, and transforming our ways of doing anti-racism work. However, I want to bring the attention to some red flags raised by Collins (1998), McKittrick (2006), and Carastathis (2016) about using the expression "centering the margins" in a decontextualized, abstract, and universal sense that could be "applied to all sorts of power relations" (Collins, 1998, p. 129). According to these authors, "centering the margins" should not become a mere "literary metaphor" that embellishes liberal discourses about intersectionality and diversity. As pointed out by Collins (1998), "groups already privileged under hierarchal power relations suffer little from embracing the language of decentering denuded of any actions to decenter actual hierarchical power relations in academia or elsewhere. Ironically, their privilege may actually increase" (p. 137).

I started this chapter by highlighting the difficulty for all racialized persons to tell their stories about racism in Quebec. I conclude by emphasizing that the situation is even worse for those at the intersection of multiple formations of difference; they "live in a territory between voice and silence: if they continue to speak from their experience, they may find their voice is out of relationship, too loud, off-key. If they remain silent, they are in immediate danger of disappearing" (Taylor, Gilligan, & Sullivan, 1995, p. 202). For these individuals, "being able to speak out becomes either an abnormality or a distant dream," points out Couldry (2010, p. 120). Through our several months of organizing for the IPCSR, we had the ambition to bring this dream of speaking out a little bit closer. But as mentioned by Melissa, "A consultation is hard work. It is a lot of work. It is rolling up your sleeves and trying to find a way to bring people in" (June 20, 2018). This difficulty is inherent to all anti-racist organizing in a political and social context that is not yet ready to hear about racism.

Notes

1 The premier said that "political backlash against the consultations contributed to his party's dismal results" in the Louis-Hébert by election and that he was reconsidering the mandate of the consultation as a result (Montgomery, 2017, para. 8).
2 The name of the initiative and those of the activists have been changed for reasons of confidentiality.
3 In French, there is no equivalent to "people of colour," thus "racialized people" is often used to refer to non-White minorities in Quebec. The expression "racialized people" highlights the constructed and processual quality of racism that operates through racialization. In this chapter, I will also use the term "people of colour," since it was used by some English-speaking activists during my ethnography.
4 This chapter is part of my broader doctoral research on the anti-racism movement in Quebec funded by the Social Sciences and Humanities Research Council (SSHRC).
5 This public consultative commission took place in Quebec in 2007 and dealt with a big controversy about religious symbols—especially Muslim women's head scarves—in public spaces.
6 "Witnesses" (*témoins*) is the term used to identify the citizens who give their testimonies in public consultations.
7 Following Ashcraft (2011), I use the term "formation of difference" to bring to light the social and historical reproduction of those categories that are sometimes considered as fixed and given categories or identities.
8 Like Luft and Ward (2009), I apprehend intersectional practice as "the application of scholarly or social movement methodologies aimed at intersectional and sustainable social justice outcomes" (p. 11).
9 Like Couldry, I do not limit voice to speech or the ability to speak. "What matters is less the Sonic aspect of voice (deaf people's language of signing is just as much voice, in our sense, as spoken language); more important is voice's role as the means whereby people give an account of the world in which they act" (Couldry, 2010, p. 91).

10 Critical ethnography draws from feminist epistemologies that blur the traditional boundaries between "theory" and "praxis" and considers all research projects as political. What sets critical ethnography apart from other ethnographic approaches, according to Palmer and Caldas (2017), is its "focus on the way individuals within a marginalized community engage in praxis [the interaction of knowledge and experience in a cycle of action and reflection (Naples, 2003)] and on how members of the community exercise agency for cultural production and transformation" (p. 382). Critical ethnography is also an approach that begins with "an ethical responsibility to address processes of unfairness or injustices within a particular lived domain" (Madison, 2011, p. 5). My critical ethnography was a militant one since I was participating in the process of designing and building up the consultation more than merely observing it. Indeed, according to Juris (2007), a militant ethnography "means helping to organize actions and workshops, facilitating meetings, weighing in during strategic and tactical debates, staking out political positions, and putting one's body on the line during mass direct actions" (p. 165).

11 All along my involvement—from February 2018 to January 2019—I tried to juggle, on the one hand, my role as a member of the IPCSR's Coordination Committee, and on the other hand, my role as a researcher and critical-militant ethnographer. From the very start—i.e., when I submitted my candidacy for the position of co-coordinator and later during the hiring interview—I clarified that my participation was motivated both by my long-time engagement with anti-racism in Quebec and my interest as a researcher in issues of voice and representation within social movements. My activist-researcher stance also meant that I had to be reflexively conscious of the deployment of my positionality and the power dynamics my engagement led me to navigate during the organizing process. As pointed out by Madison (2011), "Positionality is vital because it forces us to acknowledge our own power, privilege, and biases just as we are denouncing the power structures that surround our subjects" (p. 8). Hence, even if I am a racialized woman within the Québécois context (because of my Arabic name and Muslim background), I still benefit from many privileges thanks to my Canadian citizenship, my light skin, and my university degrees. Also, unlike the other members of the Coordination Committee who were involved on a voluntary basis, I benefited from a scholarship that financed my doctoral research and, thus, my critical ethnography within the IPCSR.

12 Collins (1998) traces back the use of the centre/margin metaphor to the 1960s and 1970s in postcolonial/decolonial struggles and social movements in the United States. In the same period, the core/periphery metaphor was also used in critical social theories.

13 "Work" is used in the larger sense by Ashcraft (2011), who views it as "a discourse formation that evolves across many sites of cultural activity" (p. 15). Hence, work does not only occur in "formal organizations where people perform tasks, but also in families, educational institutions, popular and trade discourse, legal and regulatory agencies, labor and professional associations, and where ever else we encounter representations, negotiations, and enactments of (who does what) work" (p. 15).

14 Lily gave the example of people without status who were continually not heard because they exist in a "systemic void," and she added, "When we are thinking about centering the margins of systemic racism, we also need to think about where does the system put the voids?"

15 The Center for Community Organizations (COCo) defines White supremacy culture as "the idea (ideology) that white people and the ideas, thoughts, beliefs, and actions of White people are superior to People of

Colour and their ideas, thoughts, beliefs, and actions. White supremacy expresses itself interpersonally as well as structurally (through our governments, education systems, food systems, etc.)" (p. 7). COCo's document is an adaptation of the work initially done by Tema Okun and Kenneth Jones, both Black activist-scholars, who identified and described five qualities of White supremacy culture: perfectionism, concentrating power, right to comfort, individualism, and progress is bigger/more (see COCo, 2019).

16 Another sign of "White supremacy culture" according to some activists is the sense of urgency in the push for a timeline for the consultation and the obsession with time scales. This point has been actually brought up by some activists in several meetings besides the assembly. For example, during a meeting with the Executive Committee to discuss a draft of the consultation's design (that we had been working on in the Coordination Committee), one representative considered the document useless because it did not follow a timeline. A few weeks later, we had a meeting with another group to discuss the same draft, so in order to avoid the same criticism we indexed a timeline to the document. However, the group we were meeting with, intersectional feminist activists, considered the timeline unimportant because it added a "sense of urgency" to a project that should take all the time it needs to be accomplished. Therefore, while for some activists (like the representative in the Executive Committee) it was important to not lose the momentum of societal debate in Quebec around racism and to wrap up the consultation in a few months, for others "the constant sense of urgency makes it difficult to take time to be inclusive, encourage democratic and/ or thoughtful decision-making, to plan long-term, or to consider consequences" (COCo, 2019, p. 39). Thus, the timeline according to activists who call for centering the margins should be adapted to the needs of the consultation and not the opposite.

References

Ahmed, Sara. (2009). Embodying diversity: Problems and paradoxes for Black feminists. *Race Ethnicity and Education*, 12 (1), 41–52.

Alcoff, Linda Martin. (1991). The problem of speaking for others. *Cultural Critique*, 20, 5–32.

Arvin, Maile, Tuck, Eve, & Morrill, Angie. (2013). Decolonizing feminism: Challenging connections between settler colonialism and heteropatriarchy *Feminist Formations*, 25(1), 8–34.

Ashcraft, Karen L. (2011). Knowing work through the communication of difference: A revised agenda for difference studies. In Dennis K. Mumby (Ed.), *Reframing difference in organizational communication studies: Research, pedagogy, practice* (pp. 3–30). Thousand Oaks, CA: Sage.

Bilge, Sirma. (2013). Intersectionality undone: Saving intersectionality from feminist intersectionality studies. *Du Bois Review: Social Science Research on Race*, 10(2), 405–424.

Carastathis, Anna. (2016). *Intersectionality: Origins, contestations, horizons.* Lincoln, NE: University of Nebraska Press.

CBC News. (2017, September 28). Community groups eager to participate in Quebec's systemic racism commission. https://www.cbc.ca/news/canada/montreal/systemic-racism-commission-quebec-1.4311187

Cho, Sumi, Crenshaw, Kimberlé W., & McCall, Leslie. (2013). Toward a field of intersectionality studies: Theory, applications, and praxis. *Signs: Journal of Women in Culture and Society*, 38(4), 785–810.

Chun, Jennifer J., Lipsitz, George, & Shin, Young. (2013). Intersectionality as a social movement strategy: Asian immigrant women advocates. *Signs: Journal of Women in Culture and Society*, 38(4), 917–940.

COCo. (2019). White supremacy culture in organizations. https://coco-net.org/wp-content/uploads/2019/11/Coco-WhiteSupCulture-ENG4.pdf

Collins, Patricia H. (1998). *Fighting words: Black women and the search for justice.* Minneapolis, MN: University of Minnesota Press.

Collins, Patricia H. (2015). Intersectionality's definitional dilemmas. *Annual Review of Sociology*, 41(1), 1–20.

Collins, Patricia H., & Chepp, Victoria. (2013). Intersectionality. In Georgina Waylen, Karen Celis, Johanna Kantola, & S. Laurel Weldon (Eds.), *The Oxford handbook of gender and politics* (pp. 57–87). New York, NY: Oxford University Press.

Couldry, Nick. (2010). *Why voice matters: Culture and politics after neoliberalism.* Thousand Oaks, CA: Sage.

Crenshaw, Kimberlé. (1989). Demarginalizing the intersection of race and sex: A Black feminist critique of antidiscrimination doctrine, feminist theory and antiracist politics. *University of Chicago Legal Forum*, 1989(1), 139–167.

Crenshaw, Kimberlé. (1991). Mapping the margins: Intersectionality, identity politics, and violence against women of color. *Stanford Law Review*, 43(6), 1241–1300.

CTV Montreal. (2017, July 20). Quebec taking steps to combat systemic racism. https://montreal.ctvnews.ca/quebec-taking-steps-to-combat-systemic-racism-1.3511679

Deetz, Stanley (1995). Transforming communication, transforming business: Stimulating value negotiation for more responsive and responsible workplaces. *International Journal of Value-Based Management*, 8(3), 255–278.

Dempsey, Sarah E. (2007). Towards a critical organizational approach to civil society contexts : A case study of the difficulties of transnational advocacy. *International & Intercultural Communication Annual*, 30, 317–339.

Dempsey, Sarah E. (2011). Theorizing difference from transnational feminisms. In Dennis K. Mumby (Ed.), *Reframing difference in organizational communication studies: Research, pedagogy, practice* (pp. 55–76). Thousand Oaks, CA: Sage. http://sk.sagepub.com/books/reframing-difference-in-organizational-communication-studies/n3.xml

Dempsey, Sarah E. (2017). Voice. In Craig Scott & Laurie K. Lewis (Eds.), *The international encyclopedia of organizational communication* (pp. 1–8). New York, NY: John Wiley & Sons. https://onlinelibrary.wiley.com/doi/abs/10.1002/9781118955567.wbieoc216

Drimonis, Toula. (2017, August 15). Quebec is reviewing systemic racism. Canada should follow. *National Observer*. https://www.nationalobserver.com/2017/08/15/opinion/quebec-reviewing-systemic-racism-canada-should-follow

Halberstam, Judith. (2011). *The queer art of failure.* Durham, NC: Duke University Press.

hooks, bell. (1990). *Yearning: Race, gender and cultural politics.* Boston, MA: South End Press.

hooks, bell. (2015). *Feminist theory: From margin to center*. New York, NY: Routledge.

Juris, Jeffrey. (2007). Practicing militant ethnography with the movement for global resistance in Barcelona. In Stevphen Shukaitis & David Graeber (Eds.), *Constituent imagination: Militant investigations//Collective theorization* (pp. 164–176). Chico, CA: AK Press. http://www.jeffreyjuris.com/articles/practicing-militant-ethnography-with-the-movement-for-global-resistance-mrg-in-barcelona-pdf

Lopez, Marlihan. (2017, March 1). Enjeux et défis de l'appropriation de l'intersectionnalité au sein du mouvement des femmes du Québec. *Droits et Libertés, 35*(2). https://liguedesdroits.ca/enjeux-et-defis-de-lappropriation-de-lintersectionnalite-au-sein-du-mouvement-des-femmes-du-quebec/

Lorde, Audre. (1984). *Sister outsider: Essays and speeches*. Freedom, CA: Crossing Press.

Luft, Rachel E., & Ward, Jane (2009). Toward an intersectionality just out of reach: Confronting challenges to intersectional practice. In Vasilikie Demos & Marcia Texler Segal (Eds.), *Perceiving gender locally, globally, and intersectionally* (Vol. 13, pp. 9–37). Bingley, UK: Emerald Group Publishing. https://doi.org/10.1108/S1529-2126 (2009)0000013005

Luna, Zakiya. (2016). "Truly a women of color organization": Negotiating sameness and difference in pursuit of intersectionality. *Gender & Society, 30*(5), 769–790.

Madison, D. Soyini. (2011). *Critical ethnography: Method, ethics, and performance*. Thousand Oaks, CA: Sage.

Martínez, Elizabeth. (1993). Beyond Black/White: The racisms of our times. *Social Justice, 20*(1–2), 22–34.

Massey, Doreen. (2005). *For space*. London: Sage.

McDonald, James. (2019). Difference and intersectionality. In Anne M. Nicotera (Ed.), *Origins and traditions of organizational communication: A comprehensive introduction to the field* (1st ed., pp. 270–287). New York, NY: Routledge.

McKittrick, Katherine. (2006). *Demonic grounds: Black women and the cartographies of struggle* (1st ed.). Minneapolis, MN: University of Minnesota Press.

Montgomery, Angelica. (2017, October 4). Quebec premier casts doubt on future of consultations on systemic racism. https://www.cbc.ca/news/canada/montreal/consultations-systemic-racism-byelection-defeat-1.4327950

Mumby, Dennis K. (2011). Organizing difference: An introduction. In Dennis K. Mumby (Ed.), *Reframing difference in organizational communication studies: Research, pedagogy, practice* (pp. vii–xiii). Thousand Oaks, CA: Sage.

Naples, Nancy A. (2003). *Feminism and method: Ethnography, discourse analysis, and activist research*. New York, NY: Routledge.

Nash, Jennifer C. (2014). Institutionalizing the margins. *Social Text, 32*(1), 45–65.

Palmer, Deborah, & Caldas, Blanca. (2017). Critical ethnography. In Kendall A. King, Yi-Ju Lai, & Stephen May (Eds.), *Research methods in language and education* (3rd ed., pp. 381–392). New York, NY: Springer International Publishing. https://doi.org/10.1007/978-3-319-02249-9_28

Parker, Patricia S. (2014). Difference and organizing. In Linda Putnam & Dennis K. Mumby, *The Sage handbook of organizational communication: Advances in theory, research and methods* (pp. 619–641). Thousand Oaks, CA: Sage.

Pavoni, Andrea, & Citroni, Sebastiano. (2016). An ethnographic approach to the taking place of the event. In Ian R. Lamond & Louise Platt (Eds.), *Critical event studies: Approaches to research* (pp. 231–252). London, UK: Palgrave Macmillan.

Putnam, Linda L., Jahn, Jody, & Baker, Jane Stuart. (2011). Intersecting difference: A dialectical perspective. In Dennis K. Mumby (Ed.), *Reframing difference in organizational communication studies: Research, pedagogy, practice* (pp. 31–54). Thousand Oaks, CA: Sage.

Rancière, Jacques. (1995). *Disagreement: Politics and philosophy.* Minneapolis, MN: University of Minnesota Press.

Roshanravan, Shireen. (2014). Motivating coalition: Women of color and epistemic disobedience. *Hypatia, 29*(1), 41–58.

Smith, Andrea. (2016). Heteropatriarchy and the three pillars of white supremacy: Rethinking women of color organizing. In Janell Hobson (Ed.), *Are all the women still white? Rethinking race, expanding feminisms* (pp. 61–71). Albany, NY: SUNY Press.

Solyom, Catherine. (2017, December 2). Close-up on racism in Quebec: "I lost part of my life." *Montreal Gazette.* https://montrealgazette.com/news/close-up-on-racism-in-quebec-i-lost-part-of-my-life

Spivak, Gayatri C. (1988). Can the subaltern speak ? In Cary Nelson & Lawrence Grossberg (Eds.), *Marxism and the interpretation of culture* (pp. 271–313). Urbana, IL: University of Illinois Press.

Taylor, Jill McLean, Gilligan, Carol, & Sullivan, Amy M. (1995). *Between voice and silence: Women and girls, race and relationship.* Cambridge, MA: Harvard University Press.

Valiante, Giuseppe. (2017, August 9). Consultations on 'systemic racism' in Quebec dividing province's political left. *CTV News.* https://www.ctvnews.ca/canada/consultations-on-systemic-racism-in-quebec-dividing-province-s-political-left-1.3538853

Conclusion

Speaking with One Voice Is a Specific Form of Multivocality

Thomas Martine and Chantal Benoit-Barné

One of the reasons the relationship between univocality and multivocality is difficult to grasp is that we tend to see univocality as the opposite of multivocality: given a situation in which multiple voices coexist, speaking with one voice would be the result of excluding or silencing voices until only one remains. What the chapters of this book show is that this is not how univocality works. Indeed, they show that speaking with one voice is primarily a process of *unifying* voices, that is, of connecting voices in such a way that one voice can speak *in the name of* many. While this process may involve excluding or silencing specific voices (this is quite clear in some of the chapters), it does not—cannot—make multivocality entirely disappear. Thus, an important takeaway from this book is that univocality should not be conceived as the opposite of multivocality but rather as a *specific re-ordering* of multivocality. By way of conclusion, we propose to highlight different aspects of this process using examples from the chapters.

Univocality Is Made of Multivocality

The first thing that becomes clear when we look at univocality as (the result of) a process of unification of voices is that univocality is literally made of multivocality. It follows that traces of various voices can be found in the midst of even the most unified and compact voice (whether it is the voice of an organization, an artist, or a political movement). What makes the chapters of this book so useful is that they capture the process of unification in the making, thus revealing the irreducible multivocal dimension of univocality.

This is especially visible in Grover Golden and Bencherki's chapter. The authors study a community-based organization whose purpose is to encourage underserved African American women in New York State to obtain reproductive health screenings. To this end, the organization has developed a "peer health advocate" initiative: they hire and train women from the local community who then take the lead on community outreach. As the authors show, a key aspect of these women's work involves bridging the gap between the clinical and community voices. That is, to speak in

DOI: 10.4324/9780429297830-9

the voice of a "peer health advocate" is to be able to combine the voice of the clinical world (e.g., by showing one understands how specific contraception devices work) with that of the community (e.g., by using the language of the everyday life in the community). In other words, what makes these women's voice unique (which is also what unifies them) is precisely the ability to shift between a plurality of voices.

The multivocal nature of univocality is also clearly illustrated in the chapter by Laaksonen, Bodström, and Haavisto. The authors report on the constitution of a grassroots movement in Helsinki to help asylum-seekers facing deportation. They analyze in particular how the various participants of the movement (Afghan and Iraqi refugees and various Finnish NGOs) progressively formulated the movement's official demands. Their analysis shows that while formulating these demands certainly involves leaving out some of the participants' concerns, the final version of the demands still bear the marks of a plurality of voices. Indeed, they represent not only the refugees' most pressing concerns (esp. deportation and police brutality) but also the NGOs' knowledge of the political and legal context and their concerns for efficacy. That is, in this case again, speaking with one voice involves articulating a plurality of voices.

The question of how to value voice and allow for an articulation of voices while also maximizing the possibilities of voice for the most marginalized and silenced racialized communities is at the core of Khaoula Zoghlami's contribution. Her chapter investigates the discussions and debates among activists involved in the design of a consultation on systemic racism in Canada. She explains how the idea of "centering the margins" imposed itself as a way to conceive and favor multivocality without imposing a process of unification that would reproduce dominating power relationships. "Centering the margins" may mean, for instance, putting at the forefront those who are usually not heard and not seen, thus prioritizing their voices all along the consultative process. What is at stake then in this chapter is the very possibility to value voices and articulate voices differently, without reproducing existing systems of privilege.

Univocality Contributes to Multivocality

The second merit of studying univocality as a process of unification is that it allows us to see that univocality is not only made of multivocality, it also contributes to it. Indeed, for various voices to start speaking with one voice, something/someone needs to start binding them together. In other words, an *additional* voice must be introduced.

This aspect is especially well illustrated in the chapter by Kryger Aggerholm and Asmuß. The authors study how managers define and negotiate rationales for laying off people in a large public organization in Denmark. They analyze in particular the role that certain idioms (e.g., "there is no holds barred" or "you can't keep up with everything") play in such negotiations. They show that managers often use these idioms to suggest that the position they defend is not only theirs but also that of a collective wisdom or common sense, thus making it easier for the other managers to align with their position. For instance, when a manager sums up her rationale for downsizing by saying "we cannot keep up with everything," she implicitly says that her understanding of the situation largely derives from common sense. In this case, it is therefore by *adding* a new voice to the situation (the voice of common sense) that managers create the conditions for a common voice to emerge.

Something similar can be found in the case studied by Grover Golden and Bencherki. The authors show how the "peer health advocates" sometimes borrow from specific discursive genres to rehearse what they want to say to their community. The authors analyze in particular how they use the call and response practice from African American churches to articulate their voices into a unified whole: one peer performs the role of leader by making declarations while other group members play the role of chorus by spontaneously adding affirmations that support the leader's declarations. Here again, it is by *adding* a voice to the situation (the voice of Black Christianity in this case) that participants connect their voices, thus allowing for a common voice to emerge.

The importance of the "binding voice" (as we say of a binding agent) is also central to Decault's chapter. The author studies how hip-hop artists involved in the Black Lives Matter movement conceive of their role of artist activist. He analyses the many facets (and voices) that these artists aim to articulate through their art: lover of culture and art, disrupter of racist and eurocentric narratives, analyst of situated experiences of power, teller of the civil rights movement legacy, developer of youth imagination and creative skills, etc. Decault thus shows that these artists do a lot more than just adding their own voice to the Black Lives Matter movement: they actively contribute to connecting and articulating the many voices that flow through it. In other words, they serve as a coalescing voice within the movement.

Univocality Needs Multivocality to Make a Difference

The third benefit of studying univocality as a process of unification is that it highlights the fact that univocality needs multivocality to make a difference. Indeed, for a voice to have influence (whether it is to convince someone of something, to lead someone to act, or simply to be taken seriously), it needs to show who or what it is speaking for; in other words, it needs to show the various voices on behalf of which it is supposed to speak. This aspect is especially visible in cases of tensions or conflicts, that is, in cases in which the relevance or legitimacy of a voice is or may be challenged.

Poroli's chapter offers a good example of this. Focusing on the case of a network of cooperatives, the author studies how members define and negotiate the network's position on various matters of social responsibility.

He analyzes in particular how some members propose to adopt a nuanced position on Genetically Modified Organisms (GMOs). The network's historical position being radically anti-GMOs, these members carefully unpack the various voices that, in their view, support a more nuanced position (and voice). They thus mention: the network's need for a renewal 20 years after its first decision on the subject, the younger generation's expectation that they do so, the fact that people make fun of them for sticking to their old position, and a recent review of the scientific literature that shows that GMOs cause no harm to people's health. In other words, these members aim to give more weight or authority to their proposition by showing the various voices that are supposed to speak through it.

Something similar can be found in McClellan's and Davis's chapter. The authors report on the organization of a waste sorting initiative during a two-day concert in a US university stadium. They analyze in particular the discussions between the "sustainability team" whose mission was to develop ambitious recycling policies for the event and the facilities stakeholders who usually deal with waste management in the stadium. They show that many of the sustainability team's propositions were resisted by the facilities stakeholders who notably argued that the concertgoers were "not the kind of crowd that [was] going to recycle." However, as the authors show, the facilities stakeholders proved to be wrong as the concertgoers overwhelmingly complied with sorting policies during the event. The sustainability team thus found themselves in a much stronger position than previously to defend ambitious policies: they could speak not only in the name of ideal policies but also in the name of what concertgoers were actually prepared to do. Here again we see that the more voices express themselves through a spokesperson, the more authority or weight this spokesperson has.

To sum up, this book's chapters allow us to see that there are three main reasons why univocality is inseparable from multivocality:

1 Speaking with one voice consists in unifying voices, which means that univocality is literary made of multivocality.
2 Unifying voices cannot be achieved without adding a new voice, which means that univocality contributes to multivocality.
3 For a voice to have influence, it needs to show the voices on behalf of which it speaks, which means univocality needs multivocality to make a difference.

Thus, rather than opposing univocality to multivocality, this book invites us to reconceive univocality as a specific form of multivocality—one in which a plurality of voices becomes both "packable" (one voice may speak and be heard *instead of* many) and "unpackable" (many voices may speak and be heard *through* one).

Index

COCo *see* Center for Community
Organizations (COCo)
collective moral consciousness
124–125
Collins, P. H. 92, 102, 163, 171,
173n12
coming to voice 90–92, 99, 102
communication: (C)SR talk
130, 131; definition of 70;
environment-shaping understanding of 129; transmission view of
127; ventriloquism in 8–9, 14,
128, 131–133
communication as constitutive of
organization (CCO) 7, 13, 66–70
communicative constitutive view of
reality 128
community-based organizations
(CBOs) 41; multiple voices in 42–45,
47, 56, 58–60
community health initiative, multivocal
organization in 41–61; case setting
45–46; community-based organizations 42–45, 47, 56, 58–60; data
analysis strategy 46–47; discursive
positioning in relation to present and
absent others 49–50; management of
48–49; practical problem, addressing
58–60; presentifying the community
50–52; situated performance 56–58;
voicing multiple discursive genres
53–56
concrete and figurative texts, characteristics for 71
conversational excerpts, ventriloquial
analysis of 135–146
Cooren, F. 7–9, 11–12, 21, 68, 128,
131–133, 147; "What Makes
Communication Organizational?
How the Many Voices of a
Collectivity Become the One Voice
of the Organization" 7
coorientation 70, 71, 84
Cornelissen, J. 147
(corporate) social responsibility ((C)
SR) 127–149; concern mobilization
136–137; conversational excerpts,
ventriloquial analysis of 135–146;
information management 136–137;
multivocal nature of 129–131;
organizational co-construction
142–143; research context 134–135;
topic (re)positioning 142–143;

ventriloquism, in organizational
communication 131–133
Couldry, N. 10, 12–14, 90, 164–168,
170, 172n9
Craig, R. T. 53
Crenshaw, K. 156, 158, 167
critical education 97–99
critical ethnography 173n10, 173n11
Crossley, N. 69
(C)SR *see* (corporate) social responsibility ((C)SR)
Cullors, P. 90
cultural capital 83

Davies, B. 49
decentering the margins 166
DELTA 134, 135, 138–141, 144–146
Dempsey, S. E. 6, 9–10, 12, 157
deploying alternative identities 57
Derrida, J. 8
dialogical theory 57
dialogism 11, 128
direct democracy 67
discursive genres 180; voice multiple
48, 53–56, 58, 59
discursive positioning 48, 55, 57; definition of 49; in relation to present
and absent others 49–50
dissonance trope 22
distributed authorship 9
distributed leadership 67
Disu, J. *see* FM Supreme
Drew, P. 23

employee voice, definition of 5
environmental rhetoric 112–113
equivalence approach 129
event support practices 119–120

Feigenbaum, A. 65
Felsenthal, E. 1–2
Fenton, N. 69, 77
Finnish Immigration Service 66
FM Supreme 95, 100, 101, 104n4
Foucault, M. 111, 112
Freire, P. 96–98
Frenzel, F. 65
Fukushima, A. 94–99, 102, 104n4
Fyke, K. 70

Garza, A. 90
Genetically Modified Organisms
(GMOs) 181

Printed in the United States
by Baker & Taylor Publisher Services